◄THE TEXAS LEFT

Number Thirty-five:
Elma Dill Russell Spencer Series in the West
   and Southwest
Andrés Tijerina, General Editor

Series Board:
Alwyn Barr
James Crisp
Rebecca Sharpless
Eric Van Young

THE TEXAS LEFT

The Radical Roots
of Lone Star Liberalism

DAVID O'DONALD CULLEN AND
KYLE G. WILKISON, EDITORS

Texas A&M University Press, College Station

Manufactured in the United States of America
All rights reserved
First edition

This paper meets the requirements of ANSI/NISO Z39.48–1992
(Permanence of Paper). Binding materials have been chosen for durability.

Library of Congress Cataloging-in-Publication Data

The Texas Left: The radical roots of Lone Star liberalism / David O'Donald
    Cullen and Kyle G. Wilkison, editors. — 1st ed.
        p. cm.— (Elma Dill Russell Spencer series in the West and Southwest ;
    no. 35)
    Includes bibliographical references and index.
    ISBN-13: 978-1-60344-175-9 (cloth : alk. paper)
    ISBN-10: 1-60344-175-1 (cloth : alk. paper)
    ISBN-13: 978-1-60344-189-6 (pbk : alk. paper)
    ISBN-10: 1-60344-189-1 (pbk : alk. paper)   1. Radicalism—Texas—
History. 2. Labor unions and socialism—Texas—History. 3. Liberalism—
Texas—History. 4. Left-wing extremists—Texas—History. 5. Social
movements—Texas—History. 6. Texas—Politics and government. I.
Cullen, David O'Donald, 1951– II. Wilkison, Kyle Grant, 1960– III. Series:
Elma Dill Russell Spencer series in the West and Southwest ; no. 35.
HN79.T43R38 2010
320.5309764—dc22

                                                        2009028570

CONTENTS

ACKNOWLEDGMENTS

This work grew out of a Texas State Historical Association (TSHA) roundtable on "The Texas Left" at the 2004 meeting in Austin. We appreciate each of those who participated on that panel and members of the audience who posed searching questions. We especially thank George Norris Green, then president of the TSHA, for fitting his paper into an already unreasonably demanding schedule where he not only delivered the presidential address in public, but in private was busy fighting for the life of the TSHA.

We heartily acknowledge the historians who contributed original essays to this volume. First, this slate of historians represents the best of contemporary work in Texas history and readers familiar with the discipline will immediately recognize the all-star nature of the team. From the beginning we set out to include the most authoritative voices, and even readers less familiar with the field will doubtlessly discover that we have succeeded.

Further, the authors in this collection responded to the task with enthusiasm, self-discipline and graceful writing. When we, the editors, managed to create roadblocks and delays, the contributors all reacted with patience and understanding. We are very grateful for that patience.

Much original research went into these essays. We would be remiss not to acknowledge the ongoing debt historians owe to professional reference librarians, archivists, and others who act as guides during our research.

We are also grateful for the immediate and ongoing support of

Mary Lenn Dixon, editor-in-chief at Texas A&M University Press. We could not have had a better guide. The volume has benefitted greatly from the work of her first-rate team of editors. In matters of interpretation and argument we owe particular thanks to the rigorous reading of the manuscript by anonymous referees selected by Texas A&M University Press.

We wish to thank our talented colleagues at Collin College who act as sounding boards and who enthusiastically help keep us in touch with reality.

◀THE TEXAS LEFT

THE RIGHT "TO WORK, TO STARVE, AND TO DIE"

The Forgotten Radical Heritage of Texas

David O'Donald Cullen and Kyle G. Wilkison

In May 1886 thousands of radical Texas farmers and laborers con-vened in Central Texas, issuing a call for protecting farmers' and workers' rights. Labor unionist William E. Farmer of Bonham, soon-to-be-Populist and future founder of the Texas Socialist Party, warned his comrades that Texas had overproduced "poverty, bare-footed women, political thieves, and many liars." Farmer denied any distinction between the armed robbery of outlaws and the "legalized robbery" perpetrated by corporations. Exhorting his audience against being taken in by their social betters, he predicted: "If you listen to other classes you will only have three rights . . . to work, to starve, and to die."[1]

Only a few months after Farmer's speech in Cleburne, a court in Chicago convicted labor leader and anarchist Albert Parsons and seven others for the Haymarket Square bombing. Long before Chicago, how-ever, the young Texan had already pushed the boundaries of his cul-ture by marrying mixed-race Lucy Gonzales, participating in radical Texas politics, and publishing a newspaper that called openly for racial equality. Moving his family north, Parsons worked as a printer and spoke out for labor rights before paying the ultimate price for his radi-cal beliefs. Widowed and far from her native Texas, young Lucy Gon-zales Parsons fought on, continuing to spread the laborite message for the rest of her life.[2]

A year after Albert Parsons died on the gallows, Joshua L. Hicks wrote to a newspaper denouncing bigotry toward African Americans. A white East Texas farmer, Hicks spent the rest of his life opposing war and racism, and fighting for a greater share of the wealth for Texas workers and farmers. Hicks argued that capitalism was "a stranger to the teachings of Jesus." Radical working people like William E. Farmer, "compañera" Lucy Gonzales Parsons, and Joshua L. Hicks receive scant attention in conventional Texas history. Indeed, for most of the twentieth century the history of the Lone Star State— both academic and in popular culture—maintained the state's heroic myth of cattle and oil, ignoring dissenters from among the poor majority and the Texas Left.[3]

Just over one hundred years ago, the first scholarly history of Texas appeared, George P. Garrison's 1903 *A Contest of Civilizations*. Published ten years after Frederick Jackson Turner's "The Significance of the Frontier in American History," Garrison's work reflected the influence of that seminal article. Garrison's Texas was a product of the frontier that created values needed both to conquer a wilderness and support democracy, self-reliance, and individualism.[4] In 1908 came the first film with "Texas" in the title—*Texas Tex*—ushering in over a half-century of American films successfully linking the images of cowboys and the West with Texas. In the 1920s alone, "Texas" appeared in the titles of eighty-eight films.[5]

Historians followed Hollywood's lead. For the first half of the twentieth century the western frontier dominated historians' understanding of the state, beginning with the writings of academics Eugene C. Barker and Walter Prescott Webb, and popularizers J. Frank Dobie and T. R. Fehrenbach. Barker's biography of Stephen F. Austin viewed the Texas empresario as part of the western movement narrative of Manifest Destiny. Webb ignored the eastern half of Texas where most Texans actually lived, and won his fame with *The Great Plains* (1931), describing a land apart, a classic western frontier, distinguished by its demanding geography. He further solidified his place as the chief historian of Texas with *The Texas Rangers: A Century of Frontier Defense* (1935), a celebratory bestseller actually made into a movie. Likewise, folklorist J. Frank Dobie further strengthened Texas as popular symbol of the heroic West with his focus on the romance of the open range. His works on cattle ranching became standard reading for those interested in the state's history and culture.[6]

A later, even more powerful shaper of popular culture—television—energetically matched these previous writers' enthusiasm for the cowboy and the West. By the 1960s, the cowboy had become the most important cultural symbol in American society, driven home by such popular television shows as *Gunsmoke, Rawhide, Bonanza,* and *Tales of the Texas Rangers*. Perhaps Texas as western icon reached its cultural crescendo in 1960 with the release of John Wayne's *The*

Alamo (tragic, if anachronistic, cowboys alone on the frontier willing to die for a just and honorable cause) and the arrival of oil heir Clint Murchison's professional football franchise, the Dallas Cowboys, in a city whose historic financial foundation had been cotton.[7]

Texas elites revised historical consciousness in order to disassociate the state from the "burden of Southern history," slavery, defeat, poverty, and white supremacy.[8] In 1936, for example, the program directors of the State Fair of Texas decided to emphasize cowboys and cattle drives rather than secession and the Civil War. The most popular show at the fair was the Cavalcade of Texas, which featured numbers entitled "Frontier Follies" and "Winning the West." Later generations of Texas historians found much fodder in such moments. In *Path to a Modern South* (2001) and other writings, Walter L. Buenger well documents Texas decision makers' turning away from the reality of the state's southern history toward a self-conscious adoption of a western identity.[9]

When Texas historians did discuss topics linked to southern history, they either focused upon the military exploits of Texans during the Civil War or repeated the interpretations that dominated the historical profession for the first half of the twentieth century. Charles W. Ramsdell's *Reconstruction in Texas* (1910), for example, reflected the prevailing "Dunningite" interpretation (for Ramsdell's mentor, historian William A. Dunning of Columbia University). According to Ramsdell, Reconstruction was a failure because northern interference in Texas politics and society resulted in corruption, violence, and racial animosity. In fact, acknowledging race and the practice of white supremacy all but disappeared from the works of the state's most widely read college textbook author.[10]

Thus the defenders of the Alamo, Texans fighting in the Civil War, and cowboys riding the open range dominated the historiography of the state for over sixty years. The only other subject that managed to rival that iconography was the discovery of oil. Even that topic, when it received attention from other than a handful of notable labor historians, told the story of the winners, providing yet another triumphal example of rugged frontier individualism.[11]

Meanwhile, beginning in the late 1960s, historical writings began to reflect the work of a new generation of scholars. Revisionist accounts of U.S. history began appearing regularly in the major journals of the profession, especially concerning the origins and influence of the modern political Left, but not much regarding Texas history. Only relatively slowly has the writing of Texas history expanded beyond the Alamo, Civil War, cattle, and oil. In the last quarter of the twentieth century, historians of Texas increasingly have followed—trailed—academic trends in studying the experiences of women, African Americans, Tejanos, Mexican Americans, and even, in a few cases, the Texas working class. A generation of scholars once or twice removed from the influence of Barker, Ramsdell, and Webb, and steeped instead in American trends in social history began to research a Texas history that revealed race, gender, and class, but also the contours of a historic Texas Left, sometimes radical, more often liberal, operating in the state between the late 1860s and early 1960s.

Ruth A. Allen is the pioneering mother of Texas social history, as well as first historian of the Texas Left. While more celebrated historians wrote about wide-open spaces and fewer people, Allen actually sought to chronicle the history of the poor majority during a thirty-year career at the University of Texas. An economist by training, Allen's writings, including *The Labor of Women in the Production of Cotton* (1931), *Chapters in the History of Organized Labor* (1941), and *The Great Southwest Strike* (1942), along with Roscoe Martin's *The People's Party in Texas: A Study in Third Party Politics* (1933), laid an important foundation for future historians of Texas workers and Texas women.[12]

This reassessment continued when fiction writers challenged the myths of the state. In 1981 Larry McMurtry published "Ever a Bridegroom: Reflections on the Failure of Texas Literature" in the *Texas Observer*. The controversial essay dismissed much of Texas writing, especially the works of the writers of Dobie's generation, and insisted that the state would only produce literature of significance when writers concentrated their efforts on the harsh realities of the state.[13]

Thus, influenced by the social history produced in the rest of the country in the 1960s and 1970s, by the 1980s some Texas historians were well on their way toward a re-examination of the Lone Star State. Over the next twenty-five years their work considered Texans ignored by earlier writers: African Americans, Mexican Americans, women, the working class and rural poor. Each of these groups at one time or another challenged the economic and social system that denied them economic opportunity and political equality. From the 1860s to the 1960s different factions of the poor and disenfranchised became, at different times, Radical Republicans, Farmers' Alliance men, Populists, Socialists, labor unionists, feminists, and civil rights activists. They were, each in their time, the Texas Left.

What are the particularities of the Texas Left and did it influence the state to any significant extent? This work hopes to raise questions and provide preliminary answers. The authors of this volume hope to stimulate further research and continued scholarly discourse on the Texas Left on the whole and in its particular elements.

The first hint of notable radicalism in post–Civil War Texas came from Radical Republicans. Whatever the motives of the white leadership, the African American rank and file sought an end to white supremacy and access to the normal opportunities of life afforded by hard work and persistence. The goal that African American Radical Republicans and their most radical white compatriots aimed for was forward-looking and radical: racial equality. The overwhelming majority of Texans, southern whites, refused to accept calls for racial equality and the tide of white supremacy stopped, but did not destroy, the radical notion of human equality. On the other hand, radical social critique has been prompted as much by change as it has been a demand for change. Thus, the Texas Left also grew in response to changes brought about by the industrial revolution and the emergence of corporate capitalism. Beginning in the late nineteenth century this resulted in the formation of the Farmers' Alliance and the Populist Party. The Texas Populist Party—with its tens of thousands of votes—represents the zenith of mass dissident action in Texas, in numbers, if not in radical ideology. After Populist defeat, the most discontented moved on to the Socialist Party in their battle to restore lost communities destroyed by the marketplace, arguing that they sought to extend democracy beyond the political to the economic. But during World War I a flood of government repression and patriotic hysteria swept away Texas Socialists, and indeed Socialists around the country. All along, from the post–Civil War era onward, labor unionists among Texas industrial workers had been fighting for collective bargaining against the overwhelming political and economic power of their employers. The economic crisis of the 1930s deepened workers' suffering and led anew to attempts to organize a viable union movement. Indeed, voices on the Left argued that the nation's greatest problems—including those of Texans—in the 1930s were rooted in the very structure of industrial capitalism, and that it was the mission of the government to deal somehow with the flaws of that structure. Union leadership came to understand, however, that backing minority-party candidates rarely resulted in higher wages, shorter hours, or safer working conditions. Seizing on the opening provided by the New Deal, unionists in Texas and elsewhere attempted to graft the labor movement on to the left wing of the Democratic Party. Nevertheless, this coalition did not— for the most part—include women, African Americans, or Mexican Americans.[14] The struggle of these disenfranchised groups dominated the post–World War II political era in Texas as the leftist social activists turned more liberal. Denied access because of their very identity as blacks or Hispanics, in the 1950s these groups—in varying degrees— necessarily developed a politics of identity rather than class consciousness. On the other hand, if possible, the story of Texas women's late-nineteenth- and twentieth-century struggles for equality is even more complicated by the crosscurrents of class and ethnicity.[15]

The chapters that follow remind us that much of the struggle against white supremacy, economic injustice, and political disfranchisement in Texas was the struggle of Texas radicals. To explore the Texas Left, however, is not to say that it triumphed, although yesterday's radical position frequently became tomorrow's conventional moderation. For example, the early twentieth-century Left fought an arduous battle for racial equality; twenty-first-century conservatives pay homage to racial equality. Early-twentieth-century radical feminists fought for gender equality; today's conservative female politicians denounce leftist feminists even as they inhabit spaces created for them by the Left. It is critical to note, however, that these essays are no triumphal valedictory of a putative protracted victory for long-dead radicals. Texas radicals' most ambitious goals remain unfulfilled one hundred years after their departure. The Texas Socialist Party called for universal health care in 1912, a call that remains unanswered.

Thus, the working definition of the Texas Left for this collection of essays is twofold. First, it is a political movement with the avowed ends of a more equal and humane society through reform, restructure, or a revolution of the economic or social system. Second, we chose to emphasize in this collection movements with sufficient following to have influenced contemporary or future social change. Thus, these essays explore the history of pragmatic radicalism whose influence eventually effected actual social change.

The Texas Left has been essentially pragmatic, nurtured more by American realities than foreign ideology. But, that very American pragmatism also allowed it at times to compromise its own principles in not defying the prevailing early-twentieth-century culture of Anglo supremacy and sexism. Consequently, the post–World War II project of the Left becomes the cause of women, blacks, and Hispanics. Because these civil rights struggles had to maintain inter-class solidarity, the Texas and U.S. Left began to drift away from a class-conscious egalitarianism in favor of equality of the sexes and ethnic groups. That is the transformative moment when the direction of the Texas and U.S. Left became liberal. The goal of late-twentieth-century liberalism, after all, was never about empowering the working class. Instead it aimed for middle-class black college students and middle-class white college students to be treated equally, for women professionals to have the same career opportunities as their male professional colleagues, and for Tejanos of all classes to be able to expect first-class citizenship and due process of law. It is tempting to say, then, that when the class-conscious agenda disintegrated in the postwar era in favor of identity politics, that the Left in Texas and nationwide had run its course. But that remains to be seen.

This collection of original essays reflects the efforts of scholars over the last twenty-five years when more historians began turning their attention toward the unexplored realities of the history of the state. Of course, powerful Texas myths still dominate the state's popular history. Academic historians continue to battle the Texas carpetbagger myth of Reconstruction in which venal Yankees ravaged the virtuous Lone Star State. As Carl Moneyhon demonstrates, it was radical egalitarianism of the "home-grown" variety that produced Texas's first attempt at free and equal public schools. The post–Civil War radicals who fought to turn the ends of state government toward equality of education, equality before the law, and enforcement of African American voting rights were Texans.

Throughout most of Texas history, the vast majority of Texans lived in the eastern half of the state and, until after World War II, farmed for a living. Far from being stereotypical individualists, they lived in kinship-based communities, and tended to cooperate in their major undertakings, including politics. As Donna Barnes shows, the Texas Farmers' Alliance took a decidedly radical step in supporting the farmer-friendly, flexible-money-supply policy known as the Subtreasury Plan. Denounced by its critics as radical, the Subtreasury Plan was still able to command the following of the Texas Farmers' Alliance as it moved away from the conservative Texas Democratic Party toward the militancy of the People's Party.

Gregg Cantrell shows how a "host of sturdy patriots," as Texas Populists saw themselves, swelled to the broadest, most radical challenge the Texas elite had yet experienced. Rooted in a profound discontent with the outcomes of the end-of-the-century U.S. economy—as well as what Cantrell calls "religious zeal and idealistic devotion to principle"—Texas Populists asserted the essential leftist demand that the toiling masses ought to retain more of the fruit of their own labor. Texas Populists demonstrated a willingness to restructure both political and economic class relations in order to achieve their goals. At their peak, the Populists polled three-quarters of the Democratic vote and, indeed, denied the ruling party a majority. Such a political uprising guaranteed a determined reaction that effectively killed off the most successful leftist electoral effort in Texas—and the nation.

In the first two decades of the next century, discontented Texas radicals turned to the Socialist Party of America. Peter Buckingham chronicles radical Texans such as newspaperman "Red Tom" Hickey and Southern Baptist preacher Reddin Andrews as they led Lone Star Socialists to becoming the fastest-growing party in the state. Overwhelmingly a rural movement of small farmers and tenants, Texas Socialists outpolled the Republicans in 1912 and 1914 to become the state's second party. The tense World War I–era marked the demise of the party, but some of the radical spirit, ideals, and demands survived in new movements.

Not the least of these movements was the long-term, continuous, and radical effort by Texas workers to achieve higher standards of living through collective bargaining. No other single movement so closely conforms to the historic project of the Left than that of the ideological descendants of the original radicals, discontented working men and women who asserted a revolutionary claim to a better life. In two essays spanning the bulk of Texas history, George N. Green (with Michael Botson in the second essay) chronicles the saga of organized labor in the Lone Star State, concluding that for the period before 1920, the Texas labor movement ought to be remembered for its fight to "bring civilization to Texas." The later twentieth-century struggle saw labor's influence in Texas peak in the 1970s.

The Texas liberal-Left coalition whose members were women and ethnic and racial minorities often found themselves shut out of the traditional class-conscious leftist groups. Those Texans challenged both the conservative and leftist status quo through more liberal-oriented strategies: collective actions that worked within the legal and political system with the goal of gaining access to society and the economy, not restructuring them.

Bruce Glasrud and Gregg Andrews find that African Americans in Texas distanced themselves, with some exceptions, from existing white-run leftist organizations. Instead much of the success of black political activism came from within the African American community through the work of individuals such as Clifton Richardson Sr. (founder of the *Houston Observer*), Robert Grovey (head of Houston's Third Wave Civic Club), Antonio Maceo Smith (leader of the Progressive Voters League), and Juanita Craft (organizer of dozens of chapters of the NAACP).

Arnoldo De León argues that the activism of the Mexican American community ranged from spontaneous worker rebellions in the fields and mines of Texas to the highly organized political campaigns of groups such as the League of United Latin American Citizens, the American GI Forum, and La Raza Unida Party. Like African Americans, most Mexican American activists improvised new institutions from within their own communities in the post–World War II era to overturn the systemic obstacles blocking Tejanos from educational, economic, and political participation.

Judith N. McArthur and Harold L. Smith show that race and class deeply influenced the feminist Left. Upper- and middle-class white women's struggle for equality took place within the economic and social structures they inhabited. Poor women and women of color worked for gender and racial equality from outside the prevailing system. Ultimately McArthur and Smith conclude that most Texas women activists worked through liberal-orientated organizations. They highlight the effective work of the Texas Equal Suffrage Association, the Texas Federation of Women's Clubs, and the Texas Women's Political Caucus, and profile the political efforts of such notable figures as Minnie Fisher Cunningham, Jessie Daniel Ames, Emma Tenayuca, and Hermine Tobolowsky.

But in Texas those in power saw any challenge to their position as radicalism, and responded as if it were in fact a call to revolution. Thus political actions by African Americans and Mexican Americans resulted in the Texas establishment labeling them communists and looking the other way as acts of physical intimidation, ranging from beatings to lynching, were used to stop their challenge to the political and economic elite. Texas women found that they were portrayed as betraying traditional family values and violating both God's and nature's laws as they increased their demands for equality in the political and economic arena, and when they forced a public discussion of domestic violence and rape.

The concluding essay by Patrick Cox, however, demonstrates that the political work of African Americans, Mexican Americans, and women created a viable liberal wing within the Democratic Party in Texas, including the formation of the Democrats of Texas and an influential journal, the *Texas Observer*. Liberal Texans Ralph Yarborough, J. R. Parten, Frankie Randolph, and Henry Gonzalez presented a challenge to Texas conservatives throughout the 1950s and the early 1960s. The results of their efforts produced a political agenda that included a call for greater political and economic equality.

The Texas Left never assumed ascendancy during the hundred years between the First and Second Reconstructions. Nevertheless, the nineteenth- and early-twentieth-century radical Left in Texas did prepare a seedbed for protest and reform. Perhaps it may even be credited with creating an agenda for the liberal left of the mid-twentieth century that produced in Texas, unlike its Gulf South neighbors, a more vibrant coalition, with more influence and greater results.

NOTES

1. Fort Worth *Gazette,* May 24, 1886; cited by Lawrence Goodwyn in his *Democratic Promise: The Populist Moment in America* (New York: Oxford University Press, 1976) 76–77.

2. For a profile of the Parsons, see James Green, *Death in the Haymar- ket: A Story of Chicago, the First Labor Movement and the Bombing that Divided Gilded Age America* (New York: Anchor Books, 2007) and Albert Parsons, "Autobiography of Albert Parsons," Chicago Historical Society, Haymarket Affair Digital Collection, http://www .chicagohistory.org/hadc/manuscripts/M07/M07.htm (accessed September 6, 2008). Texas native Lucy Gonzales Parsons, radical widow of Albert Parsons, went on to help found the Industrial Workers of the World and continued her activism on behalf of the working class, the unemployed, and the homeless throughout her long life. For the ethnic identity of Lucy Gonzales Parsons, see Gary B. Nash, "The Hidden History of Mestizo America," *Journal of American History* 82, no. 3 (December 1995), 949–50.

3. Chandler Davidson, *Race and Class in Texas Politics* (Princeton: Princeton University Press, 1990), xxiv–xxviii; Kyle G. Wilkison, *Yeomen, Sharecroppers and Socialists: Plain Folk Protest in Texas, 1870–1914* (College Station: Texas A&M University Press, 2008), 140–43; J. L. Hicks and J. B. Cranfill clippings, Box 1, Folder 228-1-3, Scrapbook 1, 153–57, Joshua L. Hicks Papers, Louis H. Hicks Collection, Texas Labor History Collection, Archives, University Library, University of Texas at Arlington, Arlington, Texas; J. L. Hicks, *The Scout* [Hallettsville, Texas] 1 (September 1911), 4.

4. George P. Garrison, *Texas: A Contest of Civilizations* (New York: Houghton Mifflin, 1903); Frederick Jackson Turner's "The Signifi- cance of the Frontier in American History" was first published in the *Proceedings of the State Historical Society of Wisconsin* in 1893 but its fullest expression can be found in Turner's T*he Frontier in American History* (New York: Henry Holt, 1920); for the cultural influence of the frontier upon American history, see Richard Slot- kin, *The Fatal Environment: The Myth of the Frontier in the Age of Industrialization, 1800–1890* (New York: Atheneum, 1985), and Henry Nash Smith, *Virgin Land: The American West as Symbol and Myth* (Cambridge: Harvard University Press, 1950); also see Ste- phen Stagner, "Epics, Science, and the Lost Frontier: Texas Historical Writing, 1836–1936," *Western Historical Quarterly* 12 (April 1981), 165–81.

5. For the relationship between Hollywood and Texas, see two works by Don Graham, *Giant: Essays on Texas* (Forth Worth: Texas Chris-

tian University Press, 1998); and *Cowboys and Cadillacs: How Hollywood Looks at Texas* (Austin: Texas Monthly Press, 1983).

6. There are a number of works that discuss the influence of these writers in shaping the image of Texas both for Texans and for the rest of the nation; see, for example, James S. Payne, "Texas Historiography in the Twentieth Century: A Study of Eugene C. Barker, Charles W. Ramsdell, and Walter P. Webb" (PhD diss., University of Denver, 1972); Robert F. O'Connor, ed. *Texas Myths* (College Station: Texas A&M University Press, 1986); Larry McMurtry, *In a Narrow Grave: Essay on Texas* (Austin: Encino, 1968); Ronnie Dugger, ed., *Three Men in Texas: Bedichek, Webb and Dobie* (Austin: University of Texas Press, 1967); Tom Pilkington, *State of Mind: Texas Literature and Culture* (College Station: Texas A&M University Press, 1998).

7. For examples of Texas entering and influencing popular culture, see "Giant of the Southwest," *Newsweek* 33 (March 21, 1949); "Everything's True about Texas," *Harpers Magazine,* March 1950; Joseph Leach, *The Typical Texan* (Dallas: Southern Methodist University Press, 1952); Frank Goodwyn, *Lone Star Land: Twentieth-Century Texas in Perspective* (New York: Alfred A. Knopf, 1955). For the cowboy as an important cultural symbol for America, see Gary Wills, *John Wayne's America: The Politics of Celebrity* (New York: Simon & Schuster, 1997); Bryan Burrough, *The Big Rich: The Rise and Fall of the Greatest Texas Oil Fortunes* (New York: Penguin Press, 2009).

8. C. Vann Woodward, *The Burden of Southern History* (Baton Rouge: Louisiana State University Press, 1993).

9. For a history of the Texas State Fair, see Kenneth B. Ragsdale, *The Year America Discovered Texas: Centennial '36* (College Station: Texas A&M University Press, 1987); Walter L. Buenger, "Texas and the South," *Southwestern Historical Quarterly* 103 (January 2000): 309–26; Buenger, *The Path to a Modern South: Northeast Texas between Reconstruction and the Great Depression* (Austin: University of Texas Press, 2001).

10. For a discussion of Ramsdell and his influence, see Walter L. Buenger and Robert A. Calvert, "The Shelf Life of Truth in Texas" in their edited collection of essays, *Texas History and the Move into the Twenty-first Century* (Austin: Committee for the Humanities, 1990), xvi–xviii; Rupert N. Richardson, et al., *Texas: The Lone Star State* (Englewood Cliffs, N.J.: Prentice-Hall, 1993).

11. John S. Spratt, *The Road to Spindletop: Economic Changes in Texas, 1875–1901* (Dallas: Southern Methodist University Press, 1957); see also Graham, *Cowboys and Cadillacs.*

12. Ruth A. Allen, "The Labor of Women in the Production of Cotton," *University of Texas Bulletin,* no. 3134 (September 8, 1931); "Mexi-

can Peon Women in Texas," *Sociology and Social Research* 16 (November–December 1931), 131–42; *Chapters in the History of Organized Labor in Texas* (Austin: University of Texas Press, 1941); *The Great Southwest Strike* (Austin: University of Texas, 1942); *East Texas Lumber Workers: An Economic and Social Picture, 1870–1950* (Austin: University of Texas Press, 1961). Roscoe Martin, *The People's Party in Texas: A Study in Third Party Politics* (Austin: University of Texas Press, 1933).

13. Larry McMurtry, "Ever a Bridegroom: Reflections on the Failure of Texas Literature," *Texas Observer* (October 23, 1981): 1–18. The reassessment of Texas continued over the next few years in such high-profile events as "The Texas Literary Tradition," held in Austin in 1983. Sponsored by the University of Texas at Austin as part of the college's centennial celebration, the conference took up McMurtry's challenge by defending the literature produced by a new generation of native writers. See also Don Graham, James W. Lee, and William T. Pilkington, eds., *The Texas Literary Tradition: Fiction, Folklore, History* (Austin: University of Texas Press/Texas State Historical Association, 1983). The questions raised by McMurtry and the work of a new generation of historians of the state were the focus of a conference held in part to celebrate the state's 150th anniversary, "Texas Images and Realities: The Governor's Sesquicentennial Conference on the Literary Arts," University of North Texas, Denton. For a discussion of the conference and Texas literature see "Literature," in *Handbook of Texas* (Austin: Texas State Historical Association, 1996).

14. Minnie Fisher Cunningham would be the obvious exception, since she helped bring Texas labor unions and New Deal farmers together with her women's group in the Texas Social and Legislative Conference, in order to strengthen the Texas Left. See Judith N. McArthur and Harold L. Smith, *Minnie Fisher Cunningham: A Suffragist's Life in Politics* (New York: Oxford University Press, 2003), chapter 9.

15. For a concise history of the Left, see John Patrick Diggins, *The Rise and Fall of the American Left: The Lyrical Left, The Old Left, The New Left, The Academic Left* (New York: W. W. Norton, 1992), and Doug Rossinow, *Visions of Progress: The Left-Liberal Tradition in America* (Philadelphia: University of Pennsylvania Press, 2008); for a discussion of works on American radicalism, see Robert Cottrell, "Twentieth Century American Radicalism: A Bibliographic Essay," *History Teacher* 20 (November 1986), 27–49; for an additional source about the Left-liberal coalition in the United States, see "Liberalism and the Left: Rethinking the Relationship," published in *Radical History Review* 71 (Spring 1998).

"TEXAS OUT-RADICALS MY RADICALISM"
Roots of Radical Republicanism
in Reconstruction Texas

Carl H. Moneyhon

◀ In July 1867 the Texas Republican Party held its first statewide
convention, at Houston. The platform produced by the delegates, many of whom had roots in the state's antebellum politics, marked the new party as an organization possessing one of the
most radical agendas in the state's history. It supported a complete
reconstitution of the state's electorate when it pledged its support to
the reconstruction policy of Congress, a policy that at least temporarily enfranchised blacks for participation in a constitutional convention. The new party went further, however, placing itself in support of
continued enfranchisement and the implementation of policies that
recognized equality of all, regardless of race or color, before the law.
Subsequently that party would go even further, advocating a public
school system open to all, legislation allowing blacks access to the
state's public lands for homesteading, and equal protection for all of
the state's people before the law.[1]

Explaining the emergence of the Texas Republican Party has been
a difficult task, since unlike in other former Confederate states few
carpetbaggers played a role in its creation. Instead of ideas introduced
by outsiders, Texas Republicanism reflected the acceptance by a considerable number of white Texans who had been residents of the state
before the war of ideas, some of which were considered heretical in
those years. Scholars have paid little attention, however, to how this
took place. Charles Ramsdell, the earliest scholar of this era, recognized the change in attitudes toward black suffrage, but did not specu-
late on its cause. As to the programs of the subsequent Republican

government, Ramsdell ascribed much of the program to the designs of the men who took power, the results of the designs of a governor who was self-willed, obstinate, pig-headed almost beyond belief, and had no regard for the popular will. In similar manner, W. C. Nunn, in his *Texas under the Carpetbaggers,* saw them simply as opportunists seeking to build a political machine on black suffrage.[2]

Recent scholarship, however, has shown the earlier interpretations of Ramsdell and Nunn largely to be wrong. Texas Republicans were not unusual men. In fact, most of them had played a role in the state's antebellum politics. Some even had distinctive careers. The one characteristic most of these men held in common was their opposition to secession in 1860. Some, but not all, maintained their loyalty to the Union throughout the Civil War years. Scholars have clearly identified the type of men who became Republicans, and examined their policies, but the process by which they became radicals has remained unclear. This essay seeks to illuminate what lay behind the transition of the Unionists of the 1850s into the Radical Republican Texans of 1870.[3]

Prewar Texas Unionists hardly possessed a radical political philosophy, even in the context of the state's antebellum politics. Edmund J. Davis, later to be one of the most radical of the Republican leaders, was typical. Prior to the war he was an active Democrat, and at a party meeting in Corpus Christi in August 1855 he helped draft an address that clearly accepted the legitimacy of slavery. These resolutions stated strong opposition to congressional interference with the institution of slavery in any of the states or territories, and endorsed popular sovereignty as a solution to the territorial dispute. The resolutions provided further support for the institution of slavery when they also asked for "the acquisition of Territory when it becomes necessary for the preservation or protection of our institutions." As late as May 1860, another future radical leader, Andrew J. Hamilton, announced his candidacy for Congress as an Independent Democrat and his support of a platform that made little mention of slavery and certainly gave no support for any abolitionist goals. Instead Hamilton explained his candidacy as being based simply on his opposition to the regular Democratic nominee's support of secession to resolve the sectional crisis. Hamilton only mentioned slavery when he denounced plans to reopen the slave trade. His major appeal was for the support of all men "who are opposed . . . to *Secession,* and other Disunion issues, all who are friends to the National Democracy."[4]

In the subsequent crisis of secession and the outbreak of war, many of the future Republicans ultimately opposed secession and refused to provide their support for the Confederate war effort. This was done at considerable peril. By May 1861, Ben Epperson, a prominent Unionist from Clarksville, noted that a military spirit had taken possession of the population and that it was impossible to resist the existing sentiment. Indeed, he concluded that it had become "impolitic" to take a position against the new Confederacy or the Confederate state government. Epperson's observations reflected a growing awareness of violence directed against all who continued to support the Union, and those who refused to abandon their position on the issue suffered greatly.[5]

Events that transpired as Texas went to war played a major role in the development of Unionist attitudes toward the Confederacy and its leaders, and would be critical to their evolving political agenda. Throughout the war they confronted militancy among Confederate Texans that subjected Unionists to violence, persecution, and legal sanction. Across the state, rabid Confederates began to suppress Unionist sentiment. Typical was a violent attack that burned the offices of the pro-Union *Alamo Express* in San Antonio. The state government also moved against Unionists early. In 1862, responding to demands by Confederate district commanders, martial law was declared in the area south of San Antonio on April 24 and for the whole state on May 30. The latter required all eligible men to register for conscription and for all noncitizens to subscribe to a Confederate loyalty oath. The May 30 proclamation also made clear that any opposition to the Confederacy would not be tolerated and would be dealt with summarily.[6]

Given the choice of having to deal with violence or swearing an oath to the Confederacy and possibly having to serve in the Confederate Army, many Unionists fled the state. Those who did not experienced difficult times for the next four years. E. J. Davis was one who left the state, but his family that remained behind faced the full wrath of Confederate officials. When Elizabeth Davis tried to join her husband in Mexico, Confederate authorities ordered her back to her home at Corpus Christi. When she protested that the return would kill her as she had just given birth to her first child, she was told, "it makes no *difference* whether *you* are *killed one way or another,* and if you attempt to cross the River, you will be *shot,* and your body will float down the river, and be like so many deserters, you will never be heard of again!" Later, she was told by Confederate general Hamilton Bee that if her husband came to Texas with an army she would be sent into the interior and, in her words, "*I must be prepared to have my throat cut first.*"[7]

Those who remained in the state also faced constant scrutiny, with authorities suspicious of their loyalty. Arrest and the loss of their property were always possible. In the summer of 1862, Confederate authorities established military commissions with the authority to arrest and try anyone accused of disloyalty. One future Radical Republican, Edward Degener of San Antonio, faced typical charges when tried on the grounds that he had failed to give information on the existence of bands of men trying to escape to Mexico, had written exaggerated and slanderous statements designed to bring the Confederate government into disrepute, and corresponded with armed enemies of the Confederate States. Degener was found guilty and let go, provided he offered five thousand dollars in security, but other Unionists were forced into the army or imprisoned.[8]

Even those who fled had not really gotten out of the control of Confederate authorities. Many lost their property, as Confederate authorities confiscated it under the Confederate Sequestration Law. The Confederate Court for the Western District of Texas began trying such cases during its first session, beginning on January 6, 1862. In the next three years Judge Thomas J. Divine, judge of that court, presided over 2,774 cases. All of these but twenty-four involved the seizure of the property of those who had left the state rather than support the Confederacy. While many of these cases involved the property of Northern merchants and land speculators, other cases involved the property of the Unionists who had tried to keep the state from seceding. The courts disposed of both real and personal property, selling it to the highest bidder.[9]

These war experiences are critical to understanding the postwar actions of these Texas Unionists. The hard feelings toward their persecutors provided ample motives for their behavior. Many of them clearly believed that the men who had persecuted them should be held accountable. They also wanted their property restored. While land could be recovered, personal property would be more difficult, and only seizure of the property of their persecutors would make that possible. Edmund Davis made clear his belief that Confederates should be held accountable for their actions, in correspondence with Hamilton Bee, his wife's persecutor. Davis informed Bee that he considered him to be a war criminal and that he would be held for trial. William P. Ballinger, a Galveston attorney who had served as a receiver for sequestered property, confronted similar hostility when Unionists in New Orleans blocked his efforts to travel to Washington, on the grounds that he "had been engaged in the most odious work of the rebellion," confiscating their property while they were fighting for the Union. Texas was full of men like Bee and Ballinger, men who had visited great harm on Unionists in the state. A year after the war one outside observer concluded that their bitter feelings toward the former rebels drove Unionist politics.[10]

To punish their enemies and to reclaim their property, control over the state government was essential for Unionists. This meant that they had to control the reconstruction process. A critical issue in achieving this goal was to create policies acceptable to the federal government. This meant, above all else, that whatever form the new government took it must somehow indicate its loyalty. For the Unionists gathered at Austin this meant recognizing the results of the war, both in terms of the right of secession and also the end of slavery. This realization and the need to secure power provided the impetus toward the radicalization of Texas Unionists. The way to achieve this end was opened up for Unionists in the summer of 1865, when President Andrew Johnson appointed Jack Hamilton as provisional governor of the state, charging him with preparing the state for an election of delegates to a constitutional convention that would revise the state's constitution, making it acceptable to the victorious Union. Unfortunately, in the summer of 1865, the men who had been prewar Unionists disagreed as to what actions were necessary to indicate their full acceptance of abolition. James W. Throckmorton, a Unionist who had gone with the Confederacy, found on his visit to Austin considerable differences among men there, particularly on the question of rights for the newly freed slaves. Some favored allowing blacks to sit on juries and give testimony, others supported this and even some form of black suffrage. William Alexander, named attorney general by Hamilton, represented the more radical of the factions, holding to a belief that he later described as one that held that the right to vote is a natural right, inherent in all adults. Others may have also concluded that universal suffrage was a possibility, but at the time they remained quiet.[11]

Most Unionists were content simply to push for the guarantee of what they referred to as basic civil rights. Typically, this meant neither suffrage nor serving on juries, but did include acceptance of black testimony in the courts. Former governor and Unionist Elisha M. Pease was typical of these men, sharing his belief that the freedman had to be "treated as a freeman in regard to all personal rights," and that any hope of preserving something of the institution of slavery had to be abandoned. Pease saw this action as important because it would place Texas in the same position toward blacks held by the majority of Northern states, and would ensure their support in restoring the state to the Union. Pease also believed that recognition of these personal rights would also play a role in preventing a more radical reconstruction. If the Northern states saw that Texas conceded "all the rights that are given him by the great mass of the civilized world, the state would be able to avoid all difficulty in relation to negro suffrage."[12]

Ultimately Jack Hamilton, acting as provisional governor and having discussed the question of freedmen's rights with other Unionists, set the Unionist agenda on these matters. Hamilton appears actually to have concluded even before his arrival in Texas that the suffrage issue was too divisive to introduce in 1865. In the speech he gave in Houston on his return to the state, the governor explicitly took black suffrage off of his agenda, stating, "The black man has enough to attend to, let the question of voting alone for the present." In late November his ideas had matured further. He informed President Johnson that, not having received clear direction on what was demanded of Texans, he had concluded that the convention he had called must show ready acceptance of the abolition of slavery. To do that he hoped the delegates would pass resolutions providing that slavery would never again exist in the state, would ratify the Thirteenth Amendment, and would protect the former slaves by equal laws that allowed them to testify in the courts.[13]

Unionists had moved beyond their fellow Texans when they accepted black testimony in the courts, and Hamilton believed this was a step necessary for a return of Texas to the Union. Hamilton warned of the potential for a delay in reconstruction and further Northern intervention in the speech he gave in Austin on his arrival at the capital city. Urging acceptance of black testimony in the courts, he insisted that black testimony was not objectionable upon principle, but if more reasons for endorsing it were needed, it also was a good point of policy. If the state did not act in this way, he believed that the federal government would provide courts for the freedmen. He believed that if the state administered the same justice to blacks as to white men, "the general government will not, perhaps, think it necessary to engraft any machinery for their protection upon our present system."[14]

Governor Hamilton settled the question among most Unionists on the freedmen, and he also provided clear indications of the agenda toward their former enemies developed by Unionists. While never fully explicit about their purpose, Hamilton indicated other major goals in the same letter to the president in which he had signaled his support of black testimony. Foremost, the governor noted that he believed that the convention's work had to include a declaration that the ordinance of secession was null and void ab initio—from the beginning. He also wanted delegates to accept the idea that no constitutional right existed for secession and to repudiate all of the state debt created in support of the war. While such measures could be seen as further assuring the North of the state's loyalty, they also had a very practical purpose for the Unionists, particularly the declaration of the nullity of secession. The idea referred to through the rest of Reconstruction as "ab initio," had it ever been adopted, would have effectively made all actions of the Confederate state government illegal, and protected the right of Unionists to prosecute former Confederates for what they considered to be crimes against them and also to move against former Confederate officials personally to reclaim property.[15]

Securing support for their program proved illusive for Unionists, however. Acceptance of black testimony was hardly radical in the national context in 1865, but Unionists found that most of their opponents and especially those who had supported the Confederacy were not ready to make even this modest concession. They certainly were unwilling to take any action that would open themselves to liability for their actions during the war. By the autumn of 1865, growing awareness of a split between the president and Congress over Southern policy convinced many former Democrats that they could take advantage of the division to make as few changes relative to their former slaves as possible. Hamilton and his supporters were also aware of national politics, and remained committed to presidential reconstruction, but also kept a watchful eye on the results of the latter policy on the state's political situation. The election for delegates to the constitutional convention suggested that the impact would not be a good one for Unionists. While the majority of delegates had not been secessionists in 1861, they had supported the war. Few men who had remained loyal to the Union throughout were elected.[16] In the context of that realization, Governor Hamilton's policies began to change, and his supporters took another step toward a more radical racial policy.

At the convention, in his message of February 10, 1866, Hamilton laid out the program of action that he believed was essential for bringing about the state's restoration to the Union. The plan, for the most part, consisted of the same goals he had proposed earlier to the president. He urged the delegates to make the laws of Texas conform to the "spirit and principles, to the actual changes that attended the progress of the late war, and followed the overthrow of the rebellion." The important Unionist goal, maintaining the possibility of some sort of action against former Confederates, remained on the agenda with Hamilton's recommendation that the convention declare secession null and void ab initio. He added nothing new regarding the end of slavery and recognition of the civil rights of freedmen, still staying away from the suffrage issue even though the president had suggested some sort of qualified black voting the previous summer. He did, however, tell the convention that while he believed that the great mass of blacks were not qualified to vote, he also did not believe that they should be excluded from voting according to their race or for all time. Instead he suggested that the delegates consider creating universal rules governing suffrage that would be applied to all who sought to become voters in the future. In the end, he warned, no laws applicable solely to the freedmen would be acceptable to the North.[17]

In the convention a small group of Unionists stood with Hamilton and pushed both for ab initio and restricted black suffrage. Delegates such as E. J. Davis and Edward Degener introduced measures to achieve these goals. Degener explained that he believed reading and writing English were essential requirements for anyone who wished to vote. Conservatives, however, blocked all of these measures from ever coming to a vote on the convention floor. Worse, relative to the prospects of reunion, they restricted the rights of freedmen. As to ab initio, the delegates went out of the way to protect former Confederate officials and killed any hope of securing restitution from former Confederate officials when they passed a resolution that prohibited lawsuits against, or prosecution of, any officials who had acted under the authority of the Confederate state government. This included a prohibition against the impressment and seizure of personal property from these men to make compensation to Unionists.[18]

The convention convinced many Unionists of the failure of presidential reconstruction, but the subsequent general election provided even more proof of that fact and moved them once again toward more radical policies. Before adjourning, the convention provided for an election on June 25 to ratify the constitution and choose public officials. Unionists nominated former governor Pease, who had actively worked with Hamilton after the latter had returned. Pease campaigned on the promise of reform of government, better transportation, promotion of immigration, frontier defense, and public schools, but the main themes he and other Unionists emphasized were the need to show loyalty and to grant to the freedmen basic civil rights. In one of his speeches, Pease insisted that Congress would never readmit the state if they did not do the latter, particularly secure the rights to make contracts, bring lawsuits, and receive full and equal protection in the law, the elements of the civil rights bill being considered in Congress at the time. He even admitted that he would be willing to grant limited suffrage to blacks, on the basis of their ability to read and write, if required by Congress. On the other hand, Pease's opponent, former Unionist James W. Throckmorton, campaigned promising Texans that none of these compromises would be necessary.[19]

The election was a Unionist disaster. In fact, from the beginning of the campaign neither Pease nor other Unionists had any hope for success. As the campaign developed, Pease concluded that the former secessionist leadership still exercised considerable influence in the state. With the election only two weeks away, he informed his daughter that he had no doubt that the "secessionists are still in the majority." The election confirmed his beliefs. He and other Unionists candidates were badly defeated. Pease lost to Throckmorton by a vote of 48,631 to 12,051. While some prewar Unionists were elected to the new legislature, none who had been supporters of Pease were chosen, and no legislator secured a seat who would support the political agenda of Hamilton and Pease during the subsequent session.[20]

Unionists saw a readily apparent meaning in the election results. "The recent election," E. J. Davis wrote to Pease, "ought to satisfy every loyal man North and South that the Secession party is just as well defined and just as intensely malignant against the Union and Unionists as in the palmiest days of the Confederacy." Andrew J. Evans, a Unionist from Waco, expressed equal pessimism about the results in a letter to Congressman Thaddeus Stevens. Evans observed that in the election not a single Union man had been elected within the state. "To the same old persecuting, hell hounds of treason, we must now look for that protection to life and property we have been bereft of for six years past. Will we get it? Will the Kite protect the sparrow, will the lion protect the lamb?" Evans concluded that unless the federal government intervened to protect the lives and property of Unionists "from the assassins swords," most Unionists would have to leave the state.[21]

Such conclusions pushed Unionists further in the development of their basic political outlook, leading them to take another step toward a more radical agenda. While previously accepting the idea of limited suffrage, the majority of Unionist leaders now concluded that the only way for loyal elements to maintain power was through universal and unlimited suffrage. Ferdinand Flake, editor of a Unionist newspaper, provided insight into his own and other Unionists' thinking when he wrote, "Whenever it becomes necessary to choose between the safety of the Union, and with it, the preservation of every right belonging to Union men; and the confiscation of every disloyal estate, and unlimited negro suffrage we will be found where we are now, with the Union men." Unionist judge Colbert Caldwell believed the refusal of secessionists to make even moderate concessions led the Unionists to labor "zealously to have the President's plan set aside, and the negroes enfranchised by national authority."[22]

In their conversion to unrestricted black suffrage, Texas Unionists found themselves ahead of many Northerners in their radicalism. Jack Hamilton went to New York City shortly after the convention ended, then on to Washington on June 7. On June 20 he met with the president to discuss the situation in Texas. He afterward held a second meeting, but by June 23 Johnson had heard rumors that the provisional governor actually had come to the East at the invitation of Radical Republicans such as Speaker Schuyler Colfax and Senator Lyman Trumbull, to attack the president's policies. Whether that was his actual purpose or not is unknown, but on July 11 Hamilton addressed the Union congressional caucus and finally denounced the policy of the president, outlining all of the bad results that it had produced in Texas.[23]

That same day Hamilton and Texas Unionists Lorenzo Sherwood, a businessman from Galveston who had been a refugee in the North, and George W. Paschal Jr., a veteran of the First Texas Cavalry, joined with Unionists from other Southern states in calling for a meeting of Southern loyalists to meet in Philadelphia in September. Hamilton's role in this was critical, and the editor of the *New York Times* asserted that the governor was the man getting the convention up, although at the behest of the extreme radicals in Congress. Events associated with that convention made clear the further radicalization of Hamilton and other Texas Unionists on the issue of black suffrage. On August 31, in a speech at Philadelphia's Union League house, Hamilton denounced the "treachery" of the government and the "cruel deceptions on the Union men of the South by the present Chief Magistrate." Asserting that blacks must be included among those who had proven loyal in the past conflict, Hamilton went on to state his support for enfranchising the black man of the South. To great applause Hamilton continued: "He has proved his manhood, his integrity, his bravery. . . . You must declare this land free to all true manhood. Let us do justice though the heavens fall and then we may claim the justice of a great God."[24]

In Philadelphia, Hamilton and other Texans played major roles in managing the convention and ensuring that it ultimately approved universal suffrage. When delegates from the border states prevented passage of an appeal for universal suffrage in the report of the Committee on Address, Texas delegates were instrumental in attaching one in the report on the condition of the Southern states. "We declare," the report read, "there can be no safety for the country against the fell spirit of slavery now organized in the form of serfdom, unless the Government, by national and appropriate legislation, inforced [sic] by national authority, shall confer on every citizen in the States we represent the American birthright of impartial suffrage and equality before the law." Jack Hamilton reveled in the accomplishment, declaring: "Sir, the lightning flash of revolution has struck the tomb within which for two hundred years the body of liberty has lain and freeing the inanimate form, stands it erect to-day, advocating true equality and liberty throughout the civilized world." Greeted with cheers he went on to conclude, "And now we will unfurl our banner in the breeze, inscribed with 'Liberty, Equality and Fraternity,' and there it shall wave, falter who may, follow who dare."[25]

Afterward Hamilton and other Texans who had traveled to Philadelphia for the convention remained in the North to push for suffrage. Hamilton and the Texans became well-known as supporters of this political revolution. In his speech to the Republican state convention in Boston on September 13, Governor Hamilton indicated the extent to which he and those around him had moved. His declaration in favor of impartial universal suffrage was met by the members of the convention with "cries of 'good' and applause," and they cheered loudly at the speech's end. When General Benjamin Butler, chairman of the convention, recognized Wendell Phillips on the floor shortly afterward and asked him to come to the platform, the old abolitionist climbed to the speaker's rostrum to prolonged cheers but said he would refrain from a speech. "There is no need or place for a speech from me today," he told the crowd. "Texas out-radicals my radicalism. [Cheers.] All we need to do is to cry 'All hail!' And Amen!"[26]

As the congressional campaign progressed, the situation in Texas did little to alleviate Unionist fears. The news those in the North received from home clearly suggested that the president's policies had made it possible for their enemies to return to power, and hardened their position on black suffrage. When the legislature first met that August, it had chosen Oran M. Roberts, president of the secession convention and a wartime member of the state Supreme Court, to the U.S. Senate. Roberts could not even take the test oath. Indeed, one member of the state senate noted: "We do not want men to go there [Washington] who have already taken it [the test oath] or would do so." The subsequent passage of black codes, a vagrancy act, and apprenticeship law, and various other labor statutes designed to control the freedmen and restrict their freedom, caused one prominent Unionist to conclude that the legislature intended nothing less than to "re-enslave the negroes." The gerrymandering of congressional districts and rearranging the boundaries of judicial districts also created dismay among Unionists. One informed Pease that the congressional districts had been laid out "for the openly avowed purpose of preventing the election of any Union man or Radical." That this purpose had been achieved was clear when Texans went to the polls and elected to Congress two men who had served in the Confederate Congress, one Unionist who had joined the Confederate Army, and Confederate officer George W. Chilton who had been charged with crossing the Mexican border in 1862 to kidnap Gen. E. J. Davis. While Davis had been released, Capt. William Montgomery had also been taken and subsequently had been lynched.[27]

Hardened by such information, Texas Unionists pushed with even greater vigor for black suffrage. Aware of the limited support for suffrage in the North, Texas radicals remained concerned that Congress would somehow moderate, and pushed to keep Congress focused on the suffrage issue. General Davis wrote to Pease that he needed to explain to Northern congressmen that successful reconstruction required the full enfranchisement of the freedmen. There could be no compromise on the matter. Like other Unionists, Davis may have advocated limited suffrage initially, but now he had made up his mind that any restrictions other than very limited ones on the participation of the freedmen in the electoral process would be useless to Southern loyalists. Davis optimistically believed that the results of the congressional elections that autumn would ensure that the new Congress would come out firmly for black suffrage. Still, Davis feared that attempts to reconcile Congress and the president might water down suffrage provisions. For Davis, by the winter of 1866, there could be no compromise on the suffrage issue. Attorney General Alexander was of like mind and implored Congressman Benjamin Butler, with whom he had formed an acquaintance in Louisiana, to oust the existing government, composed "exclusively of 'public enemies,'" and extend full suffrage in order to create the majority necessary for loyal government.[28]

The Texas Unionists and their associates from the other states secured their goals when Northern voters delivered the radical vote that they hoped for. The plan of reconstruction that emerged from the next Congress gave them a form of the universal suffrage that they had sought. The First Reconstruction Act, passed over the president's veto on March 2, 1867, declared the governments that existed in the South to be provisional, and allowed the people of each state to frame new constitutions in conformity with the Constitution of the United States. Approval of these by Congress and the state's ratification of the proposed Fourteenth Amendment would result in their representation in Congress and a restoration of their normal relationship with the Union. For Unionists, the particularly significant provision of the act was its requirement that the delegates to the convention be elected by adult male citizens of the state, regardless of race, color, or previous condition. Blacks, for all practical purposes, had been enfranchised, and provisions in the proposed Fourteenth Amendment virtually ensured that this enfranchisement would be continued in the new state constitutions.[29]

On April 19, Maj. Gen. Charles Griffin, who had been appointed to direct congressional reconstruction in Texas, started the registration of voters for the proposed constitutional convention, a registration that included adult African American men. Unionists worked to secure the fullest registration of these new voters, using as their principal mechanism an organization known as the Union League. Unionist refugees had become familiar with that organization, initially a patriotic club in the North, during the war, and William Alexander had headed the executive committee of the "Loyal National League of Texas" in New Orleans. After the war, the refugees brought it to Texas and attempted to use it as a political tool in the 1866 election, but with little success. Beginning in May, Judge James Bell, one of those who had campaigned for black suffrage in the North, returned with a charter to organize a state Union League to mobilize black voters, with the first lodges created in Galveston, San Antonio, and then Austin.[30]

Accepting black suffrage and integration of black voters into the electorate proved the next step in the increasing radicalization of what would become the Texas Republican Party. The new voters were not passive in the process, and articulate black leaders emerged quickly who would participate actively in state politics for the rest of Reconstruction. Already in 1867 men such as George T. Ruby of Galveston and Shep Mullins of McClennan had emerged to become spokesmen for blacks, and were active leaders in the Union League and encouraging black registration. Both of these men would serve in the subsequent constitutional convention and in the Twelfth Legislature. The Union League also provided the vehicle for the development of long-term Republican leaders such as future legislators Richard Allen from Houston, Stephen Curtis from Brazos County, and Scipio McKee. Their success and the desire for blacks to take part in the state's political process was reflected clearly in the results of their registration efforts. By the following January, 49,497 African American men had registered, possibly as much as 98 percent of those eligible.[31] The participation of such men helped to shape the Republican agenda for the state.

Through April, blacks and whites participated in mass meetings held in Austin, Brenham, Corpus Christi, Galveston, Prairie Lea, Lockhart, San Antonio, and Waco, to organize local Republican parties. All of these meetings endorsed the same program. They avowed their support of the "National Republican Union Party," the new reconstruction acts passed by Congress, the military, and the call issued by members of the Austin meeting for all like-minded men to meet in Houston to organize a state party on July 4, 1867. The Houston meeting saw Republicans, for the first time, articulate the broad agenda that had emerged quickly in response to the new political environment. Many of the resolutions of the Houston convention had to do with national politics, and were what would be expected. Delegates pledged their support to Congress, offering their appreciation to the military commanders of the district, and asserting their belief that the National Republican Party was the only means of saving the country. They also asked for the removal of all public officials who had participated in the rebellion or who were hostile to the goals of Congress. The emergence of a biracial coalition, however, prompted new domestic demands that would become central to Texas Republicanism. Central to the program would be the promise of support for free schools for the benefit of all children, "without distinction of race or color." In another appeal directed at blacks, delegates pledged support for a homestead law that would allow the state's citizens to acquire land. Again, the plank promised a law "without distinction of race or color."[32]

At Houston another future Republican goal began to take shape. By the summer of 1867 the party's leaders had recognized that any successful biracial coalition in Texas would require protection of the newly enfranchised freedmen. While registration proceeded, party leaders discovered that their political opposition was willing to sanction violence to break up efforts at organizing blacks as voters, and to discourage participation in the political process by the freedmen. The freedmen had been the object of some violence since the war's end, but contemporaries recognized a steady increase in attacks upon freedmen who had become politically active as the registration process moved forward. In July, the military commander in Texas informed Gen. Philip Sheridan that lawlessness and outrages, including the shooting of two voting registrars in Washington County, had increased over the previous two months, and complained that few of the public officials in the state would "turn or raise his hand against the scoundrels." A Republican in eastern Texas found blacks to be the subject of widespread intimidation, threatened with the loss of their jobs unless they voted as demanded by their employers, and warned to "look out for danger" if they voted with the Yankees.[33]

An understanding of the fragility of black voter participation became all the more clear during the convention elections and in subsequent months. Republican opponents had organized in early 1868, and bands of horsemen identifying themselves as the Ku Klux Klan preyed upon black political leaders throughout the state. This clearly cut into African American voter participation. In the convention vote, despite Republican efforts to ensure a large turnout, 18 percent of registered black voters stayed away from the polls. Republican leaders realized that something had to be done, although they could not agree precisely on what action should be taken. The party's regular leaders, men like Pease and Jack Hamilton, already were looking for means to attract white voters to the party, and feared that too strident an action might threaten their efforts.

In June, blacks took control of the matter themselves. Black lead-

ers of the Loyal League, concerned with what they perceived as a reluctance to prosecute white terrorists, combined with a failure to take
a stronger stand on civil rights and also to recognize black aspirations
for political office, determined to take over leadership of the League.
At the League's annual state meeting in Austin, Ruby seized control of
the state organization with black support, replacing Judge Bell as state
president. As leader of the party's primary tool for mobilizing black
voters, a black man was in position to ensure that the party pursued a
more radical agenda regarding the rights of African Americans. In July,
at the Republican state convention, the white leaders of the party split
on a variety of questions. Ruby led the League to support the bolters,
led by General Davis and Jack Hamilton's brother Morgan, because
they promised a more rigid enforcement of the laws. By the end of the
summer of 1868, for at least one faction of the Republican Party, the
intention of protecting the rights of all races had become a central Republican idea.[34]

In the state elections of 1869 the Republican faction led by Gen.
Edmund J. Davis became the representative of the most radical ideas
that had emerged since the war's end. Davis had long accepted the idea
of full suffrage for blacks, and he now promised to protect their rights
as citizens and voters, and also to ensure that they had equal access to
the institutions provided by the state. In the end, a pledge of law and
order, and the opportunity for a public education for all were at the
center of his campaign, and promised a Texas that would be considerably different from what it had been. Davis's opponent, Jack Hamilton,
differed little in his campaign promises. He did, however, move away
from his support of blacks, condemning Davis for trying to create a
"Negro party" in his concessions to black politicians. When the votes
were counted, Davis had won. The radical promise of the Republican
program now was realized fully in his election.[35]

Davis's perception of the situation and his intentions were made
clear in his inaugural address on April 28, 1870. For the state, a new
day had arrived. He saw the return of Texas to the Union as a time for
a "fresh departure in political affairs" and one in which the American
Revolution's proclamation that "all men are created equal" would be
fulfilled. He believed events over the past years reflected a message of
Providence to Texans that there was no neutral ground between right
and wrong, and that Texans could not "afford to be unjust to the weak-
est of God's creatures. Let us be wholly right." The new Texas that he
perceived would be one in which free speech and thought would prevail, and policies would be in place that would produce a citizenry that
was law-abiding, temperate, intelligent, industrious, and prosperous.[36]

In the message that he delivered to the Texas legislature on the following day, April 29, Davis put forward the specific measures that he sought, and provided the rationale for them. Given the biracial character of the Republican coalition and the violence of the era, he not surprisingly made the establishment of law and order his first priority. While recognizing the general problem of violence, he pointed specifically to "mobs of lawless men assembling and operating in disguise," whose actions were generally "directed against the recently enfranchised," as a problem that had to be dealt with when local authorities failed to act. To establish law and order, the governor recommended that the legislature implement a militia system that included within it a national guard, armed and ready to act quickly; a state police force; state support for the construction of jails; restrictions on carrying personal firearms; and authority for the governor to temporarily establish martial law in lawless districts.[37]

Next only to the establishment of law and order, Davis urged the legislature to take steps to ensure the constitutional provision to provide for the education of all children of scholastic age with a system of universal public education. "No money discreetly expended in promotion of universal public education," he asserted, "can be considered lost in an economical point of view." He went further, however, to insist that education not only served an economic function, but also would help to quell the crime that beset the state. Ultimately, however, he argued that education was a "special necessity" in a country where government depended on the will of the people. Republican institutions and "universal suffrage" would work only if universal education was provided. In the next three years, many of the programs sought by Davis were implemented. Although the Republicans had seized control of both houses of the state legislature, many white Republicans turned out to be relatively conservative on questions of law and order and civil rights. Davis achieved success, however, in large part because he found strong allies for his program among the black members elected to the legislature. In the Senate, George Ruby, who had been elected from Galveston, proved a steady supporter of the governor, and Matthew Gaines from Washington County, while sometimes a critic, added his vote. Twelve African Americans served in the House of Representatives. They did not vote as a unit, but the majority helped ensure that Texas moved ahead with the agenda that had been put forward by Davis. African Americans ultimately held the balance of power that kept Texas on the radical path.[38]

Despite contemporary controversy and early scholarly criticism of Davis and the Republican agenda, recent scholarship has shown that the program that grew out of this early biracial coalition promised to achieve exactly what Davis and others thought that it would, a major change in the very culture and character of Texas. The crowning achievement would be the system of education. The system represented a radical departure from past efforts, with funding based primarily on state revenues distributed to counties on the basis of their student population. This ensured an equal share of educational monies for students in all districts. The Republican state school superintendent supervised a system with a standardized academic year and a common curriculum to ensure that all students received the same opportunities for schooling and also acquired the same basic knowledge. The plan even required that teachers be certified before they could teach in the schools. By December 1871, 1,324 schools had been opened under the new program, enrolling 28 percent of the school-aged population. The numbers grew by the end of the spring term in 1872 to 2,067 schools, attended by 56 percent of potential students. Critically, in terms of the long-range development of radical ideas, the state, while segregated, nonetheless provided schools for black Texans. Unfortunately, within a year, the schools had become the target of the Republicans' political opponents, starved by the refusal of taxpayers to pay their school taxes, and consequently unable to realize their full potential. At the end of Reconstruction, the system would be replaced by a decentralized system with all of the inequities inherent in such a plan.[39]

The Republican state police and militia, institutions surrounded with controversy in their day, actually appear to have achieved considerable success in suppressing the lawlessness and banditry that plagued postwar Texas. Under the command of Adjutant General James Davidson, the state police began compiling lists of men at large, subject to arrest. In the first seven months of operation of the State Police, its officers arrested 978 criminals. During 1871 another 3,602 were captured. The State Guard was used in conjunction with Governor Davis's declaration of martial law in two instances to assist local law enforcement officers unable to maintain order, and on two occasions, in Freestone and Limestone counties, to stop election-related violence. While these institutions suppressed crime and violence in general, they also were unique in their efforts in providing protection to blacks as well as whites. Like the schools, however, both the State Police and the State Guard became objects of opposition criticism, and in 1872 the legislature repealed the police bill and also moved to destroy the power of the Guard.[40]

In the end, despite initial success, the Republican revolution failed. Its opponents, criticizing the taxes necessary to implement it and the very idea that African Americans should share some part of the largesse of the state or its protection were able to mobilize white voters and terrorize black voters to the point that by 1872 they had gained control over the legislature and in 1873 the governor's office. They effectively prevented the protection of the frontier by undermining efforts at financing frontier military companies with bonds. They dismantled the State Police. They destroyed the school system with a taxpayer's revolt that starved the schools and their teachers. When fully in power, they did nothing to replace these institutions. They would leave frontier protection to the federal government. They created a new police force known as the Texas Rangers, but did not use it to protect the civil rights of the newly enfranchised African Americans. They created a school system that discriminated against African Americans and provided an inferior education to the state's white children. As a result, Texas would remain a land of cotton and cattle into the twentieth century, a land untouched by the revolution that appeared to have been unleashed by war and Reconstruction.

What had unleashed this potential revolution? The development of the radical Republican Party in Texas clearly did not represent the carrying out of Northern policy in the state by unscrupulous office seekers. Instead, it was to a large degree a homegrown party produced by the outrages of the Civil War and the efforts of the war's victims to secure political power in its wake. The course that they took to a large degree was determined not by what was happening in the North, but rather by the actions of those who they opposed. Texas Republicans embraced the need for radical policy even before the majority in Congress, responding to their own experiences with policy and programs they believed necessary to sustain loyal government in the South. In the spring of 1866, the future radical Colbert Caldwell had warned Texans that policies toward blacks would change if Texans refused to accept the results of the war. "The same causes which provoked and rendered necessary their emancipation, are now at work, and will end in their enfranchisement, and if it shall ever occur, its real authors will be the radical secessionists, as they are of emancipation."[41] Caldwell was writing about black suffrage, but his perception proved prophetic for all aspects of race relations, and white intransigence spurred the development of the entire program of the Republican Party in Texas. Texas radicalism was to a great extent homegrown.

NOTES

1.　*Flake's Daily Bulletin* [Galveston], July 6, 1867.
2.　Charles W. Ramsdell, *Reconstruction in Texas* (New York: Columbia University Press, 1910), 166, 317 (first quote), 318 (second quote);

W. C. Nunn, *Texas Under the Carpetbaggers* (Austin: University of Texas Press, 1962), 4.

3. For works that sought the origins of Texas Republicanism, see James Alex Baggett, "Birth of the Texas Republican Party," *Southwestern Historical Quarterly* 79 (July 1974): 1–20, (hereafter cited as SWHQ), and "Origins of Early Texas Republican Leadership," *Journal of Southern History* 40 (August 1974): 441–50; Dale A. Somers, "James P. Newcomb: The Making of a Radical," *SWHQ*, 72 (April 1969): 449–69; Randolph B. Campbell, "George W. Whitmore: East Texas Unionist," *East Texas Historical Journal* 28 (1990): 17–28.

4. *State Gazette* [Austin], September 8, 1855 (first quote); *Southern Intelligencer* [Austin], May 25, 1859 (second quote); John L. Waller, *Colossal Hamilton of Texas: Andrew Jackson Hamilton, Militant Unionist and Reconstruction Governor* (El Paso: Texas Western Press, 1968), 19; Llerena Friend, *Sam Houston: The Great Designer* (Austin: University of Texas Press, 1954), 323.

5. B. H. Epperson to E. M. Pease, May 22, 1861, Pease-Graham-Niles Papers, Center for Austin History, Austin Public Library, hereafter cited as CAH, APL.

6. B. H. Epperson to E. M. Pease, May 22, 1861, Pease Papers, CAH, APL; H. E. McCulloch to S. B. Davis, March 3, 25, 1862, *Official Records of the War of the Rebellion* (Washington: Government Printing Office, various), Ser. I, vol. 9, 704–705 (hereafter cited as OR); General Orders, No. 45, May 30, 1862, in OR, Ser. I, vol. 9, 716; G.O. No. 1, December 30, 1861, in San Antonio *Herald*, January 25, 1862; G. O. No. 3, April 24, 1862, OR, Ser. I, vol. 9, 709, announced Bee's assumption of command; P. O. Hébert to S. Cooper, October 11, 1862, OR, Ser. I, vol. 53, 892, indicates that Bee declared martial law shortly after assuming command; see also Hamilton Bee to S. B. Davis, October 21, 1862, OR, Ser. I, vol. 53, 454–55.

7. Lizzie Davis to Dear Friend, September 14, 1871, clipping, Lizzie Davis Civil War Scrapbook, David and Harriet Condon Family Collection, Middleburg, Virginia.

8. Alwyn Barr, "Records of the Confederate Military Commission in San Antonio, July 2, October 10, 1862," *SWHQ* 73 (October 1969), 47–48. See also George W. Paschal, *The Handbook of Texas Online*, http://www.tshaonline.org/handbook/online/articles/PP/fpa46_print .html (accessed May 2, 2009). For a description of violence aimed at pro-Union sympathizers in northeastern Texas, see Richard McCaslin, *Tainted Breeze: The Great Hanging at Gainesville, Texas, October, 1862* (Baton Rouge: Louisiana State University Press, 1994), and David Pickering and Judy Falls, *Brush Men and Vigilantes: Civil*

War Dissent in Texas (College Station: Texas A&M University Press, 2000).

9.   T. R. Havins, "Administration of the Sequestration Act in the Confederate District Court of the Western District of Texas, 1862–1865," *SWHQ* 43, passim.

10. H. P. Bee to A. J. Hamilton, November 6, 1865, Hamilton Papers, Governors Papers, Texas State Library and Archives (hereafter cited as TSLA); Ballinger Diary, June 10, 1865 (quote), William P. Ballinger Papers, Center for American History, University of Texas at Austin (hereafter cited as CAH, UTA); *New York Times*, April 1, 1866, p. 1.

11. Alexander letter quoted in *Flake's Daily Bulletin*, June 21, 1866; Colbert Caldwell to Ferdinand Flake, *Flake's Daily Bulletin*, April 13, 1867.

12. Elisha M. Pease to J. H. Starr, August 19, 1865, James Harper Starr Papers, CAH, UTA.

13. "Hamilton Speech," *Galveston Daily News (Supplement)*, August 6, 1865, (quote); J. W. Throckmorton to B. H. Epperson, August 6, 27, 1865, B. H. Epperson Papers, CAH, UTA; William Alexander to Francis P. Blair Sr., June 8, 1865, and A. J. Hamilton to A. Johnson, November 27, 1865, Andrew Johnson Papers, Library of Congress.

14. Speech quoted in *Galveston Daily News*, September 20, 1865.

15. A. J. Hamilton to A. Johnson, November 27, 1865, Andrew Johnson Papers, Library of Congress.

16. *New York Times*, April 1, 1866.

17. *Journal of the Constitutional Convention of 1866*, 16–27, 21 (quote).

18. E. Degener to John Sherman, John Sherman Papers, Library of Congress; Benjamin C. Truman to *Times*, February 10, in *New York Times*, March 5, 1866; Benjamin C. Truman to *Times*, February 14, 1886, *New York Times*, March 11, 1866, 1; Benjamin C. Truman to *Times*, March 24, 1866, *New York Times*, April 1, 1866, 1; C. Caldwell to editor, March 29, 1867, *Galveston Daily News*, April 1, 1867; C. C. Herbert to editor, June 3, 1866, *Galveston Daily News*, June 8, 1866; *Journal of the Constitutional Convention of 1866*, 81.

19. *Flake's Daily Bulletin*, April 11, 1866; *Galveston Daily News*, May 11, 1866; E. M. Pease to the People of Texas, *San Antonio Express*, May 24, 1866; J. W. Throckmorton to B. H. Epperson, April 25, 1866, Ben H. Epperson Papers, CAH, UTA.

20. E. M. Pease to Carrie Pease, June 10, 1866 (quote), May 18, 1866, CAH, APL; Mike Kingston, Sam Attlesey, and Mary Crawford, *The Texas Almanac's Political History of Texas* (Austin: Eakin Press, 1992), 61; Patsy McDonald Spaw, ed., *The Texas Senate, Volume 2,*

Civil War to the Eve of Reform, 1861–1889 (College Station: Texas A&M University Press, 1999), pp. 53–77.

21. E. J. Davis to E. M. Pease, July 14, 1866 (first quote), Pease-Graham-Niles Papers, AHC, APL; A. J. Evans to Thaddeus Stevens, July 8, 1866 (second quote), Thaddeus Stevens Papers, Library of Congress.

22. *Flake's Daily Bulletin*, February 4, 1866 (first quote); C. Caldwell to editor, March 29, 1867, (second quote), *Galveston Daily News*, April 1, 1867.

23. *Galveston Daily News*, July 5, 1866; *New York Times*, June 22, 1866; *New York Herald*, June 6, 1866, quoted in *Flake's Daily Bulletin*, July 4, 1866; *New York Tribune*, July 12, 1866.

24. "Address of Southern Loyalists," July 11, 1866, *New York Tribune*, June 12, 1866; *New York Times*, July 11, 1866; *Philadelphia Inquirer*, September 1, 1866 (quotes).

25. *Philadelphia Inquirer*, September 8, 1866.

26. *New York Tribune*, September 14, 1866; T. H. Duval to E. M. Pease, August 9, 1866, Pease-Graham-Niles Papers, CAH, APL.

27. R. K. Gaston to O. M. Roberts, August 24, 1866 (first quote), and see also W. M. Neyland to Roberts, September 29, 1866, Oran M. Roberts Correspondence, CAH, UTA; J. L. Haynes to E. M. Pease, October 4, 1866 (second quote), November 28, 1866 (second quote), Pease-Graham-Niles Papers, CAH, APL; Patsy McDonald Spaw, ed., *The Texas Senate, Volume 2 , Civil War to the Eve of Reform, 1861–1889* (College Station: Texas A&M University Press, 1999), 65.

28. E. J. Davis to E. M. Pease, November 24, 1866, Pease Papers, CAH, APL; William Alexander to B. F. Butler, November 23, 1866, Benjamin F. Butler Papers, Library of Congress; George W. Paschal Jr., to Thaddeus Stevens, January 7, 1867, Thaddeus Stevens Papers, Library of Congress.

29. George P. Sanger, ed., *The Statues at Large, Treaties and Proclamations of the United States of America from December, 1865, to March, 1867*, vol. XIV (Boston: Little, Brown, 1868), 428–29.

30. General Order, April 19, 1867, in *Flake's Daily Bulletin*, April 21, 1867; Citizens of Texas to Nathaniel Banks, March 7, 1865, Nathaniel P. Banks Papers, Library of Congress; E. B. Cushing to E. M. Pease, Mar. 24, 1866, Pease Papers, AHC, APL; J. W. Throckmorton to B. H. Epperson, April 17, 25, 1866, B. H. Epperson Papers, CAH, UTA; *Flake's Daily Bulletin*, July 24, August 26, 1865, January 12, 1867; *Galveston Daily News*, July 25, 1865, June 29, July 25, 1866; T. H. Duval to A. J. Hamilton, May 29, 1867, A. J. Hamilton Papers, CAH, UTA.

31. *Flake's Daily Bulletin*, July 5, 6, 7, 1867, February 8, 1868; *Galveston*

Daily News, July 7, 19, 1867; Carl H. Moneyhon, *Republicanism in Reconstruction Texas* (Austin: University of Texas Press, 1980), 71.

32. *Flake's Daily Bulletin,* April 30, May 5, 15, 16, 22, June 1, 9, July 6 (quote), 1867; *Galveston Daily News,* May 23, 1867.

33. Charles Griffin to Philip Sheridan, July 15, 1867, Philip Sheridan Papers, Library of Congress; C. Caldwell to E. M. Pease, August 20, 1867, Pease Gubernatorial Papers, TSLA.

34. *Flake's Bulletin,* June 28, August 13, 15, 16, 19, 1868; *Austin Republican,* August 15, 1868; *San Antonio Express,* August 21, 1868; *Galveston Daily News,* June 23, 1868; Republican State Executive Committee, *Proceedings of the Republican State Convention Assembled at Austin, August 12, 1868* (Austin: Daily Republican Book & Job Office, 1868), passim; U.S. Congress, *Senate Executive Documents,* 40th Cong., 2nd. Sess., no. 53 (Serial 1317).

35. E. J. Davis to J. P. Newcomb, July 4, 1869, Newcomb Papers, CAH, UTA; *Flake's Bulletin,* September 22, 24, 1869; *Galveston Daily News,* September 16, October 10, 1869.

36. Texas Legislature, 12th Leg., 1st Sess., *House Journal,* 14–15, quote 14.

37. *Austin Republican,* May 2, 1870.

38. *Austin Republican,* May 2, 1870. Of all topics related to Texas Republicanism, the one that has received the most attention has been the emergence and actions of African American leaders. See in particular Alwyn Barr, "Black Legislators of Reconstruction Texas," *Civil War History* 32 (December 1986), 340–52; Barry Crouch, "Self-Determination and local Black Leaders" *Phylon* 39 (December 1978), 344–55; and "Self-Determination and Local Black Leaders in Texas," *East Texas Historical Journal* 31 (Spring 1993), 41–58; Merline Pitre, *Through Many Dangers, Toils and Snares: The Black Leadership of Texas, 1868–1900* (Austin: Eakin Press, 1995), "The Evolution of Black Political Participation in Reconstruction Texas," *East Texas Historical Journal* 26 (1988): 36–45, and "Richard Allen: the Chequered Career of Houston's First Black State Legislator," *Houston Review* 8 (1986): 79–88; J. Mason Brewer, *Negro Legislators of Texas and Their Descendents: A History of the Negro in Texas Politics from Reconstruction to Disenfranchisement* (Dallas: Mathis Publishing, 1935); Monroe N. Work, "Some Negro Members of Reconstruction Legislatures: Texas," *Journal of Negro History* 5 (1929): 111–13; Carl H. Moneyhon, "George T. Ruby and the Politics of Expedience in Texas," in *Southern Black Leaders of the Reconstruction Era,* ed. Howard N. Rabinowitz (Urbana: University of Illinois Press, 1982), 364–78; and Ann Patton Malone, "Matt Gaines: Reconstruction Politician," in *Black Leaders: Texans for Their Times,* ed., Alwyn Barr

and Robert A. Calvert (Austin: Texas State Historical Association, 1981), 49–81.

39. Carl H. Moneyhon, *Texas after the Civil War: The Struggle of Reconstruction* (College Station: Texas A&M University Press, 2004), 146–50. Little has been written about the Republican school system. For an overview of the basic operations, see Frederick Eby, *The Development of Education in Texas* (New York: Macmillan, 1925).

40. Moneyhon, *Texas After the Civil War,* 139–43; Ann Patton Baenziger, "The Texas State Police during Reconstruction: A Reexamination," *SWHQ* 72 (April 1969): 470–91; William T. Field Jr., "The Texas State Police, 1870–1873," *Texas Military History* 5 (Fall, 1965): 131–41; Otis Singletary, "The Texas Militia During Reconstruction," *SWHQ* 60 (July 1956): 23–35.

41. C. Caldwell to editor, *Houston Telegraph,* April 29, 1866, in *Galveston Daily News,* May 3, 1866.

REBEL FARMERS
The Texas Farmers' Alliance

Donna A. Barnes

The Farmers' Alliance had its beginnings in a time of great hardship for farmers. Beginning in the mid-1870s, crop prices began to fall sharply. Texas farmers were hit hardest by the decline in cotton prices. Prior to 1875, cotton prices had fluctuated between $.12 and $.18 per pound. In 1875, the price fell below $.12 per pound and at one point fell as low as $.046 per pound. Profit margins were under pressure since production costs ranged between $.05 and $.08 per pound—the cost varying by soil quality.[1]

It is important to note that poor economic conditions do not inherently create viable protest groups. Groups that seek to mobilize protest often encounter difficulties. Such groups must develop a consensus on two fronts—first, in regard to the diagnosis of the causes of their problem, and, second, in regard to which strategies hold the most promise of redressing those causes. The nature of the derived consensus can, in turn, be used by scholars in determining whether group members are best viewed as reformers or radicals. Reform groups are those that contend that their problems can be effectively addressed with relatively modest structural or cultural changes in society. In contrast, radical groups conclude that some aspect of society needs to be completely changed or circumvented. Their ideologies usually contain elements of class consciousness wherein they argue that society as presently constructed favors the elite and works against the best interests of the working class. The Farmers' Alliance is an interesting organization because it contained both reform and radical factions, with a persistent tension between those two factions and changes over time in which faction was dominant.

There are only two major works on the Farmers' Alliance in Texas. No account of the Texas Alliance can ignore Lawrence Goodwyn's seminal book *Democratic Promise*,[2] which is heavily based on his research of the Alliance in Texas. Goodwyn highlighted the early cooperative strategies of the Alliance movement, identifying them as the primary impetus to the mobilization successes of the movement. He also correctly identified the Alliance as the crucial precursor to the third-party movement now best known as the Populist movement. The other close analysis of the Alliance in Texas is my own work, *Farmers in Rebellion*,[3] from which this chapter extensively borrows.

The birthplace of the Farmers' Alliance was Lampasas County, Texas, where in September 1877 farmers gathered to discuss their economic plight and to form a "Grand State Farmers' Alliance." They, however, held diverse views on what strategies to adopt. Some argued that their problems stemmed from misguided government policies. While one faction felt these misguided policies were best addressed through third-party politics, loyal Democrats within the group insisted that reforms were possible through pressure politics within the Democratic Party. Others argued that the Alliance should limit itself to nonpartisan, educational efforts to promote more efficient farming practices. Still others were strong advocates of purchasing and marketing cooperatives.[4]

Given the complexities of society, there often are diverse views concerning who or what to blame for social problems and what strategies to adopt when seeking redress. Unless some consensus can be reached, a protest group cannot thrive. Certainly this was the case in the early history of the Alliance in Texas. When one faction pushed for the Alliance organization in Lampasas County to endorse independent Greenback Party candidates in the 1880 elections, a fatal schism developed.[5]

The nascent, organizational branches of the Alliance in surrounding counties were spared the intense political disputes and survived the 1880 elections intact. Growth was slow, however, and enthusiasm was hard to maintain as time passed and little was accomplished. The state organ of the Alliance in its early years, the *Rural Citizen*, made very few references to strategies for addressing the agricultural crisis. Aside from a few articles on scientific farming methods to increase crop yields, the paper was filled with insipid articles on topics such as color coordination in clothing, proper sleeping positions, the courage of Southern women, and the origins of the stars and stripes.[6]

By 1883, the Alliance was struggling to survive. Only thirty of the one hundred local Alliance groups bothered to send delegates to the annual convention. It was clear that if something were not done, the Alliance would die. Recognizing this, Alliance president W. L. Garvin created a full-time, salaried position for a traveling lecturer, and appointed S.O. Daws to the position, instructing him to travel around the state to infuse vitality into existing local Alliances and to organize new local Alliances.[7]

Daws revitalized the Alliance by facilitating a discussion of what strategies might best help farmers. This discussion carried over to the semiannual Alliance convention in February 1884. When the annual state convention was held in August 1884, 180 delegates attended— a stark contrast to the paltry number attending previously. More than six hundred delegates attended the annual convention in 1885, and a formula had to be devised to limit the number of delegates from each county at future conventions.[8]

The growth of the Alliance was largely the result of the hope created by its newly proposed strategies for alleviating the problems of farmers. The strategies focused on both the purchasing and marketing systems. The first strategy adopted was the trade agreement, a rather conservative strategy that attempted to address perceived problems in the purchasing system. In fact, had the Alliance not moved on to other strategies, it would not have qualified as an example of Texas radicalism. The trade agreement required no major change in the structure of the purchasing system within agriculture. It worked as follows: a local Alliance committee conferred with local merchants to see who would charge the lowest markup on wholesale prices in return for a guarantee of the retail business of county Alliance members. Since losing the bid for a trade agreement meant a decline in customers, there was a strong incentive for merchants to secure trade agreements.

While such agreements at least marginally improved the economic well-being of many Alliance farmers, it was not long before Alliance leaders began criticizing the strategy. Several problems undercut its effectiveness: First, a trade agreement only affected cash prices for supplies. Therefore, it did not help Alliance farmers who could only buy goods on credit. Second, a trade agreement stipulated a predetermined charge above wholesale cost. Farmers, however, did not have access to wholesale cost information. This made it difficult to confirm compliance with the terms of the agreement. Finally, problems occurred when cooperating merchants were pressured by wholesalers to repudiate the agreements. Since most retail merchants bought from wholesalers on credit, the latter had a stake in retail profits. When trade agreements threatened the viability of retailers without such agreements, wholesalers retaliated by threatening to cut off credit to merchants cooperating with the Alliance.[9]

Given the limited success of the trade agreement strategy, the Alliance called for the creation of Alliance-owned cooperatives to circumvent the existing retail system. The creation of cooperatives, amidst tirades about the excessive pricing and greed within the existing retail system, qualified the Alliance for inclusion within the ranks of Texas radicalism.

The capitalization features of Alliance cooperatives varied. In one approach, farmers had to own a minimum number of shares of stock in the cooperative in order to buy from it. But no stock dividends were paid so that goods could be sold at close to cost. Other cooperatives utilized a dividend-paying approach. Both approaches had advantages and drawbacks. Operating costs were lower in the no-dividends approach, allowing for rock-bottom pricing. There was no monetary incentive, however, to buy more than the minimum number of shares required for trading at the co-op. Cooperatives utilizing this approach struggled to achieve adequate capitalization. While dividend-paying cooperatives had an easier time securing capital, the dividends added to operating costs. Consequently, prices were not reduced much more than with the earlier trade agreement strategy.[10]

An additional problem was that co-ops were irrelevant to farmers who depended on credit. The co-ops lacked the capital to extend farmers lines of credit, and attempts to deviate from cash-only transactions were unsuccessful.[11]

Limitations aside, cooperatives played an important role in mobilizing Alliance support, with some cooperatives selling goods up to 30 percent below pre-co-op prices. As time passed, however, more cooperatives struggled. Competing merchants began cutting their cash prices and compensated for their losses by increasing credit prices charged for goods. This action not only undermined the cooperatives, it also intensified the troubles of indebted farmers. The Alliance found itself pitting the interests of indebted farmers against farmers with the financial means to make cash purchases.[12] By late 1888, the Alliance was questioning the utility of cooperatives: "Reports of local cooperative stores, with few exceptions, do not encourage such ventures. They doubtless can be successful, but experience proves they generally are not."[13]

In regard to strategies of the Alliance addressing the marketing system, some contextual detail is necessary. In the nineteenth century, brokers at the various cotton exchanges bought and sold cotton for a flat rate per bale. Only very large orders were handled through the exchanges. Small farmers had to sell to their local merchant or a traveling cotton buyer. The latter bought cotton and stored it in warehouses until enough was amassed that it could be sold to exchange brokers. The traveling cotton buyer sent grade, quantity, and asking-price information to brokers who then negotiated deals with buyers, after which the cotton was shipped from the various warehouses directly to the buyers.

Alliance leaders hoped to gain leverage in the cotton market by having county Alliances establish cotton yards that would bulk the cotton of their members. The reasoning was that bulked cotton sales would attract multiple buyers, thereby introducing competition into the bidding process, and that the convenience of buying in bulk would justify higher prices as well. Should prices not rise, Alliance leaders urged farmers to withhold their cotton from market.[14]

County Alliances embraced the strategy, bulking up to over a thousand cotton bales. Early reports of success drew media attention. At one widely touted sale, farmers received about $.85 more per bale than the average market price.[15] Many local Alliances, however, struggled to make the strategy work. The most serious problems with the bulking strategy were experienced in areas where many farmers depended on crop-lien loans. These loans were granted by local merchants throughout the year for supplies and food, collateralized by the farmer's cotton. Much of the cotton crop had to be turned over to merchants to satisfy the terms of the crop liens, making bulking and withholding impossible.[16]

Sometimes the bulking strategy faltered because of the difficulty attracting multiple buyers. If traveling cotton buyers could easily accumulate cotton, they had little incentive to pay a premium for bulked cotton. They made their best profit by buying at the lowest price, then bulking the cotton themselves to sell. For the Alliance bulking strategy to work, it had to corner enough of the available cotton to make it difficult for traveling cotton buyers to get sufficient quantities of cotton through individual sales, a very daunting challenge.[17]

By 1887, with its strategies floundering, the Alliance called a special convention in order for the dynamic Alliance president, Charles Macune, to propose a new strategy. Macune had already become one of the most important leaders within the Alliance in Texas, and he would eventually play a major role on the national scene as the Alliance spread throughout the southern states and beyond. His challenge in 1887 was to keep the Alliance in Texas from self-destructing. He did this by proposing an "Alliance Exchange," which would coordinate the marketing of the cotton crop of Alliance members throughout Texas and act as a central purchasing house for supplies and dry goods. It was a bold attempt to bypass the existing purchasing and marketing systems in agriculture. The hope was that with large-volume purchasing, the Exchange could act as a wholesaler and purchase goods directly from manufacturers at considerable savings. In bulking cotton state-wide, the Exchange planned to bypass both traveling cotton buyers and exchange brokers, and market cotton directly to textile mills.[18]

Macune also spoke of the need to organize the entire Cotton Belt to offset the existing power of corporations. He proposed a merger with the Louisiana Farmers' Union, a similar organization. After the merger, the Alliance adopted the official name of the National Farmers' Alliance and Cooperative Union. The plan was to merge with other similar state farmer organizations and, in states where they were absent, to create such organizations. If the Alliance Exchange proved its success, it could be expanded across the cotton-producing states of the South.[19]

The Alliance Exchange opened for business in Dallas in September 1887. To function as planned, it needed an estimated $500,000 to underwrite purchasing and marketing contracts. To raise this amount, each Alliance member was assessed two dollars.[20] As Exchange assessments began trickling in, cotton harvesting was beginning. So the Exchange focused on its marketing program. County Alliances throughout the state began bulking cotton. The plan called for them to send quantity and grade information, along with cotton samples, to Exchange headquarters where buyers could view them. There were some early successes. In one transaction, fifteen hundred bales were shipped to Europe from various Alliance cotton yards throughout Texas.[21]

There was a serious limitation to the Exchange marketing program, however, one that had long characterized Alliance strategies. Farmers dependent on debt financing could not participate; they had to turn over much of their crop to the merchants to whom they were indebted. If the goal of mobilizing most small cotton farmers was to be realized, an innovative strategy was needed. To address this need, Macune devised a joint-note program whereby members of local Alliances would collectively make a joint note to collateralize the amount of money needed to supply farmers from each locality. Each signer would specify the number of acres cultivated in cotton and grains, as well as any cattle owned. The joint note was then sent, along with the order for supplies, to a county Alliance agent who examined the joint note and, if acceptable, signed and mailed it to Exchange headquarters. The joint note was then examined by a committee at the Exchange. The proposed charge for approved notes, 1 percent interest per month on the loan balance, represented huge savings for farmers, given that interest rates on crop-lien loans held by local merchants typically were at least 20 percent annually.[22]

Following the announcement of the joint-note program, membership in the Texas Alliance soared. Farmers seemed to believe that they had finally harnessed their collective power to challenge the prevailing purchasing and marketing systems in agriculture. Membership doubled from about seventy-five thousand to one hundred fifty thousand.[23] Initially, Macune planned for the joint notes to remain at the Exchange. The slow rate of collecting Exchange assessment fees, however, did not allow this to happen. The Exchange authorized joint notes worth over $200,000 in the fall of 1887, yet had collected only about $20,000 in assessment monies. There was no choice but to use the joint notes as collateral for bank loans, which could then be used to purchase supplies.[24]

Dallas bankers, however, refused to loan money to the Exchange, and Macune claimed that they also poisoned the possibility of securing loans in other cities. Alliance leaders called an emergency meeting of local Alliances to rally behind the Exchange. They set Saturday, June 9, 1888, as the day to redeem the Exchange. Macune proposed that each Alliance member be assessed an additional two dollars, with the entirety of this money being prorated among various creditors.[25] After receiving ample pledges of financial support during the June 9 meetings, the Alliance claimed that the Exchange was finally on solid financial footing. The optimism, however, was unfounded. The Exchange never received more than $78,000 in capitalization. The joint-note plan had to be suspended before the 1888 harvest. Cash-only purchases were once again the only option. By the end of 1889, creditors foreclosed, and the Exchange building in Dallas was sold at auction.[26]

In his book *Democratic Promise: The Populist Movement in America*, historian Lawrence Goodwyn has attributed the collapse of the Exchange to the hostility of established businesses, which is consistent with the claims made by the Alliance at the time of the collapse. Michael Schwartz has also drawn a similar conclusion in his book, *Radical Protest and Social Structure: The Southern Farmers' Alliance and Cotton Tenancy, 1880–1890*.[27] The "business-hostility" explanation, however, overlooks a significant factor in the collapse of the Exchange: its poor capitalization made it a very risky venture. The joint notes did not help. City banks had always resisted granting crop-lien loans to farmers far removed from the banks' operations: it was difficult to assess the risk entailed in such loans, and in cases of default city bankers would be turned into cotton merchants.[28]

If the Exchange had been properly capitalized, it never would have been put in the difficult position of seeking bank loans. The crucial question is: Why was it so poorly capitalized? The membership of the Alliance in Texas peaked in 1888, with reported figures varying from two hundred thousand to three hundred thousand.[29] Using the lower figure, the two-dollar Exchange assessment should have produced $400,000 in capital reserves.

Goodwyn argued that many Alliance members were too poor to pay the Exchange assessment. There is some merit to this argument. Some members claimed that they were unable to pay the assessment, but wished the best for the struggling Exchange.[30] Poverty, however, is not a sufficient explanation. While the Exchange was struggling to survive, some local Alliances focused instead on funding local cooperative enterprises, such as gins and grain mills.[31] One Alliance member complained: "Six months ago I was as zealous for cooperative stores as any man, but today I wish there was not one in existence. Why? Because they do not work in harmony with the Exchange."[32] Another Alliance member wrote: "We are friends of the Exchange, but local interest in our mill and cotton yard has kept us back, and many good men are overtaxed."[33]

Why did the Exchange have difficulty competing with other Alliance endeavors for needed capital? Some of the answer lies in its approach to financing: a flat two-dollar assessment per Alliance member. Macune had insisted on this approach, arguing that it ensured that all farmers benefited, not simply those with surplus money to invest in dividend-paying stock. Without dividends, lower prices were possible. Unfortunately his choice of capital procurement failed. Many poor farmers were unable to pay the Exchange assessment. Yet there was no monetary incentive for farmers in better financial shape to pay more than the required assessment. The self-interest of the more prosperous farmers led them to support more generously the dividend-paying Alliance projects underway at the local level.[34]

Another neglected factor in the Exchange's collapse is the internal dissension over the explanation for the Exchange crisis. At the onset of the crisis, Alliance circulars blamed merchant-banker collusion. This explanation was soon challenged by an incriminating article in the *Texas Farmer*, which argued that the directors of the Exchange were hiding their business incompetence and inexperience behind misrepresentations.[35] Prospects for saving the Exchange were undercut further when an internal Alliance investigatory committee, the Committee of Five, harshly criticized the business acumen of the managers of the Exchange.[36]

Sensitive to the decline in Alliance membership after the attack on the Exchange, Alliance leaders met to discuss a course of action. A new investigatory Committee of Eleven was formed, with one member from each congressional district of Texas. This committee eventually issued a report vindicating Macune and other Exchange officials of wrongdoing. The report placed blame for the Exchange crisis squarely on the shoulders of the Alliance membership, arguing that members had inadequately capitalized the Exchange. An independent accountant who audited Exchange transactions concurred with the Committee of Eleven report.[37]

The damage done by the earlier accusations, however, was irreversible. The survival of the Alliance may well have been at stake if it had not been for the struggle with the large corporations that manufactured jute, the primary material used to wrap cotton bales. Jute bagging was essential to preparing cotton for sale. Each cotton bale was held together with over six yards of jute bagging. In the summer of 1888 the price of jute had increased almost 60 percent. The price increase had come to symbolize the ability of large manufacturers to manipulate prices and unfairly extract greater profits to the detriment of small farmers. This perception was strengthened by a government investigation that concluded that jute prices had soared as a result of the creation of a jute-bagging consortium. The eight major jute-bagging corporations had signed an agreement binding each of them to a selling price set by a majority vote of the members of the consortium.[38]

The annual Alliance convention in 1889 was dominated by a discussion of the jute consortium. The Alliance, which had by now grown into a national organization with local Alliances throughout the South, served as an excellent organizational vehicle whereby farmers could be quickly galvanized to develop a strategy to undermine the jute trust. Talk of a jute boycott swept through the Alliance. Local Alliances throughout Texas began to pass jute boycott resolutions. With the cotton harvest season of 1888 rapidly approaching, a jute bagging substitute was needed for a boycott to be viable. Cotton could not be marketed without protective bagging. The president of the Alliance in Texas, Evan Jones, called for farmers to withhold their cotton from the market until a suitable alternative to jute bagging could be provided. By October 1888, he arranged for Lane Cotton Mills in New Orleans to manufacture a bagging substitute made of cotton. On such short notice, however, the mill could not supply enough of the alternative bagging, so many farmers had no choice but to use jute bagging.[39]

In anticipation of the next cotton harvest, Alliance leaders worked to inform farmers of the advantages of the alternative bagging. First, manufacturing enough cotton bagging to fully replace jute bagging would consume about 125,000 bales of cotton, thereby, increase the demand for cotton. Second, the contract with Lane Mills ensured that cotton bagging would be manufactured in the South, providing employment for thousands. Third, cotton bagging was less flammable than jute, more impervious to moisture, and more resistant to sand

and dirt; therefore, Alliance leaders hoped to secure lower insurance rates.[40]

However, in order to replace jute as the preferred bagging material, the Alliance needed a sufficient supply of cotton bagging. This problem was more difficult to address than Alliance leaders had anticipated. An Alliance committee appointed to study the bagging issue reported that existing looms in most mills were incapable of producing cotton bagging in the dimensions needed. The mills either did not have the capital to invest in new looms or considered such looms too risky an investment. If the boycott ended, the mills would be stuck with expensive looms that they no longer needed.[41]

To ensure a successful boycott, talk turned to the possibility of building an Alliance cotton bagging mill in Marble Falls, Texas. The idea was appealing. It would not only address the problem of securing a reliable supply of cotton bagging, but would also place the bagging supply under the control of the Alliance, ensuring that there would never be price gouging. The Alliance, however, was unable to secure sufficient capital to build such a mill.[42]

The problem of an inadequate supply of alternative bagging was compounded by its price. Alliance leaders warned farmers that cotton bagging would initially be expensive since its production required the purchase of new looms. In 1889, cotton bagging sold for the same price as jute bagging.[43] Nevertheless, the Alliance continued to support the boycott, which had become a symbol of the ability of small farmers to thwart corporate America.

The boycott was sufficiently threatening to entice jute manufacturers to offer the Alliance a deal: jute would be reduced to $.087 per yard if the boycott ended. Alliance leaders refused the deal, arguing that if it would leave farmers vulnerable in the future to renewed price collusion. The goal of the boycott was to kill the jute trust once and for all by promoting the development of cotton bagging.[44]

Despite the Alliance's refusal to end the boycott, jute producers went ahead with their price reduction. By the summer of 1889, jute bagging was less expensive than alternative bagging.[45] As if this were not sufficiently problematic, another issue emerged. Cotton bagging weighed less than jute bagging. When cotton bales were weighed, a standard 6 percent was deducted to determine the weight of the cotton without the bagging. This deduction, known as a "tare," reflected the weight of jute bagging. If a bale were wrapped in alternative bagging, the standard tare would underestimate the weight of the cotton. Thus, farmers using alternative bagging would lose money both by paying more for the bagging and as the result of the tare formula.[46]

By the harvest of 1890, the jute boycott had faltered. Like earlier strategies, it had failed to deliver significant economic relief. In desperation, the leaders now turned from a focus on economic, self-help strategies to politics. It is important to note that there had always been a faction within the Alliance interested in political remedies. In 1886, tension between political insurgents and conservatives within the Alliance rose over what became known as the Cleburne Demands. The backdrop of this conflict was the Great Southwest Strike of 1886, initiated by the Knights of Labor against the Gould rail corporation. The union had won a reversal of a wage cut. Unfortunately, Jay Gould retaliated by firing employees who had played a prominent role in the strike. In response, the Knights of Labor initiated a boycott of goods shipped over Gould rail lines and asked the Alliance to support the boycott. Some Alliance leaders, such as William Lamb, strongly identified with the Knights of Labor and called on the Alliance to support the boycott. Lamb drew parallels between the plight of railroad workers and farmers, arguing that both groups were victimized by business.[47]

Political conservatives within the Alliance were alarmed by the tone of the discussion. They opposed unions such as the Knights of Labor, arguing that their wage demands would increase the price of commodities for farmers who were already economically struggling. While wholesalers and retail merchants could pass price increases along to their customers, farmers did not have enough market control to ensure that their increased costs would be offset by higher prices for farm commodities.[48]

The state Alliance convention, held in August 1886 in the town of Cleburne, served as the battleground for the dispute. The political conservatives insisted that the Alliance focus exclusively on its economic, self-help strategies. The political insurgents wanted the Alliance to pursue both economic strategies and political action. A committee was created to address the dispute. The committee sided with the political insurgents, arguing that the Alliance should push to "secure to our people freedom from the onerous and shameful abuses that the industrial classes are now suffering at the hands of arrogant capitalists and powerful corporations."[49] The committee recommended specific legislative actions and its recommendations became known as the Cleburne Demands. Five of the demands related to labor issues highlighted by the Knights of Labor conflict. Other demands addressed agrarian grievances. By far the most controversial of the Cleburne Demands related to monetary reform. With the decline in farm commodity prices, many farmers were struggling with debt incurred through high-interest, crop-lien loans. To address this problem, one of the Cleburne Demands called for an expansion of the currency supply and a revamping of the entire monetary system. Specifically, farmers demanded a federally administered banking system that issued legal tender based on a predetermined per capita currency supply. Such a system would end the existing gold-backed currency system, which allowed private financiers to manipulate the currency supply to maximize profits.[50]

The monetary reform demand thrust the Alliance into a hotly debated issue. During the Civil War, the nation had abandoned the gold standard to relieve the financial drain of the war on the U.S. Treasury. After the war the resumption of the gold standard was fiercely debated. Hard-money advocates were convinced that paper currency had to be backed by metal reserves. Fiatists, also known as Greenbackers, countered that metal reserves were unnecessary and that the amount of money in circulation should be dictated by the needs of the country, not the availability of gold and silver. They believed the contraction of the currency supply, a result of the resumption of the gold standard, was the primary cause of the recession in agriculture.[51]

The fiatist stance of the Cleburne Demands placed the Alliance in direct conflict with the Democratic Party, which officially endorsed the hard-money position. In the 1882 gubernatorial election in Texas, Greenbackers had formed a third party and had captured 40 percent of the vote. Democratic loyalists within the Alliance feared that the monetary reforms of the Cleburne Demands would lead to another third-party challenge. They fought hard to convince Alliance delegates to vote down the Cleburne Demands. Despite their efforts, the final vote was 92 to 75 in favor of the demands. A minority faction issued a dissenting report and threatened to establish a rival organization.[52]

Little came of the threat to bolt, largely because shortly after the Cleburne convention Macune had proposed the bold idea of the Alliance Exchange. As long as economic strategies were the major focus, this minority faction tolerated the undercurrent of political insurgency. But after the Alliance Exchange collapsed and the jute boycott faltered, growing numbers of Alliance members believed that economic self-help strategies had been exhausted and that a political approach was essential.

At the national convention of the Alliance in 1889, the shift toward politics was evident. In convention speeches, Alliance leaders argued that low crop prices were a symptom of a deepening economic depression caused by an inadequate currency supply. Their argument was reminiscent of the monetary ideas of the Cleburne Demands. Convention delegates created a committee to develop a specific Alliance plan to address the currency problem. The relief strategy proposed by this committee, which was headed by prominent Texas Alliance leader Charles Macune, became known as the Subtreasury Plan.[53]

THE SUBTREASURY PLAN

The Subtreasury Plan called for a halt to the government's practice of using national banks as depositories for U.S. Treasury monies because these banks had used their leverage to contract the money supply to maximize their profits. Under the Subtreasury Plan, the federal government would regulate the supply of currency to ensure the health of the economy. The latter required a flexible currency that could be contracted and expanded to meet fluctuating demand. Alliance leaders argued that low crop prices were the result of the great demand placed on an inadequate currency supply when the bulk of crops were harvested and marketed within a fairly narrow period of time.[54]

To ensure a flexible currency, the Alliance proposed that the federal government initiate both land-loan and commodity-loan programs. The basic purpose of the land-loan feature was to expand the currency supply. These loans were to be made until the volume of money in circulation reached $50 per capita. The commodity-loan program was aimed at providing a flexible currency system, while also serving as an alternative to the hated crop-lien financing system. Federal warehouses, or subtreasuries, were to be established in every county that annually produced farm products worth at least $500,000. Farmers could then store their nonperishable crops in these warehouses and borrow money, at low interest rates, collateralized by their warehoused crops.[55]

The subtreasury plan was touted as having far-reaching benefits for farmers, and those promised benefits were a major factor in the popularity of the subtreasury plan among farmers. The subtreasury plan would help farmers who depended on high-interest, crop-lien loans. It would also get farmers a better and fairer price for their products. To move the cotton crop alone required about one-sixth of the total U.S. currency in circulation, which placed tremendous strain on the money market. The tight money supply resulted in serious deflation, with many farmers unable to sell their products at a price that covered production costs. The subtreasury warehouses, serving as inexpensive storage facilities and extending affordable loans, would allow a staggering of sales of farm products and reduce the pressure at any given moment of time on the money supply. The money supply would also be flexible. When subtreasury loans were granted, the money supply would expand; as the stored crops were sold and the loans terminated, the money supply would contract.[56]

The shift of the Alliance to politics was decisive. Alliance newspapers were filled with discussions of the subtreasury and political issues in general. Contention now centered on the manner in which the Alliance would be political. Many Alliance members argued that necessary changes could be achieved through the existing two-party system. Others Alliance members argued that a new party was crucial since reform demands, such as the subtreasury, required action at the federal level. If farmers north of the Mason-Dixon Line remained loyal to the Republican Party and southern farmers remained loyal Democrats, farmers would be divided and would inevitably lose their fight for change. Initially, Democratic Party loyalists were the largest faction in the Alliance, so third-party advocates had to bide their time.

Many Alliance members in Texas saw significant potential for reform through the state Democratic Party, which nominated James Hogg for governor in 1890. As a former attorney general, he had gained popularity by addressing questionable economic practices of major railroad companies. In his gubernatorial campaign, he endorsed the notion of a railroad regulatory commission. On Election Day, he easily won over his Republican opponent.

Democratic loyalists within the Alliance argued that Hogg's victory and the railroad commission reform demonstrated the usefulness of working for reform from within the Democratic Party. Other Alliance members, however, were angered by the explicit rejection of the subtreasury plan by the state Democratic Party. At the state Alliance convention in 1890, a vote was taken on whether the Alliance should insist that the Democratic Party support its subtreasury proposal in order to receive Alliance support. The debate extended over two days. In the final vote, seventy-five delegates voted yes, twenty-three voted no, and sixteen abstained.[57] Thus, two-thirds of the delegates had declared themselves in opposition to the Democratic Party on a fundamental issue.

The Democratic Party, however, remained firmly against the subtreasury plan. Its leaders deemed it a radical proposal that entailed an unprecedented and dangerous intervention by the federal government into the agricultural commodities market. The prospects for its adoption were also affected by the fact that it called for radically changing the existing monetary system in a manner that undercut the economic interests of powerful groups, such as bankers and retail merchants. Party leaders began a concerted media campaign to discredit the subtreasury proposal, referring to it as an absurd heresy, a wild idea that would exacerbate the economic problems facing the nation. Some leaders even voiced the suspicion that it was a ploy of the Republican Party to wrest Alliance loyalty away from the Democratic Party.[58]

Alliance leaders launched an educational campaign in defense of the subtreasury. They were well aware of the challenges protest groups face when their ideas are labeled as radical or extreme in the mainstream news. They realized the importance of creating cultural support for what was being labeled by opponents as a heretical idea. Traveling Alliance lecturers gave speeches to hundreds of local Alliances. Alliance newspapers were full of articles advocating the subtreasury and explaining why it was the answer to the economic problems of farmers. Alliance newspapers also advertised "encampments" where Alliance members congregated in a revival-like atmosphere to hear speeches promoting the subtreasury. Some of the encampments in Texas were reported to be spectacularly successful, drawing from five thousand to fifteen thousand participants.[59]

The subtreasury proposal, however, was not without its critics within the Alliance. In Texas, critics issued the Austin Manifesto, which declared that the subtreasury was a scheme of radical third-partyites within the Alliance who knew that the Democratic Party would never support the proposal. These third-party radicals, the Manifesto alleged, had concluded that the only way to get most Alliance members to sever ties with the Democratic Party was to make support of the subtreasury a political litmus test. The Manifesto was signed by eleven Alliance members, eight of whom were state legislators. Tension rose; one of the Manifesto signers even got in a fistfight with a prominent subtreasuryite in the corridors of the state capitol.[60]

An Alliance convention was held in April 1891 to discuss the Manifesto. Of the hundreds in attendance, all but about a dozen strongly favored the subtreasury proposal. A resolution denouncing the Manifesto easily passed. Another question put before the convention, however, was not easily answered: it concerned whether to continue seeking change through the Democratic Party or to support the more radical step of forming a third party. After extended debate, the third-party approach was defeated in a 95 to 83 vote.[61] Third-party sentiment was strong, but it had not yet become the majority sentiment within the Texas Alliance.

A third party was, nevertheless, formed at the national level in May 1891. To entice the reluctant Alliance to join the third-party movement, delegates at the founding convention of the new party—the People's (or Populist) Party—voted to adopt a platform identical to that of the Alliance.[62] Given the steadfast refusal of the Republican and Democratic parties to endorse the entirety of the Alliance platform, especially the controversial subtreasury plan, Alliance members faced a crucial choice: remain loyal Democrats or remain loyal to Alliance principles and endorse the People's Party. As the political direction that the Alliance had taken beginning in 1889 came to its apex, the Alliance as an organization faded into the shadows of the newly formed People's Party and what is broadly known as the Populist movement.

NOTES

1. U.S. Department of Agriculture, *Yearbook of Agriculture, 1901* (Washington, D.C.: Government Printing Office, 1902), 754.
2. Lawrence Goodwyn, *Democratic Promise: The Populist Movement in America* (New York: Oxford University Press, 1976).
3. Donna Barnes, *Farmers in Rebellion: The Rise and Fall of the Southern Farmers Alliance and People's Party in Texas* (Austin: University of Texas Press, 1984).
4. Goodwyn, *Democratic Promise*, especially chapters 5 and 7.
5. Ibid.
6. Barnes, *Farmers in Rebellion*, 53.
7. W. L. Garvin and S. O. Daws, *History of the National Farmers' Alliance and Co-operative Union of America* (Jacksboro, Texas: J. N. Rogers and Co., 1887).
8. Ibid.
9. Michael Schwartz, *Radical Protest and Social Structure: The Southern Farmers Alliance and Cotton Tenancy, 1880–1890* (New York: Academic Press, 1976), 205–6.
10. Barnes, *Farmers in Rebellion*, 57–58.
11. Ibid., 58.
12. Ibid., 59.
13. *Southern Mercury*, January 10, 1889.
14. Garvin and Daws, *History of the National Farmers' Alliance*.
15. *Dallas Morning News*, October 8, 1885 and October 10, 1885.
16. Barnes, *Farmers in Rebellion*, 62.
17. *Dallas Morning News*, October 9, 1885.
18. Garvin and Daws, *History of the National Farmers' Alliance*.
19. Ibid.
20. Charles Macune, *Farmers Alliance Narrative*, Barker Texas History Archives, University of Texas at Austin, 1920.
21. Ibid.; *Southern Mercury*, September 4, 1890.
22. *Report on the Industrial Commission on Agriculture and Agricultural Labor*, House Document 179, 57th Congress, 1st Sess., 1901–1902.
23. *Southern Mercury*, August 22, 1895.
24. *National Economist*, May 25, 1889; *Southern Mercury*, September 4, 1888 and January 9, 1890.
25. Macune, *Farmers Alliance Narrative*.
26. *National Economist*, May 25, 1889; *Southern Mercury*, September 4, 1889 and January 9, 1890.
27. Goodwyn, *Democratic Promise*, 129–39 and 145–46; Schwartz, *Radical Protest and Social Structure*, 225–30.

28. Barnes, *Farmers in Rebellion*, 87–88.

29. *Southern Mercury*, December 13, 1888, and August 22, 1895; Macune, *Farmers Alliance Narrative*.

30. *Southern Mercury*, August 22, 1889.

31. Barnes, *Farmers in Rebellion*, 89.

32. *Southern Mercury*, December 27, 1888.

33. *Southern Mercury*, July 11, 1889.

34. Barnes, *Farmers in Rebellion*, 90–91.

35. Reprinted in *Ft. Worth Gazette*, May 31, 1888, and June 5, 1888.

36. *Southern Mercury*, September 11, 1888.

37. Barnes, *Farmers in Rebellion*, 95.

38. Ibid., 99–100.

39. Ibid., 100.

40. Ibid., 100–101.

41. *Southern Mercury*, April 18, 1889, and May 2, 1889.

42. *Southern Mercury*, December 12, 1889.

43. *Southern Mercury*, June 6, 1889.

44. *National Economist*, June 1, 1889.

45. *National Economist*, June 15, 1889.

46. *National Economist*, March 14, 1889; *Southern Mercury*, May 30, 1889.

47. Goodwyn, *Democratic Promise*, 52–66.

48. Barnes, *Farmers in Rebellion*, 71; Goodwyn, *Democratic Promise*, 55–58.

49. Ernest Winkler, *Platforms of Political Parties in Texas* (Austin: University of Texas Press, 1916).

50. Ibid.

51. Irwin Unger, *The Greenback Era: A Social and Political History of American Finance, 1865–1879* (Princeton: Princeton University Press, 1964).

52. Barnes, *Farmers in Rebellion*, 75.

53. Macune, *Farmers Alliance Narrative*; *National Economist*, December 14, 1889.

54. Barnes, *Farmers in Rebellion*, 111–12.

55. Ibid., 112.

56. Macune, *Farmers Alliance Narrative*; *National Economist*, May 3, 1890.

57. Goodwyn, *Democratic Promise*, 223.

58. Barnes, *Farmers in Rebellion*, 120–23.

59. Ibid., 123–26.

60. *Dallas Morning News*, March 19, 1891.

61. *Galveston Daily News*, April 24, 1891.

62. Barnes, *Farmers in Rebellion*, 137.

"A HOST OF STURDY PATRIOTS"
The Texas Populists

Gregg Cantrell

◀ Despite claims to the contrary, it was really no coincidence that two separate conventions were being held on consecutive days in Dallas in August 1891. One was the annual gathering of the state Farmers' Alliance, the massively popular self-help organization that, although officially nonpartisan, had increasingly served as a political protest vehicle for struggling farmers over the previous several years. The other was the founding convention of the Texas People's (or Populist) Party. "I want to emphasize the fact that the alliance has nothing on earth to do with the people's party convention," declared Alliance leader Harry Tracy, "and is in nowise responsible for its being held in Dallas at the time of the meeting of the state alliance." Tracy was speaking a bit disingenuously, and former Alliance state lecturer William Lamb—now a Populist organizer—knew it. When a *Dallas Morning News* reporter pointed out to him that the Alliance had "adopted demands that can only be secured through legislative enactments," Lamb admitted that this was indeed the case. "Will those demands be granted by either of the old parties?" asked the reporter. "They will not," Lamb replied. "That being the case," continued the reporter, "what remains for the alliance as a non-partisan organization but to vote with your party?" "That's all that is left for it," Lamb forthrightly conceded.[1]

And so it was. Most of the founders of the Texas People's Party were indeed Alliancemen, and the platform they adopted incorporated all of the Alliance's political demands. It is an oversimplification, though, merely to say that the Alliance "went into politics" in 1891. The Populist platforms of the 1890s may have been forged over the previous decade by the various state and national conventions of the Farmers' Alliance, but these in turn had borrowed heavily from the platforms of the Greenback, Independent, and Union Labor political insurgencies of the 1870s and 1880s, and also from the Knights of Labor. Not surprisingly, most Populist leaders had been active in the Alliance, the Knights, or in various third-party political campaigns. Many had been involved in more than one of these movements, and some in all of them. The birth of the Texas People's Party, then, was the culmination of a quarter-century of political insurgency in the Lone Star State.[2]

Nationally, the central document of the People's Party was the Omaha Platform, written in 1892 at the party's first national convention—a gathering in which Texan delegates played conspicuous roles. This brief but eloquent document called for sweeping reforms in three broad categories: finance, transportation, and land. Of these, the financial planks received the most attention. They demanded "a national currency, safe, sound, and flexible, issued by the general government"—in other words, a system of paper (or "fiat") money, not redeemable in gold or silver. The platform also endorsed the controversial Subtreasury Plan (or "a better system") of the Farmers' Alliance, whereby farmers would store staple crops in government warehouses, use the crops as collateral for low-interest government loans, and then have the crops released onto the market in an orderly fashion when prices were best, thus relieving the yearly harvest-season price collapse. The platform called for the free and unlimited coinage of silver, a graduated income tax, economy in government, and the establishment of postal savings banks. By increasing the amount of money in circulation and thus causing inflation, these measures would provide relief to debt-strapped farmers who for years had been forced to repay loans in appreciated dollars at harvest time. These measures would also remove the country's financial system from the hands of private bankers and place it under the control of the government.[3]

Recognizing the monopolistic nature of the nation's railroad industry, the Populist transportation plank called for government ownership of the railroads, a measure backed by Texas Populists, who had witnessed the failure of mere government regulation to control predatory pricing and other unfair practices. Similarly, the plank called for government ownership of the telephone and telegraph systems, which by their very nature tended to be monopolistic.[4]

The land plank also echoed the antimonopoly theme of the financial and transportation planks, calling for a prohibition on alien landowning and demanding that all lands held for speculative purposes by railroads and other corporations be "reclaimed by the government and held for actual settlers only." Commenting on the Omaha Platform, 1892 Texas Populist gubernatorial candidate Thomas L. Nugent declared it "a plain, simple enunciation of true democracy." The document became the bible of Texas Populism, the standard against which Populists were measured. If they stood by the Omaha Platform in full, they were said, in Populist parlance, to be "in the middle of the road."[5]

Populist platforms at the state level incorporated the major demands of the Omaha Platform, elaborating on some of those demands and adding others that were strictly of state interest. For example, a call for free public schools with a mandatory six-month term and free textbooks became a standard feature of the state platforms. Free and fair elections, featuring a secret ballot, likewise characterized the state documents. As we shall see later in this chapter, the state platforms prominently featured planks intended to address issues important to organized labor, and beginning in 1894 the party added demands of specific interest to African Americans.[6]

From our modern perspective, then, it is easy to see why Populists are considered "liberal," "progressive," or even "radical." The unprecedented willingness of Populists to embrace public (i.e., government) solutions to widely shared public problems clearly marks them as belonging to what we today call the political Left. Many of their policy positions indeed foreshadowed later liberal/progressive causes. The farm-loan and price-support components of the Subtreasury Plan, for instance, found expression in New Deal farm programs. The call for a nonmetallic-based paper currency issued and controlled by the federal government later came to fruition with the creation of the Federal Reserve system. While the federal government never nationalized U.S. railroads, the interstate highway system embodied much of the spirit of the Populist transportation plank. The income tax favored by the Populists became the law of the land with the passage of the Sixteenth Amendment in 1916. Populist electoral reforms, including the direct election of senators, voter registration, and the secret ballot, likewise gained widespread acceptance in the twentieth century. And two progressive causes that were championed by many individual Populists but that never became part of the party's official platform—woman suffrage and prohibition—also later became law, as did Populist labor demands, including the eight-hour workday and the right to strike. At the state and local level, Populist causes such as greater funding for public schools, free textbooks, and abolition of the notorious convict-lease system all eventually became the successful objects of liberal or progressive reform. And the Populists' efforts to reach out to African Americans and accord them a meaningful, dignified place in the party's councils further cemented their reputation as forerunners of today's political Left.

Interestingly, though, relatively few Populists thought of themselves as "liberals," much less as "radicals." Of course, the "liberal" label had not yet been applied generally to a political ideology in American politics; to most Americans in the 1890s the term simply suggested a certain broadness in outlook, a tolerant and generous spirit. Nor were the terms "progressive" or "Left" commonly used in Texas or Southern politics. "Radical" was somewhat better known, but most Populists eschewed the label. Indeed, the adjective that Populists most often applied to themselves was the word "conservative." When asked about the 1892 state platform, Thomas Nugent was quoted as saying "that the people's party state platform is in his opinion conservative enough to suit every man of whatever calling within the state" and that he was "confident of rallying the conservative element of the state to his support." During that same campaign, the *Dallas Morning News* reported that Nugent would prevail against incumbent Democrat James S. Hogg "because the conservative population is bound to vote for Nugent because of his recognized conservatism." When Nugent lay dying in late 1895, Populist leader Harry Tracy sang the praises of Jerome Kearby, Nugent's successor as the party's standard-bearer, declaring that Kearby's "well-known conservatism will bring thousands of wavering democrats to us." The *Morning News* likewise described an 1892 speech by the African American Populist orator John B. Rayner as being "conservative, sensible and logical." And at the start of the 1894 campaign, state party chairman H. S. P. "Stump" Ashby proudly announced "that our ranks are being rapidly filled with the conservative, justice-loving people of our State."[7]

Democrats and Republicans, of course, scoffed at the notion of Populists as conservatives. To old-party stalwarts, the Populists were indeed dangerous radicals, if not socialists, communists, or anarchists. African American Republican leader Norris Wright Cuney voiced a typical opposition opinion, charging that Thomas Nugent was but "a few steps removed toward socialism and communism" for his support of the Subtreasury Plan and government ownership of the railroads. In a similar vein, the Democratic editor of the *Kaufman Sun* denounced "populistic heresies" as "surely tending to socialism, confiscation of property, disorganization, political tyranny, social debasement, [and] commercial ruin." So common did these slurs become that Populists spent a significant amount of time and energy rebutting them. During the 1894 campaign, the *Texas Advance,* the People's party's state organ, dismissed "the silly and false cry that 'the people's party is a set of socialists, anarchists and revolutionists,'" calling all such charges "bosh." To most Populists, opposing the monopolistic corporate combinations that had arisen since the Civil War was an eminently conservative policy.[8]

Instead, the Populists consistently portrayed themselves as champions of Jeffersonian, Jacksonian, and Lincolnian democracy, with occasional nods to Benjamin Franklin, James Madison, John C. Calhoun, Henry Clay, and Daniel Webster. Jefferson, of course, held a revered place in Populist thought because of his apotheosis of the independent, freeholding farmer, and his opposition to Alexander Hamilton's pro-bank, pro-business ideas. "The idea that Jefferson had of republican government," explained Alliance and Populist leader Evan Jones, "was a government in which the people ruled. Hamilton, on the other hand, believed in a centralized government." James H. "Cyclone" Davis, the most famous Texan in national Populist circles, typically mounted the campaign podium with ten volumes of the works of Jefferson, after which he proceeded to demonstrate how the Sage of Monticello held Populist views. "The republican and democratic parties to-day support Hamilton's policies, and the populists the true Jeffersonian party," Davis declared in a typical stump speech, whereas Hamiltonians said that "government should be taken from the masses and placed in the hands of classes and the Jeffersonian theory was that the people can be trusted with self-government, that they are the source of all political power, and the powers of government as now exercised should be wrested from the classes and restored to the masses."[9]

The other patron saint of Texas Populism was Andrew Jackson. Although Populists would not have agreed with the specifics of Jackson's hard-money policies, they viewed his battle against the Bank of the United States and his advocacy of the rights of the common man as the embodiment of Populist ideals. "[T]he industries of the country are growing under the iron heel of monopolies and the people need another such man as 'Old [H]ickory' Jackson to regulate our finances as he did in opposition to the United States banking system, for there is but little difference in the way our present banking system is oppressing the people and the system then proposed," Evan Jones contended. Or as prohibitionist-turned-Populist E. L. Dohoney put it, "We want a democratic party like that inspired by Jefferson and organized by Jackson, which will align itself on the anti-monopoly side of the branch and stand on the doctrine of 'equal rights to all; exclusive privileges to none,' and will fight the battle of the producing classes against monopoly in all its varied forms."[10]

Given the large number of Confederate veterans in their ranks, it is interesting that the third statesman whose political thought Texas Populists most admired was Abraham Lincoln. His name could be invoked in a number of ways. One was Lincoln's willingness to join a third-party movement (the antebellum Republicans) when he perceived that the established parties had abandoned their principles. "How long think you it would have taken Abraham Lincoln and his associates to have emancipated slavery and remain in the whig and democratic parties?" asked Jerome Kearby in 1896. "To reform a party and remain with it is a delusion and deceit, the seductive appeal of the demagogue." But Populists were also drawn to Lincoln because of his humble origins and his pro-labor ideology. "Abraham Lincoln said 'Labor is prior to and independent of capital,'" the *Southern Mercury* editorialized. "Labor is much more important than capital or capitalists." Populists seized upon an alleged 1864 quote from Lincoln in which Lincoln declared that "corporations have been enthroned" by the war and that "the money power" now threatened the survival of the republic.[11]

The Populists' roots in the Farmers' Alliance, their admiration of, and advocacy for, the small producer, and their invocation of Jefferson, Jackson, and Lincoln have led some scholars to see them not as forward-looking progressives but rather as rustic provincials yearning for an imagined agrarian past of sturdy, independent yeomen. It is but a short step from this image to a conclusion that Populists were hicks and hayseeds, or, at their worst, even bigots and reactionaries. In this view, Populists' narrow-minded nostalgia for an idealized bygone era led them to embrace anti-intellectualism, anti-Semitism, nativism, and Anglophobia. Cut off from the modernizing mainstream of American society, socially, economically, and geographically isolated farmers embraced first the Alliance and then Populism because they failed to understand the complexities of the modern world—a world that kept them marginalized and poor.[12]

There were certainly Texas Populists who fit this description, but on the whole it gives a distorted picture. In reality, at both the grassroots and the leadership levels, and in both geographic and economic terms, Populists were a remarkably diverse lot. In the Lone Star State, the People's Party did well in several of the poor, isolated, Piney Woods counties of deep East Texas and in the hardscrabble Cross Timbers region of West Central Texas—patterns that would seem to support the social-isolation/hayseed thesis. And it is true that they generally fared better in rural areas than in towns. But Populists also found significant support in many counties that were relatively prosperous, that boasted rich soil, and that were well connected to the outside world. And while Populists may have invoked the names of Jefferson, Jackson, and Lincoln, and longed for a time of more principled politics, they did so not in an attempt to turn back the clock and recapture some idyllic agrarian past, but rather they devised policies that they believed would curb the excesses of modern commercial and industrial capitalism and allow them a fair share in the bounty of modern America. As Evan Jones contended, "the present system of our government finances is divorcing capital and labor. . . . The question of finances is affecting all classes of our people—the man that wields the hoe, the business man and the professional man; it affects all alike." Harry Tracy likewise believed that "the people's party is not the enemy of any necessary industry or class, but that its object will prove to be the salvation of the commercial world, and we urge all classes to analyze the principles involved in our Omaha platform." Democrats, he explained, had "made it a point to endeavor to get merchants and manufacturers to believe that the people's party was their enemy, seeking to destroy their business." Not true, he claimed: "the people's party is the friend and not the enemy of legitimately invested capital."[13]

Even African American Populists in Texas, who might have been expected to be more radical than whites in their critiques of capitalism, agreed that Populism was not meant to interfere with the proper functioning of America's capitalist system. John B. Rayner, the foremost black leader of the party, argued that neither capitalism nor wealth were inherently evil. Rather, he suggested that the leaders of the major parties had pitted the classes against one another for their own corrupt purposes. In order "to carry out their fiendishness," Rayner stated, "the two old parties . . . will make the banker intimidate the merchant and manufacturer, and the merchant will intimidate the small farmer, and the farmer will bribe or intimidate the laborer and tenant farmer." The Populist program, then, aimed to restore each of these necessary groups to its proper relationship with the others. Corruption and monopoly, not capitalism per se, were the enemies of all.[14]

When couched in these terms, it becomes clear that Texas Populists were not pursuing radical goals such as overthrowing capitalism or abolishing private property; they simply wanted a system that would reward hard work and secure to each the deserved fruits of his or her labor. In short, they strove to create a fairer, more humane form of capitalism. Their experience in groups like the Alliance and the Knights of Labor had proven to them that self-help and collective bargaining would never secure to them the reformed capitalist system that they desired, so the rise of the People's party marked the next phase of their struggle. To win that struggle they would use the only power available to poor people in a democracy—the power of the ballot. They would take back their government from the corrupt, monopolistic powers that had controlled it for the previous twenty years, and then use the government to restore equity to an exploitative system.

The genius of Populism, then, lay not in any of its specific reforms but in the simple realization that widely shared public problems demanded public solutions. The *Dallas Morning News* captured the essence of the Populist worldview shortly after the party's first election, noting that the new party "is composed of those who cherish the general principles of democracy so far as they are applicable to present problems, but do not hesitate to ignore democratic traditions in seeking remedies for modern ills. . . . [T]hey take the ground that democracy is whatever the people will, and that it is part of democracy to solve present problems with present means. They measure public policies not by party standards, but by the people's needs. . . . They look for the accomplishment of reform and seek their object through whatever channel is more promising. . . . [T]hey marched to the polls a host of sturdy patriots, each resolved to cast his ballot in the best interests of his family and his country. Such a movement is a great moral influence, a threat to party power and a rebuke to party greed."[15] Armed with this worldview and an elaborate set of political demands for achieving their goals, the Populists set out to win elections. The move on the part of dissident Alliance men and their allies to found a third party the previous year had further complicated an already-chaotic political scene in the Lone Star State. As the dominant party in an essentially one-party state (the black-dominated Republican Party was never competitive), Texas Democrats had long been divided into a conservative wing and a more progressive faction. The incumbent governor, James Stephen Hogg, had won the office in 1890 with the support of Alliance men, who backed his promise to create a railroad commission. Despite his hostility to the Subtreasury Plan, which alienated the more doctrinaire Alliance men, Hogg's promise to regulate the railroads kept Alliance men in the party, but when the legislature failed to make the commission elective, and then Hogg refused to appoint an Alliance man to the agency, angry Alliance men rose in revolt and created the People's Party.[16]

If this were not trouble enough, Hogg faced yet another rebellion from the conservative wing of his own party. When the Democrats met in August to nominate their state ticket, the losing conservatives bolted the convention and nominated railroad attorney George W. Clark for governor. Republican leaders decided to endorse Clark rather than nominate their own ticket, meaning that there would be two Democratic tickets in the general election.[17]

By the time the Democrats split, the Populists had already nominated Thomas L. Nugent, a lawyer and former state judge from Fort Worth, for governor. Nugent's nomination gave the Populists instant credibility, for he was almost universally respected. A former Confederate officer and delegate to the 1875 state constitutional convention, he had been a staunch Democrat until early 1892, when he concluded that a third-party movement finally had enough strength to win. The *Dallas Morning News* spoke for many Texans when it sized up the Populist candidate: "Judge Nugent for governor forms an eminently respectable head. A quiet, self-contained, intellectual and scholarly man, and an accomplished lawyer withal, his enthusiasm for his cause is not less because not boisterous and stormy. His presence at the front is certainly calculated to impart peculiar features of controversial dignity and moral elevation to the campaign." Populist papers quoted with glee an admiring Democratic editor's description of him as "the William Tell of Texas." The Fort Worth correspondent of the *Morning News* declared, "If elected governor he will probably be the most cultured man who has ever occupied that position in the state. He has the courage of a gentleman and is in perfect sympathy with the masses of the people, and all the material interests of the State can be safely trusted to his care."[18]

Despite Nugent's strength at the top of the ticket, the Populists realized that they faced daunting challenges. First there was the issue of financing the campaign. A party with struggling farmers as its core constituency could not hope to compete in the fundraising game with Hogg, who enjoyed the backing that comes with major-party incumbency, or Clark, with his strong ties to railroads and other corporate interests. The Populists counted on grassroots organization to spread the party gospel, and by September they boasted 2,800 Populist clubs statewide. It was not enough. When the campaign was over, they lamented that the recent contest had been conducted "literally without a campaign fund, save as one could be gathered during the canvass in penny contributions from a people already reduced to the extremities of poverty," and that the Democrats, by contrast, had been "sustained by all the wealth and social prestige of the state."[19]

If overcoming the Democrats' massive financial advantage were not obstacle enough, the Populists also had to battle against deeply entrenched Southern political traditions. While it is true that many of the party's leaders and voters came to the Populist revolt as veterans of earlier third-party and independent political movements, none of those movements had ever attracted the numbers needed to seriously threaten Democratic hegemony. Most white Texans, like most white Southerners, regarded the Democratic Party as the "party of the fathers," the party that had "redeemed" the South from the "evils" of Republican rule during Reconstruction, the sole repository of time-tested political principles, and the main bulwark against racial mixing and "social equality" of the races.[20]

The act of publicly leaving the Democratic Party clearly was not something undertaken lightly. Democrats abandoning their party for Populism often published solemn statements explaining how the Democratic Party had ceased to champion the principles of Jefferson and Jackson, how the party had fallen under the sway of corrupt party bosses, and how there had ceased to be any meaningful difference between Democrats and Republicans. Melvin Wade, one of Populism's most popular African American leaders, employed humor in his appeal to Democrats to abandon their party. "Young feller says he's a Democrat because his father was one," Wade joked. "According to him I ought to want to be a slave because my father was one." Wade's logic notwithstanding, Populists never succeeded in breaking the emotional attachment that many Texans felt toward the Democratic Party. After the downfall of Populism, black leader John B. Rayner bitterly noted that "the faith the South has in the Democratic party is stronger than the faith the South has in God."[21]

Even if the Populists could manage to finance their campaigns on a competitive basis and break the stranglehold of Democratic tradition, the party still had to broaden its appeal beyond its core constituency of white farmers and Alliancemen. Early on, the party identified two blocs of voters who might not be automatically drawn to Populism but whose votes were vital to its success. One of these was, as previously mentioned, African Americans.

Texas Populists could look at the political landscape in Texas and see the importance of the black vote; African Americans comprised about 22 percent of the state's population, which meant that if whites were ever less than united, blacks might hold the balance of power. It was not, however, a case of Populists simply deciding that they would invite African Americans to support the People's Party. A complex calculus of racially charged factors had to be taken into account. Would Populists appeal to blacks simply on the grounds of shared economic interest, or would the party include planks designed specifically to win over black voters? Would African Americans hold positions of authority in the party? Would the party welcome black candidates? Would it try to make "fusion" arrangements with the Republicans, whereby black Republicans could stay with their traditional party but agree to support Populist candidates as some sort of a quid pro quo bargain? In each case, white Populists had to conduct a delicate balancing act: if they appeared *too* friendly toward blacks, they exposed themselves to Democratic charges of racial treason and ran the risk of alienating white voters. If they kept African Americans at arm's length, ignoring specifically "black" issues and excluding blacks from positions of leadership within the party, they were unlikely to attract the numbers of votes needed to ensure victory. If they chose the fusion route and cut deals with the Republican Party, they became vulnerable to charges of crass political opportunism—the very lack of principle of which they accused the Democrats.[22]

Given these complexities, it comes as no surprise that the Populists sometimes took a tentative, halting approach to the problem of race. The 1892 governor's race exposed the problem in stark terms when incumbent progressive Democrat Jim Hogg denounced lynching, winning many black votes. The black-dominated Republican Party, meanwhile, cynically endorsed conservative Democrat George Clark. The Populists soon found that appeals to blacks' economic self-interest were not enough to offset these two factors, and the bulk of the African American vote went to the two Democrats. The Populists learned that they would have to do more to specifically address black interests if they were to win future elections. As a consequence, in 1894, with ex-slave John B. Rayner holding a position on the platform committee, the party added a plank demanding that "each race shall have its own [public school] trustees and control its own schools." Another plank that year called for the state to "provide sufficient accommodation for all its insane without discrimination in color."[23]

The other bloc of voters that Populists sought to win over was the urban labor vote. By the 1890s, with the rapid growth of towns and cities and the ongoing diversification of the Texas economy, that vote was growing increasingly important. In 1886 the Farmers' Alliance had supported the Knights of Labor in its bitter strike against the Jay Gould railroad lines in Texas, and relations between the two groups had remained warm, even after the strike was crushed. The problem was that the interests of farmers were not always identical to those of laborers. Populist monetary policy, with its emphasis on increasing the supply of circulating currency and thus creating inflation, offered little to urban laborers who would have to pay higher prices for food and other necessities. Populist land reforms, such as the prohibition on alien ownership, likewise held little appeal for workers, and it was difficult for many laborers to evaluate how government ownership of the railroads might affect them. The 1892 Omaha Platform, in its "Expression of Sentiments" section, did denounce the use of Pinkerton strikebreakers, vaguely "sympathize[ed] with the efforts of organized workingmen to shorten the hours of labor," and expressed support for the Knights of Labor in its dispute with the clothing manufacturers of Rochester, but it was short on specific pro-labor planks.[24]

With so little in their national platform to help them woo the labor vote, Texas Populists determined that they would remedy the situation in their state platform. All of the party's platforms included calls for an eight-hour workday, a fairer mechanics' lien law, reform of the convict-lease system in order to take convict labor out of competition with free labor, and a demand that railroads pay employees promptly and in "the lawful money of the country." The 1892 platform added a plank calling for a state bureau of labor statistics and a state board of arbitration "to adjust all differences between corporations and employees." These demands remained mainstays of Texas Populist platforms for the remainder of the party's existence, and their inclusion helped the party win urban votes.[25]

The Populists lost the 1892 election, running third in the three-man race for governor. Still, having polled 108,483 votes their first time out and electing scores of officials at the local level, party leaders were little short of jubilant. During the critical period between the 1892 and 1894 elections, Texas Populists honed their message and mounted a massive organizing campaign confidently looking forward to victory in 1894. It was during these two years that Populism in Texas emerged as more than just a political movement; it began to take on the dimensions of a religious crusade.[26]

Populism in Texas and elsewhere was thoroughly imbued with an evangelical zeal and sense of mission, not merely bordering on the religious but with Protestant religious ideas actually at its very core. Populists exhibited no shyness in their conspicuous mixing of politics and religion. Ministers played prominent roles in the party and the Populist press. H. S. P. "Stump" Ashby, for example, who chaired the state executive committee and ran for lieutenant governor in 1896, was a former Methodist minister who frequently invoked the Bible in his speeches. John B. Rayner came to Populism from a background as a Baptist preacher. Reddin Andrews, a prominent Baptist minister and former president of Baylor University, likewise converted to Populism. "Politically I am a populist," Andrews explained. "In fact, I am a Jeffersonian, Madisonian, Jacksonian democrat." When asked why he had become a Populist, he replied, "I vote as I pray." He went on to state that being "a Baptist after the Pauline type," he would not worship his denomination "with a Big D," just as he refused blindly to follow any political party. "I wear no political nor ecclesiastical collar," he stated. In virtually the same breath that he denounced the "monopolists" and "money lords" he likewise castigated the "ecclesiastical corruptions, corners, cliques, combines and machines" which "curse the world to-day." Clearly he saw Populism and Christianity as intimately related. Andrews received the Populist nomination for Congress in the Ninth District in 1896, finishing a distant third in the race, but in 1910 he reappeared on the political scene as the Socialist Party nominee for governor.[27]

Although Ashby was a Methodist, and Andrews and Rayner Baptists, Populism appears to have appealed most strongly to adherents of "restorationist" denominations such as the Primitive Baptists, the Methodist Protestant Church, and the Disciples of Christ, all of which had broken away from larger denominations, much as Texas Populists had broken off from the Democrats. Restorationists saw themselves as reformers, struggling to restore the ancient purity of the first-century church. Generally rejecting creeds and narrow sectarianism, they valued freedom of conscience and distrusted anything that tended toward hierarchy. They looked at the state of religion in America and saw it as decadent and corrupt, bringing American society itself ever closer to the brink of calamity. Believing as they did that religion could not be separated from the broader society, it was logical that religious restorationists would also be political restorationists. Just as Christianity had fallen away from the purity of the early church, so had American politics fallen away from the alleged purity of the Jacksonian era, an era when the virtuous common people, through their tribune Old Hickory, had kept monopolists at bay and ensured (as the Jacksonian slogan went) "equal rights for all and special privileges for none." In both their political and religious views, then, Populists could be conservative and countercultural at the same time—conservative in the sense that they sought to restore "pure" religious and political values of a bygone era, and countercultural in the sense that their efforts to do so ran counter to the corruption of the dominant culture of the late nineteenth century.[28]

In Texas the most prominent restorationist denomination was the Disciples of Christ, and Disciples played highly visible roles in the People's Party. North Texas in particular was a hotbed of Disciple Populists. Elder W. L. Thurman, a Disciples minister who stumped the county for the Populists, found himself the target of malicious falsehoods spread by Democrats, who claimed he had been kicked out of the church. The Populist press exulted when a local Democratic paper apologized for repeating the charges and retracted its critical statements. In the same county, Elder J. C. Lowry, a Disciples minister, ran for the state legislature in 1896. The local paper described him as "a very successful preacher" and "one of the 'Old Guard' of greenbackers" dating back to 1876. But most noteworthy was the nomination by North Texas Populists of U. M. Browder, minister of the Disciples of Christ congregation in Gainesville, who ran for congress against the charismatic incumbent Democrat Joseph Weldon Bailey. Despite their conspicuous ideological mixing of religion and politics, Populists strenuously supported the constitutional separation of church and state, and Browder resigned his pulpit when he accepted the nomination. In one of the dirtiest campaigns of the entire Populist era in Texas, Bailey won handily, but Browder remained a hero for local Populists. After the election he left Texas for a pastorate in Indiana, but local papers continued to follow his career, publishing one sermon that summarized his—and the religious Populists'—attitude toward religion and politics: "If my pulpit is not for the uplifting of poor, distressed and suffering humanity, it's good for nothing and has no right to the respect of an oppressed people." Texas Populists would have heartily agreed with this Social Gospel position, and moreover, they would have added that politics served the same purpose.[29]

As one of its principal campaign devices, the Populists adopted an institution borrowed from evangelical Protestant culture and from Alliance practice: the camp meeting. These gatherings, which attracted thousands of Populist families, were particularly popular during the summers between election years, and they combined politics, entertainment, and the opportunity for isolated farm families to socialize during the slack times between planting and harvesting. Democrats marveled at the elaborate preparations for the camp meetings and immense crowds that they drew, and Democratic politicians usually felt compelled to accept Populists invitations to participate in the joint debates that were the highlight of the meetings.[30]

As the 1894 elections drew nearer, the Populists felt certain that they would finally wrest control of the state from the Democrats. At their state convention in Waco in June, some twelve hundred delegates converged upon a large tent erected in the Waco city park to nominate candidates, write a state platform, and plan for the upcoming campaign. The convention was a virtual love feast, as Nugent was renominated for governor by acclamation and the platform was adopted with little dissent. As previously noted, the party made much more concerted efforts to woo the votes of organized labor and of African Americans. "[T]he colored brother was a conspicuous figure," reported the *Waco Evening News*, noting that "a hearty welcome was accorded him." The Democrats, now genuinely fearful of losing power, papered over their internal differences, agreeing upon the nondescript "harmony" candidate Charles Culberson for governor and adopting a platform that straddled on the issue of silver coinage.[31]

When the votes were counted in November, the Populists again fell short of victory statewide, but their gains were apparent for all to see. Even though the Republicans fielded a ticket, Nugent polled 159,676 votes to Culberson's 216,373. The Republicans and Prohibitionists combined for 83,746 votes. Nugent's vote had increased by over fifty thousand since 1892. Clearly, if the party continued to grow at its present rate, and if all anti-Democratic votes could be combined on the Populist ticket, the Democrats would be ousted in 1896. Even more cheering for the party faithful was the fact that Populists won hundreds of local offices and elected twenty-four members of the state legislature.[32]

The upcoming 1896 election cycle, however, presented new challenges for Texas Populists. In the United States, state and local party politics cannot be separated easily from national politics, and developments on the national stage were troubling. Despite party leaders' attempts to appeal to urban voters, Populism had failed to gain much of a foothold outside the party's agrarian strongholds in the South, the Mountain West, and the Great Plains states. And even in many of these states, Populists had sought power—often successfully—through the expedient of fusion. In Kansas, for example, Populists formed a winning coalition with Democrats at the state level. In North Carolina, they fused with Republicans to capture the state. Those who opposed fusion, including a large majority of Texas Populists, believed that such combinations constituted a betrayal of Populist principles. For several years Populists had watched the growing rift in the national Democratic Party over the monetary issue. The dominant wing of the national party followed the lead of President Grover Cleveland and endorsed the gold standard, a position that was anathema to "middle of the road" (anti-fusion) Populists. Still, many national leaders of the People's Party from states that had experienced electoral success with fusion believed that if the Democrats were to embrace free silver and abandon the gold standard, the Populists would be justified in joining forces with the Democrats. By early 1896 it was becoming more apparent that members of the Populist national executive committee were seeking, as one Texas Populist put it, "to lead the Populist party, bag and baggage into the camp of the enemy" when the party's national convention met in July 1896. "Is it possible," he asked, "that they can succeed in carrying out their treasonable design?"[33]

Not only was it possible, it is exactly what happened. Middle-of-the-road Populists had made a fatal miscalculation. Believing that the Democrats would nominate another conservative, gold-standard candidate, they were banking on the defection of the pro-silver, "reform" wing of the Democratic Party into the ranks of the Populists. But when the Democrats met in Chicago for their national convention, the silver faction of the party engineered the surprise nomination of Nebraska's William Jennings Bryan, whose famous "Cross of Gold" speech had captivated the assembled delegates.

Now the stage was set for the fusionist Populists to execute their plan. Depicting Bryan as a Populist in everything but the name, Populist leaders placed his name in nomination at the St. Louis convention, eliciting howls of protest from the Texas delegates. The best the Texans and other mid-roaders could do was to reverse the normal order of nominations and engineer the nomination of Georgia Populist Tom Watson for vice president, hoping that it would force Bryan to repudiate the nomination. Bryan cleverly remained quiet, and the Texan delegation, now dubbed the "Immortal 103" by the Populist press, returned home in bitter disappointment. Facing the impossible task of explaining to Texas Populists how their national party could have nominated a hated Democrat who supported only one minor plank in the Populist platform, the Texans now had to devise a way to win the upcoming state elections.[34]

The Populists held their state convention in Galveston the following month. Now that fusion with the Democrats had been perpetrated at the national level, many Populists believed that they owed no further allegiance to their national party. Desperate to salvage the statewide election, they entered into secret negotiations with Texas Republicans for a fusion deal that would trade Populist votes for the Republican national ticket in exchange for Republican support for the state candidates of the People's Party. They faced two problems. First, they opened themselves up to charges of hypocrisy, having so staunchly opposed fusion with the Democrats as being a sacrifice of principle. Second, they knew they would run headlong into the thorny issue of race. The Republican Party in Texas was overwhelmingly African American, and to openly advocate supporting Republican William McKinley for president exposed Populists to charges of racial treason. Memories of Reconstruction still burned strong in the minds of white Texans, and any vote for a Republican conjured up the old bugaboo of "negro domination." In the end, the Texas Republicans acceded to the informal deal and did not place a state ticket in the field, and both Populists and Republicans quietly sought to convince their voters to cast ballots for the Republican national ticket and the Populist state ticket.[35]

It was not to be. In a campaign marked by bitter demagoguery, race-baiting, voter intimidation, and outright violence, the Populist state ticket, now headed by the charismatic Dallas lawyer Jerome Kearby, managed only 44 percent of the vote. Worse still, Populist candidates at the local level suffered widespread defeats, as white Populist voters expressed disgust with their leaders' actions at both the state and national levels. For a movement that had been based on religious zeal and idealistic devotion to principle, enough Texas Populists now believed that their party had succumbed to the same corrupt machine politics that had led to the Populist revolt in the first place.[36]

After the debacle of 1896, the People's Party rapidly withered away in Texas and elsewhere. Many disillusioned Populists simply dropped out of politics, although some of the more radical party members who could not stomach a return to the Democrats joined the Socialist Party, which before World War I outpolled the Republicans in Texas. Most eventually returned to the Democratic Party, contributing to the rise of the progressive wing of that party in the early years of the 1900s. Ironically, it was the progressive Democrats, including ex-Populists, who succeeded in enacting the state's poll-tax amendment and other "clean government" election reforms, thus disfranchising thousands of the poorest ex-Populists, especially African Americans. Progressivism in Texas may have drawn some of its reform impulse from Populism, but it was a distinctly white, moderate, business-friendly variety of reform.[37]

With the hindsight of a century's time, certain perspectives on Populism in Texas emerge. Far from being a backward-looking last gasp of rustic agrarians longing for an imagined preindustrial utopia, the People's Party was a remarkably modern and innovative reform movement seeking to rein in the excesses of a social, political, and economic system that had trampled on the rights and aspirations of thousands of Texans. Populists employed the language of Jacksonian, Jeffersonian, and Lincolnian democracy in their crusade to empower ordinary citizens, but in doing so they were only drawing upon an American political tradition that recognized the incompatibility of monopoly with true democracy. Few Populists ever advocated overthrowing capitalism, but they recognized the corrosive toll that that concentrated wealth had taken on the nation's political system. They understood that in a modern industrial democracy, the ballot—wielded in the hands of an informed electorate—furnished the only effective check on the corrupting influence of monopoly. "I have never been frightened by that scarecrow, strong government," Texas Populist Charles Jenkins wrote at the zenith of the movement in 1894. "I believe in a government strong enough to protect the lives, liberty and property of its citizens." Jenkins recognized that in a society where great disparities of wealth and power exist, government was the only weapon that could counterbalance private, corporate influence. And while Jenkins and his fellow Texas Populists would have deprecated the role played by money and corporate interests, and bemoaned the lack of grassroots participation in modern liberal politics, their recognition that public problems demand public solutions links them with the political Left of our own time.[38]

NOTES

1. *Dallas Morning News*, August 17, 18, July 19, 1891 (first and second quotations); July 2, 1891 (subsequent quotations).
2. The two principal monographs on Texas Populism are Roscoe Martin, *The People's Party in Texas: A Study in Third Party Politics* (Austin: University of Texas Press, 1933), and Donna A. Barnes, *Farmers in Rebellion: The Rise and Fall of the Southern Farmers Alliance and People's Party in Texas* (Austin: University of Texas Press, 1984). Although it is a study of national Populism, Lawrence Goodwyn's *Democratic Promise: The Populist Moment in America* (Oxford: Oxford University Press, 1976) heavily emphasizes the Texas roots of the agrarian revolt. For the influence of previous labor and third-party movements on Populism, see Matthew Hild, *Greenbackers, Knights of Labor, and Populists: Farmer-Laborer Insurgency in the Late-Nineteenth-Century South* (Athens: University of Georgia Press, 2007). The 1891 state platform can be found in Ernest Willim Winkler, ed., *Platforms of the Political Parties of Texas* (Austin: Bulletin of the University of Texas, 1916), 293–99.
3. The Omaha Platform can be found in Sheldon Hackney, ed., *Populism: The Critical Issues* (Boston: Little, Brown, 1971); 1–6.
4. Ibid., 4–5.
5. Ibid., 5 (first quotation); Dallas *Southern Mercury*, June 23, 1892.
6. For the Populist state platforms of 1891, 1892, 1894, and 1896, see Winkler, *Platforms*, 293–99, 314–16, 332–35, 379–84.
7. *Dallas Morning News*, August 6, 1892 (first and second quotations), August 9, 1892 (third quotation), December 5, 1895 (fourth quotation), August 27, 1892 (fifth quotation); *Houston Post*, January 19, 1894 (sixth quotation).
8. *Dallas Morning News*, October 5, 1892 (first quotation); *Kaufman Sun*, quoted in *McKinney Democrat*, February 27, 1896 (second and third quotations); *Texas Advance* [Dallas], February 24, 1894 (fourth quotation).
9. *Dallas Morning News*, September 7, 1892 (first and second quotations), October 29, 1893 (third and fourth quotations). For Populist invocations of Franklin, Madison, Calhoun, Clay, and Webster, see *Dallas Morning News*, September 7, 1892; *Dublin Progress*, February 7, 1891; *McKinney Democrat*, June 2, 1892; *Southern Mercury*[Dallas], October 30, 1888, March 13, 1890, April 14, October 27, 1892; *Texas Advance* [Dallas], April 28, December 2, 1894.
10. *Southern Mercury* [Dallas], November 13, 1888 (first quotation); July 16, 1891 (second quotation). For other examples of Populists' use of Jackson, see *Southern Mercury* [Dallas], November 28, 1889, June 18,

1891; *Dallas Morning News*, September 7, 1892; *McKinney Democrat*, August 8, 1895.

11. *McKinney Democrat*, July 2, 1896 (first and second quotations); *Southern Mercury* [Dallas], Oct. 27, 1892 (third and fourth quotations), August 23, 1894 (fifth and sixth quotations). While the 1864 quote was a favorite of Populists and of liberal bloggers since (a quick Internet search uncovers hundreds of hits for the quotation), experts seriously question its authenticity; see Thomas F. Schwartz, "Lincoln Never Said That," *For the People: A Newsletter of the Abraham Lincoln Association* 1, no. 1 (Spring 1999), 4–6.

12. The classic expression of the Populists-as-reactionaries view is Richard Hofstadter, *The Age of Reform: From Bryan to F.D.R.* (New York: Alfred A. Knopf, 1955). For an interpretation that stresses the social, economic, and geographical isolation of Populists, see James Turner, "Understanding the Populists, "*Journal of American History* 67 (September 1980): 354–73.

13. *Southern Mercury* [Dallas], November 13, 1888 (first quotation); *Dallas Morning News*, November 22, 1894 (subsequent quotations). Martin emphasizes the farmer-laborer base of Populist support, and finds Populism strongest in the poorer rural areas, but he concludes that the party "rested on divers social and economic bases" and that "it welcomed and to some extent received the support of other classes." See Martin, *People's Party in Texas*, 58–88 (quotes on p. 87).

14. *Southern Mercury* [Dallas], April 9, 1896 (quotations).

15. *Dallas Morning News*, December 1, 1892.

16. Alwyn Barr, *Reconstruction to Reform: Texas Politics, 1876–1906* (Austin: University of Texas Press, 1971), 116–30; Martin, *People's Party in Texas*, 36–41; Barnes, *Farmers in Rebellion*, 120–35; Goodwyn, *Democratic Promise*, 234–43.

17. Barr, *Reconstruction to Reform*, 125–38.

18. Martin, *People's Party*, 115–17; *Dallas Morning News*, quoted in *Southern Mercury* [Dallas], July 7, 1892 (first and third quotations); *Palestine Times*, quoted in *Southern Mercury* [Dallas], Decenber 1, 1892 (second quotation).

19. *Dallas Morning News*, September 12, 1892; *Southern Mercury* [Dallas], December 22, 1892 (quotation).

20. Goodwyn, *Democratic Promise*, 8–9; *Southern Mercury* [Dallas], December 6, 1894.

21. *Waco Evening News*, June 21, 1894 (first and second quotations); "Wise Sayings of J. B. Rayner," undated item in Rayner Papers, Center for American History, University of Texas at Austin (third quotation). For representative statements illustrating the hold that the Democratic Party had on white Southerners and the ways in

which Populists justified their abandonment of the old party, see *Southern Mercury* [Dallas], October 20, 1892, December 6, 1894; *Dallas Morning News*, June 7, 1892, October 28, 1894; *McKinney Democrat*, October 17, 1895, May 7, 1896.

22. Gregg Cantrell and D. Scott Barton, "Texas Populists and the Failure of Biracial Politics," *Journal of Southern History* 60 (November 1989), 659–92.

23. Gregg Cantrell, *Kenneth and John B. Rayner and the Limits of Southern Dissent* (Urbana: University of Illinois Press, 1993), 205–15; Winkler, *Platforms*, 333 (first quotation), 334 (second quotation).

24. Goodwyn, *Democratic Promise*, 52–65; Martin, *People's Party*, 53, 67–69; Matthew Hild, *Greenbackers, Knights of Labor, and Populists: Farmer-Labor Insurgency in the Late Nineteenth-Century South* (Athens, Ga., University of Georgia Press, 2007), 66–78; Ruth Allen, *The Great Southwest Strike* (Austin: University of Texas Press, 1942); Hackney, *Populism: The Critical Issues*, 5 (quotation).

25. Winkler, *Platforms*, 297 (first quotation), 315 (second quotation).

26. Barnes, *Farmers in Revolt*, 142; Martin, *People's Party*, 222; *Dallas Morning News*, November 28, 1892; *Southern Mercury* [Dallas], December 22, 1892.

27. *Dallas Morning News*, April 24, 1894 (quotations); *Biennial Report of the Secretary of State of the State of Texas, 1896* (Austin: Ben C. Jones & Co., 1897), 62.

28. Joe Creech, *Righteous Indignation: Religion and the Populist Revolution* (Urbana: University of Illinois Press, 2006), xxii–xxiv, 10–13, 20–21, 100–102, 128–29,144–45, and passim. This work focuses on North Carolina but its interpretation applies well to Texas. Thomas Nugent's Swedenborgian religious beliefs subjected him to a great deal of criticism, and his responses reinforce the notion of Populists holding countercultural religious opinions; see *Dallas Morning News*, November 5, 12, 1892, March 14, 1894; *Dublin Progress*, June 8, 1894.

29. *McKinney Democrat*, May 31, July 26, November 1, 1894, October 22, 1895 (first and second quotations), September 19, 1895 (third quotation); *Dallas Morning News*, October 2, 1894.

30. Martin, *People's Party*, 134, 168–72. For examples of press coverage of Populist camp meetings, see *Dallas Morning News*, July 22, August 7, September 3, 1892, July 30, 1893, July 13, 31, 1894, June 20, August 17, 18, 1895; *McKinney Democrat*, August 8, 1895, August 20, 1896.

31. *Waco Evening News*, June 20 (quotation), 21, 1894; *Southern Mercury* [Dallas], June 28, 1894; *Dallas Morning News*, June 20, 1894; Barr, *Reconstruction to Reform*, 154–60.

32. Barr, *Reconstruction to Reform,* 157; Martin, *People's Party,* 210–11.
33. *Southern Mercury* [Dallas], April 16, 1896 (quotations). All major national-level studies of Populism have dealt with the crucial 1896 campaign and the politics of fusion, although they provide widely differing interpretations as to the motives of the fusionist and middle-of-the-road factions; see for example John D. Hicks, *The Populist Revolt: A History of the Farmers' Alliance and the People's Party* (Minneapolis: University of Minnesota Press, 1931), 340–79; Robert F. Durden, *The Climax of Populism: The Election of 1896* (Lexington: University of Kentucky Press, 1965); Goodwyn, *Democratic Promise,* 426–514; Gene Clanton, *Populism: The Human Preference in America, 1890–1900* (Boston: Twayne, 1991), 148–61; Robert C. McMath Jr., *American Populism: A Social History, 1877–1898* (New York: Hill and Wang, 1993), 193–205. For a perceptive recent explanation of the 1896 Populist-Democratic fusion, see Peter H. Argersinger, "Taubeneck's Laws: Third Parties in American Politics in the Late Nineteenth Century," *American Nineteenth Century History* 3 (Summer 2002), 93–116.
34. Cantrell, *Kenneth and John B. Rayner,* 225–26.
35. Cantrell and Barton, "Texas Populists," 673–85.
36. Ibid., 685–90. On Kearby, see Gregg Cantrell and Kristopher B. Paschal, "Texas Populism at High Tide: Jerome C. Kearby and the Case of the Sixth Congressional District, 1894," *Southwestern Historical Quarterly* 109 (July 2005), 30–70.
37. Cantrell and Barton, "Texas Populists," 690–92; Worth Robert Miller, "Building a Progressive Coalition in Texas: The Populist-Reform Democrat Rapprochement, 1900–1907," *Journal of Southern History* 52 (May 1986), 163–82.
38. *Southern Mercury* [Dallas], August 9, 1894.

THE TEXAS SOCIALIST PARTY

Peter H. Buckingham

Thousands of Texans turned to the Socialist Party during the first two decades of the twentieth century in the hope of attaining a brighter future. Under the leadership of former Populists, the Socialist movement grew slowly at first. The party sponsored political rallies and educational campaigns, and further broadened its appeal through Socialist encampments. Irish-born "Red Tom" Hickey reorganized the Lone Star Socialists, publishing a highly effective weekly newspaper, *The Rebel.* Farmers and workers, united under the banner of the Texas Socialist Party, challenged the Republicans as the second party in the state. Brave opposition to the U.S. entry into World War I, the failure to break the Texan fealty to the Democratic Party, and internal schisms combined to wreck the movement in short order after it had barely begun the process of setting down political grass roots.

While the great economic crisis of the middle 1890s passed eventually, life did not improve for ever-increasing numbers of landless farmers, trapped in a nightmare of debt and poverty. Some of the former Populists, including William E. Farmer, Jake and Lee Rhodes, and G. B. Harris, became interested in the single tax idea of Henry George and the Americanized socialism of J. A. Wayland, who argued in the pages of his newspaper *Appeal to Reason* that public operation and control of the trusts (including corporate agriculture) and continued private holdings by small farmers would bring prosperity to the countryside. William Farmer broke with the Populists in 1898 to found an independent Socialist Party in Texas and a party newspaper, *Social*

Economist. The next year, the executive board of the fledgling Social Democratic Party (SDP), led by labor leader Eugene V. Debs (another recent convert to socialism) met with Farmer to merge their organizations.[1] The *Social Democracy Red Book* exclaimed in 1900, "No man living will have a better right to rejoice at the overthrow of capitalism which is sure to come, than comrade W. E. Farmer, and we hope he may be one of the elect who will be permitted to live to see this grand transformation. His address is Bonham, Texas."[2]

The Social Democratic Party competed for a short time with Texas affiliates of the Socialist Labor Party (SLP), dominated from New York by the doctrinaire Marxist, Daniel DeLeon. The SLP state platform of 1900 denounced their rivals as "the residuary legatee of moribund Populism" and pledged to overthrow capitalism in favor of a cooperative commonwealth.[3] The document had nothing to offer to farmers except that the revolution would abolish privately held land. The SDP endorsed the national candidacy of Eugene Debs for president and the basic doctrine of international socialism: "ownership of the means of production and distribution." Immediate demands included abolition of child labor where it interfered with education, a ban on women and children in unhealthy occupations, government health-and-safety inspections of workplaces, an eight-hour day for work, and measures to allow the people to initiate laws. There was to be no fusion with capitalist or middle-class political parties, a strategy that had doomed the Populists in 1896. Every support would be given to any and all labor unions.[4]

The SDP proved to be an intermediate step for the many former Populists in their shift to a more permanent and broad-based organization, the Socialist Party of America (SP), a national organization founded in 1901 out of the SDP and the "kangaroos" (critics of DeLeon) of the SLP. "Battling Bill" Farmer chaired the state executive committee and wrote the founding platform in 1902, which reaffirmed the most basic problem to be faced as "the triune curse—interest, profit, and rent." The Socialists asserted that two-thirds of the people were tenants in a vast area where wealthy corporations controlled much of the land. The working class was more poorly protected than any other state in the union and simply had to be freed from economic slavery. Progressive trust busting had no relevance for the new party. It also welcomed the endorsement of the American Labor Union, an arm of the militant Western Federation of Miners.[5]

In the early days of the SP, the national office could not spare enough authorized organizers to blanket Texas and the neighboring Twin Territories (Indian and Oklahoma Territories), so former Populists, sympathetic preachers, and even traveling salesmen carried the water for the Socialist cause at times. This led to confusion and incon-sistency in the party line. German Marxist Karl Kautsky observed that while Southern farmers might be "ripe for a revolt of desperation. . . . it seems to me impossible to found a permanent party organization with them."[6] But Kautsky had never met J. A. Wayland, publisher of the *Appeal to Reason,* of Girard, Kansas, who agreed to send a trained organizer to Texas to bring farmers to the movement *if* the party sold enough subscriptions to his paper. He tried to goad Texas trade union-ists into action in the wake of the state attorney general filing suit to halt a union boycott. "Wake up, you foolish virgins, you union men," he thundered. "Do you not see how the bogey man is getting you? You need and must have the powers of government and get on the right end of the injunction and a high-grade rifle. Vote the Socialist ticket and stop this farce and humbuggery."[7]

As promised, Waylands's organizer arrived in the spring of 1904. Frank P. O'Hare had graduated from an *Appeal* school for Socialist agi-tators in Girard, Kansas, a few years earlier, where, for good measure, he had wooed and won a wife, Kate Richards. He created something of a sensation in Waco when he passed out thousands of slips of paper to students, promising to give one dollar to the best answer to the ques-tion "What is Socialism?" "Considerable literary work and economic research" was carried out that week by parents and students alike, ac-cording to the *Laborer* of Dallas. At his lecture, O'Hare read out the best answers, and the audience voted little Ada Hall as the winner for the best definition: "Socialism is a condition under which the means of production and distribution collectively used shall be collectively owned; and those individually used shall be individually owned."[8]

In August 1904, the Rhodes brothers organized a Socialist encamp-ment just outside of Grand Saline in Van Zandt County, modeled on Populist and religious camp meetings. "Speakers of National promi-nence" attended, including *Appeal* organizer O'Hare, Benjamin Frank-lin Wilson of Kansas, and Texan Stanley Clarke. While the weather did not cooperate, tenant farmers from all over Northeast Texas came by wagon to hear the speaking. O'Hare later remembered speaking on a practical level, avoiding theory while denouncing the big old political parties. He was impressed enough with the encampment as an orga-nizing tool that he brought the idea with him to Oklahoma, where it became a way of educating southwesterners in an Americanized Marx-ism, and sowing the seeds for a grassroots movement. Richey Alexan-der, a local lawyer, held yearly encampments in Grand Saline for years thereafter. No coincidence that Van Zandt County became an early center of support for the SP.[9]

At the conclusion of the first Texas Socialist encampment, the party held its state convention. Eschewing immediate demands this time, the new platform presented a long-term plan of action, beginning with education of workers "to a consciousness of their identity of interests as proletarians, their possessing themselves of the powers of government, and then using the government to inaugurate the social revolution."[10] That fall, SP gubernatorial candidate W. H. Mills received 2,847 votes, far outdistancing the SLP candidate (552 votes), but well short of the Populist (9,301) and the Prohibitionist (4,509) men, not to mention the Democrats and Republicans. Clearly, the new party had its work cut out, especially in light of newly enacted poll taxes, arcane rules for party nominations, and a law that allowed the party in power sole discretion in the counting of votes.[11] Running on the Democratic ticket, Socialist newspaper publisher E. O. Meitzen won a judgeship in Lavaca County, another early party stronghold.[12]

The nascent SP ran into problems exercising the right of free speech at times. Acting temporarily as a party newspaper until the real thing came along, *Appeal to Reason* reported that armed thugs threatened party organizer Laura B. Payne with rotten eggs as well as hot lead for any man who defended her if she spoke as advertised in Point, Texas, in July 1906. State secretary W. J. Bell wired for reinforcements, who arrived in time to confront several armed men "led by an old sinner who claimed special authority as a hard shelled baptist and democrat." Armed with twin .44's in his belt, a local party man introduced Payne and the speech went on as planned. The *Appeal* guffawed that the incident served only to arouse new interest in the party "by waking up people who have been too sound asleep for anything but day dreams of dead democracy."[13] It was more difficult in Galveston, where police announced a ban on public soapboxing by Socialists. When SP organizer H. L. A. Holman tried to speak in a hired hall, the city cut off the electricity, so the meeting moved into the street, where police arrested Holman. Another speaker filled in until he obtained release from jail and finished his speech.[14]

Determined to improve its showing at the ballot box in 1906, the party nominated for governor George C. Edwards of Dallas: a school teacher, secretary of the Federal Labor Union, and editor of the *Laborer.* Instead of a nominating convention, the party held a mass meeting to affirm the candidates chosen earlier in a referendum. The platform endorsed the national party's pledge to end the capitalist system. Immediate demands called for higher wages and shorter hours; workmen's compensation; government pensions; public ownership of transportation, communication, and exchange; the abolition of child labor and poll taxes; more democracy; and universal adult suffrage. *Appeal to Reason* was confident enough on the eve of the election to note, "Socialists are becoming numerous in the Lone Star state."[15]

Months of hard work did not seem to have paid off as Edwards received only 111 more votes than the SP gubernatorial candidate had two years earlier. Still, party secretary W. J. Bell found "cause for congratulation in the results," arguing that a party investigation revealed massive and obvious voter fraud in several counties. Many votes were thrown out because poll taxes had not been paid. In central and western counties, cotton pickers stayed in the fields on Election Day as the harvest had not been finished. The ballots used were "new and strange and complex." Under these circumstances, the Texas SP proved to be the only party that actually recorded an increase in votes, however modest. Bell pointed out that the party had gone from fifth to third place behind only the Democrats and Republicans. "If we can avoid needless petty dissensions and keep our faces to the future," he concluded, "the outlook for telling results is flattering indeed."[16] Petty dissensions must have already become a distraction for Bell, and the problem of holding a party of Texas farmers and workers together would only get worse in the short term.

Farmers and workers alike thrilled to the words of Mary Harris "Mother" Jones during her extended swing through Texas in 1907. Still without a party newspaper, W. J. Bell continued to use the pages of a special Southwest edition of the *Appeal* to speak directly to volunteer organizers. He urged them to load up on application cards and present new members to party locals as soon as possible. "We do not mean," Bell wrote, "that you should take in every Tom, Dick and Harry . . . seek out those known to be in accord with the party and who will remain attentive and faithful members." Find a trustworthy unemployed Socialist. Then, "put him on a horse and let him go to every nook and corner of your county, and solicit members, take subs [to the *Appeal*] and sell books, and he will nearly make a living off the profits of book sales." Knowing that Frank O'Hare had used the Socialist encampment idea, that he had first seen in Grand Saline, to build an extraordinary, united party organization in Oklahoma, Bell urged his readers to start encampments up in the summer when farmers had time before the harvest. Finally, the state secretary addressed "every weak-kneed comrade," worried that the boss will fire him for being Red, to have the courage to help overthrow capitalism and its cowardly lackeys.[17]

Detailed instructions on how to manage an encampment followed a few weeks later: delegate by committee, find a suitable spot at least a mile from a town with lots of clean water for both people and stock, and do lots of advertising well ahead to give people something to look forward to. Get discounts from railroads. Build a platform and lots of board seats. Sell privileges for everything from balloon sales to airplane rides and have the party local run some simple attractions like a greased pole (or pig) and sack races. Bell understood how important these encampments could be for retaining party members, spreading the gospel of socialism to those not yet converted, and also showing participants a good time. In such a folksy atmosphere, socialism could be made relevant to landless farmers, explained in terms that were as American as a sermon on Sunday, not as frightening alien Marxist dogma. Poor farmers had little disposable income and free time, but if the party could attract enough rural folk to spend a week with them, then they could build a movement with roots—one that would last long enough to bring about a peaceful revolution.[18]

As the Texas party faithful prepared to improve on a disappointing showing at the polls, Bell continued to hammer away at them. "Our prospects for the future are flattering beyond description," he observed, except that the party needed more members and money.[19] In June he wrote: "It looks as though the bottom had been reached and that from now on the movement and the organization in Texas would bound forward. . . . We must have more encampments."[20] Two weeks later, several encampments were taking shape in Throckmorton, Young, Palo Pinto, Erath, Comanche, Eastland, Callahan, and Shackleford Counties with plans for Texarkana and Hallettsville too. Playing on Texas chauvinism, Bell reminded his state's *Appeal* readers that Oklahoma already had more than five thousand dues-paying members, so the Lone Star party ought to at least shoot for three thousand. The more members, the more money to fund full-time organizers like Reverend M. A. Smith and Laura B. Payne, not just for the campaign season but year-round. In midsummer, the party secretary made no apologies for not writing his column in the *Appeal* for a while. Why? No money for his rent and the butcher—and the grocers wanted something on their bills too—and not enough had come into the party office for him to make ends meet. So Secretary Bell picked up his tool kit and spent several weeks on construction jobs as the work piled up in SP headquarters.[21]

Bell also took some time off because, at long last, the Texas SP had its own party newspaper, *American Manhood*. When many of the comrades did not rush to subscribe, Bell and the editor of the new sheet took them to task. Good party members simply had to read it because the *Appeal* did not have enough space to publish Texas news and the latest information from the National Executive Committee (NEC) in Chicago. Several socialist papers had come and gone in Texas, so, Bell wanted to know, "Is this to be the fate of the 'American Manhood' also?"[22] It was a question with a double meaning, for many socialists, including Eugene Debs, sought to redefine the whole notion of American manhood not in terms of the self-made man but fighters for justice and equality. The paper continued to languish, perhaps owing to a rumor among party members that *Manhood* was not even a Texas paper. Not true, publisher J. C. Thompson wrote in the *Laborer*. He lived in Texarkana, one mile inside the Texas line; the paper was merely written and published in Arkansas. Not for much longer, it turned out.[23]

A feud between the state office and the Dallas-based *Laborer* came out into the open in 1908. Three years earlier, at the behest of "Battling Bill" Farmer and others, the Dallas local of the SP hastily convened a convention in Fort Worth to amend the "very crude" party constitution to comb out possible sources of corruption and conflict of interest. The *Laborer* objected to Bell's appointment of Stanley Clark as a Texas SP organizer because he was working for the national party concurrently, a move that seemingly violated the constitution. The newspaper, friendly to the interests of conservative craft unionism (including the American Federation of Labor—AFL) and an advocate of a "soft" socialism espoused by the Center-Right of the national SP, objected to Clark because he was close to the Industrial Workers of the World (IWW). Clark dismissed the criticism as a technicality invented by "a rump convention." The *Laborer* replied that Clark had made his rebuttal while in New Orleans during Mardi Gras and wondered aloud what he was doing there. The paper also attacked Laura B. Payne, like Clark a tireless organizer, who also held two party appointments, both of them within Texas.[24] Bell would have his way for the moment, but the party would stay divided underneath the surface, a fair reflection of the national organization.

The summer of 1908 witnessed bigger and better encampments all over the state, featuring national party leaders like standard-bearer Eugene V. Debs, "Big Bill" Haywood of the IWW, and "Mother" Jones. Texans Clark, Payne, M. A. Smith, W. S. Noble, and Dan C. Crider crisscrossed the state, speaking and organizing new locals. Reddin Andrews proved to be the favorite among the Texas speakers. Former Confederate scout, Baptist preacher, Populist, one-time president of Baylor University, writer, and editor, Andrews argued that the ethos of socialism and Christianity were virtually synonymous. Another former Populist, J. C. Rhodes, campaigned hard for governor. Meeting in Waco, the state party simply readopted the platform from two years earlier. The results, though, were anything but a repeat of 1906. Rhodes received 8,100 votes, an increase of 5,142 from the last election. Still, the Democratic candidate received almost seventy thousand more votes than two years earlier and the Republican office seeker, although a distant second, got seventy-three thousand votes.[25]

Then along came Hickey, Thomas Aloyisius Hickey of Dublin, who, according to a very friendly article in the *International Socialist Review*, burst dramatically on the scene to bring disparate factions together under what he called the "Texas Plan." In point of fact, Hickey had been well-known in the Lone Star State for some years as a national party organizer working out of Arizona. With "much experience in party rows," Hickey proposed to State Secretary Bell that all party locals have more or less complete autonomy "to do their own work in their own way; adapting their propaganda to local conditions, settling their own disputes and depending on themselves rather than a centralized state organization." Strict term limits would be observed by state and county secretaries. Most of the dues would stay with the locals to spend as they saw fit. Bell drew up a new constitution based on the plan, while party members debated its merits in the Abilene *Farmers Journal*, a Socialist sheet edited by J. L. Hicks. Most of the comrades did not realize it at the time, but "Red Tom" had begun to push the party far to the left from its Populist beginnings to a syndicalist form of organization favored by the IWW.[26]

In 1910, Tom Hickey's friend, E. R. Meitzen, son of Judge E. O. Meitzen, and editor of the *New Era* of Hallettsville, took the reins as state secretary, vowing to implement the new party constitution. In his *Appeal* column, Meitzen included reports on several encampments and street meetings that had taken place in early August. Eugene Stevens, a "live wire" electrical worker of El Paso "is waking up a dead town," Meitzen wrote, speaking on the street, selling literature, and recruiting a Spanish speaker as well. A party local would soon be formed there, he promised. Another comrade, C. W. Stewart, took on a Democratic congressman, who made "the same old venomous tirade," but was bested by the logic of socialism. The secretary of the Wichita Falls local wrote that a lecture by "Big Bill" Haywood there had been very effective. An African American of his acquaintance told him that the socialists were stirring things up and said that "with a few more Haywoods turned loose in Texas we would stir things sure enough."[27]

A mass meeting nominated the Confederate hero Reverend Reddin Andrews for governor in 1910. The party had a net gain of at least twelve hundred dues-paying members since the first of the year. Seventeen organizers were in the field, with much attention given to farmers. Urban activism, "heretofore weak," was however "gaining ground very fast," especially in Fort Worth and Houston. Seventeen encampments graced the countryside. The gathering at Groesbeck seemed especially memorable, with the owner of the grounds, W. H. Wilson, writing that Haywood, Hickey, Andrews, and O'Reilly "'made good' before great crowds" and saying that he wanted them all back next year. Most of East Texas seemed to be en route to Tyler to hear "the Fighting Editor" of the *Appeal*, Fred Warren, speak at the final encampment of summer, where "all kinds of privileges" were still available at reasonable rates.[28] Once again the party improved on its performance at the ballot box, as the Andrews ticket garnered 26,207 votes, an increase of 3,538. Democrat Oscar Colquitt received twenty-five thousand fewer votes than his immediate predecessor, while the Republicans had forty-seven thousand less ballots.[29] The fortunes of the Texas SP never seemed brighter, not just at the ballot box, for the culture of socialism seemed to be taking hold at the local level.

Hickey created a socialist newspaper, *The Rebel*, based in Hallettsville, which contained hard-hitting articles on the evils of capitalism, socialist sermons to the faithful, columns boosting subscription sales patterned after the *Appeal*, and news of the movement in Texas and Oklahoma. Quickly the *Rebel* became the most important regional radical weekly in the country. It was not an official party newspaper (that would have violated the spirit of the Texas Plan), but it proved to be just what the SP needed. Membership tripled in just four years. Running again for governor in 1912, Reddin Andrews received 25,268 votes, 2,179 more than the Republicans. When E. R. Meitzen ran in 1914, he did almost as well, easily beating out the GOP for second place.[30] Seemingly, the Texas SP had arrived and Hickey deserved a share of the credit for making the party competitive with the Republicans. His friend Covington Hall half-jokingly referred to him as "not only the uncrowned king of Texas Socialism, but its despot and 'pope' as well."[31]

He insisted that the land question be paramount. When a Fort Worth newspaper asked in an editorial, "Why are you here, Tom?" Hickey replied that "a true Celt would sooner wield his shillelah on the hide of a landlord than kiss a colleen or take a libation of potheen. Where then . . . could one of my glorious stock cross the seas to find landlords more plentiful than in this glorious Lone Star State of ours?"[32] Academics and agricultural experts had paid attention to the growing tenant problem but state and national government officials had not. In November 1911, a Renters' Union came into being in Waco at Socialist Hall. Hickey remained behind the scenes to give the organization a nonpartisan flavor, but the founding platform repeated the *Rebel* mantra: tax the land and grant land titles based on actual use and occupancy. The delegates vowed to get rid of politicians who would not agree to their demands. Still the Democrats ignored the land question until 1913, when James Ferguson decided to harvest votes in the Democratic Party primary race for governor by pledging to protect land renters and sharecroppers through a new law enforcing customary rents. "Take away the abuses of the present rent system," he promised, "and the Socialist would not have a leg to stand on."[33] Hickey fought back against Ferguson, who, once safely elected, settled for a watered-down version of his proposal, which was quickly declared to be unconstitutional.

In 1915, the United States Commission on Industrial Relations came to Dallas to hear testimony on rural unrest and the exploitation of landless farmers. Chairman Frank Walsh and his chief investigator, Charles Holman, worked with Hickey, E. O. Meitzen, and W. S. Noble, head of the newly reconstituted Renters' Union, the Land League. A parade of witnesses provided compelling evidence of the miseries faced by rural landless people. Levi Stewart explained that while he paid his poll tax, he seldom bothered to vote because "it did not look like it done any good. It seemed like it went their way, anyhow."[34] When Stewart's wife was asked if the family bought medicine for their surviving children, she replied that all they could afford was "Dr. Miles' Nervine; I used to keep that all the time."[35] Noble testified that the Stewarts faced blacklisting for speaking out and that renters who dared to declare themselves socialists were harassed at every turn.[36] Hickey and the Meitzens had urged *Rebel* readers to send them detailed descriptions of their lives as tenant farmers, which the Commission published as part of its final report. All of this stood as a powerful indictment of landowners and their allies in high places.[37]

Although he had become "the uncrowned king" by uniting disparate factions under the Texas Plan, Hickey was not a healer. At first he aimed most of his appeals at sharecroppers, tenant farmers, and itinerant workers such as cotton pickers, then turned his attention to oil and timber workers in East Texas. If he thought of himself as a Socialist Party leader, it was of the "Red" faction, supporters of militant trade unionism and the direct action (including sabotage) of the IWW. The "Yellows," believers in evolutionary socialism and the craft unionism of the AFL (centered in Dallas, Ft. Worth, and Houston) were the frequent objects of ridicule in the *Rebel*. Hickey evidenced little interest in the fate of rural, landless African Americans, spewing out a brand of racism that sometimes matched that of the lily-white Democratic Party. The relative narrowness of the Texas Socialist appeal caused the party to be less successful (by percentage of votes received) than Oscar Ameringer's "Yellows" in nearby Oklahoma or, for that matter, in at least ten other states. Hickey had no interest in building bridges to middle-class Texans. Threats of violence, recurring migration, and the poll-tax payments combined to make it very hard for the Texas sp to organize the landless. By 1916 the Republicans had regained the place they had occupied since the end of Reconstruction as the distant second party of Texas. This might have just been a temporary setback had it not been for U.S. participation in the Great War—and the excuse it afforded to crush the Socialist Party.[38]

Like most Socialists, Hickey opposed U.S. entry into World War I. So did millions of German-Americans, Irish-Americans, and assorted pacifists, anarchists, and iww members. As Hickey saw it, the war merely distracted from the crucial land question. What counted, he wrote in early 1915, was the "war from within" against capitalism, "a secretive, elusive, Janus-faced foe that besmirches our judiciary, corrupts our congress, debauches our legislatures, muzzles our press, mammonizes our teachers and preachers, and even seeks to degrade the electorate."[39] A few months later, Hickey warned that President Wilson should realize that he would have a fight on his hands at home if he committed the United States to the European conflict. Resistance to war dominated the columns of the *Rebel* throughout the final crises with Germany, the declaration of war, and initial mobilization. Hickey thundered against Wilson, calling him "the only Czar left in the world" since Nicholas II had been toppled in Russia.[40] By the time most of his subscribers read Hickey's May 19 editorial denouncing conscription, he was sitting in an Abilene jail, arrested on suspicion of conspiring to abet draft resistance.[41]

By the time Hickey met bail, more than fifty members of the Farmers' and Laborers' Protective Association (flpa) had been jailed on suspicion of seditious conspiracy for opposing conscription. Founded in 1915 as an offshoot of an Oklahoma scheme to boost prices for farmers, organizers of the flpa hoped to create better lives for tenant farmers and small producers by running their own cotton gins, mills, and cooperatives. Only founder George T. Bryant had ties with the much-feared iww. Bryant also appeared as Tom Hickey's invited guest at the convention of the Texas sp in November 1916, making, as the *Rebel* reported, "an earnest and eloquent talk. . . . The address was received with much enthusiasm by the membership present."[42] In early 1917, with U.S. participation in the European war fast approaching, delegates representing the eight-thousand-member flpa approved resolutions pledging their refusal to fight overseas at the behest of the ruling class, vowing instead to "fight for Liberty and Justice and the Brotherhood of Man."[43] Subsequently a divided convention voted to resist selective service through peaceful means if Congress authorized a military draft. On May 19, two days after Hickey's arrest, government agents announced the first arrests in "an armed uprising against the conscription plan" by the FPLA.[44]

Government officials "have made a mistake," Hickey explained coolly. "The American Farmers' and Laborers' Association was not organized to fight conscription or oppose the government in any manner. The facts will come out at the proper time."[45] His friend, labor leader and poet Covington Hall, wrote that Hickey had obviously been "framed" for his work to provide land to the exploited lower classes.[46] In the end, federal and state officials declined to indict him, but the veracity of Hall's comment that, in effect, Hickey had been persecuted for his militant socialism, meant more serious trouble.

"Red Tom" had made powerful enemies among Texans in high places over the years, including Postmaster General Albert Sidney Burleson, a feud that began in April 1915 when the *Rebel* published a transcript of testimony by E. O. Meitzen before the Commission on Industrial Relations in Dallas. Burleson and his brother-in-law together owned the Day Ranch in Bosque County that had long been home to a community (complete with a school and a church) of thirty tenant farmers and their families. When the landowners discovered that using convict labor meant higher profits, they threw the weeping tenants off the property on New Year's Day. As Oscar Ameringer later wrote: "Tom Hickey . . . who hated landlords and landlordism more than any devil could possibly hate holy water, printed abstracts of that testimony in the *Rebel*, which explains why of all the many hundreds of publications, the *Rebel* was the first to walk the plank."[47]

In April 1917, local postmasters began forwarding copies of the *Rebel* to U.S. Solicitor General William H. Lamar, a man who once explained: "You know, I am not working in the dark on this censorship thing. I know exactly what I am after. I am after three things and only three things—pro-Germanism, pacifism, and 'high-browism.'"[48] Lamar did not explain which of these categories applied to the *Rebel*, except to say that he had seen material "of a treasonable character."[49] Following Hickey's publication of Jack London's "Good Soldier," word came down from Washington to take away the *Rebel*'s second-class mailing privileges, a weapon designed to throttle a paper that could not afford to spend fifty-two cents to mail subscriptions that cost fifty cents a year. The next week Lamar declared another issue to be unmailable under the Espionage Act because of an article entitled "Don't Buy Bonds," and then the issue after that, which turned out to be the last *Rebel* ever printed.[50]

In mid-July, Hickey joined a battery of Socialist Party lawyers, including Clarence Darrow and Frank Walsh, in three-hour sessions with

Espionage Act enforcement attorney Judge William C. Herron (another Texan) and Burleson. Walsh told Burleson that he found it incredible that the postmaster general had apparently let his underling Lamar make life-and-death decisions about suppressing the radical press.[51] By September, Hickey admitted, "We could receive no satisfaction at their hands. They refused to say what was mailable and what was unmailable; they refused to construe the espionage act. They would not say why the *Rebel* was stopped on June 9, under a law that was not passed until June 15, 1917. . . . These high officials simply stood pat saying in effect what are you going to do about it."[52] The only thing left to do was let go of the *Rebel* and start all over again, in Dallas, it was hoped.[53]

Back in late May, when authorities had released Hickey from jail on bond, he went immediately to his German-American in-laws' farm outside of Brandenburg. Hearing of Hickey's return, a mob burned the family's utility barn to the ground. Stonewall County residents had been inclined to let socialists and Germans live and let live when the war broke out, but that attitude ended with negative publicity surrounding Hickey, and shortly thereafter the discovery that some of the arrested members of the FLPA had been locals. The county's only newspaper, the *Aspermont Star*, called for the creation of a self-defense organization. When a socialist speaker appeared at the end of the summer, the paper warned, "You had better move to the country that you are in sympathy with or keep your chops shut."[54]

On July 4, 1918, the *Star* reported that residents of Brandenburg had presented a petition to the Post Office Department to change the name of their town to Old Glory. Once the change became official, the paper reported "that [while] most of the people of that place are of German descent, they are loyal Americans, and wanted the name changed. And to the few who were opposed to the name being changed, we would suggest that you keep very quiet or pack your 'duds' and move to Brandenburg, Germany."[55]

By the time Brandenburg turned into Old Glory, the Socialist Party of Texas had also been cleansed out of existence. The Socialists had, for a brief time, become the second party of Texas because the other political movements had not spoken to the needs of the majority of the state, who were hungry, landless, and exploited. The party had attempted to set down social roots through electioneering, encampments, and renters' leagues. Hickey tried to lead the movement in a different direction by pushing his comrades to the left and challenging the establishment directly, both in person and through the *Rebel*. A majority of white adult males stuck by the Democrats, "the party of the fathers," and chose to close ranks with the state and national governments when the country went to war in 1917. The spirit of the movement would live on in other ways, though, that continued to reverberate in politics, schoolhouses, college campuses, and union halls for the rest of the century.

NOTES

1. James R. Green, *Grass-Roots Socialism: Radical Movements in the Southwest, 1895–1943* (Baton Rouge: Louisiana State University Press, 1978), 3–20; Elliott Shore, *Talkin' Socialism: J. A. Wayland and the Role of the Press in American Radicalism, 1890–1912* (Lawrence: University of Kansas Press, 1988), 32–54; and *Social Democracy Red Book, 1900* (Terre Haute: Standard, 1900), 71–74, 111. Socialist newspapers are valuable primary sources for information on the Texas Socialist Party, 1900–1917. Complete runs of *Appeal to Reason* of Girard, Kansas, and the *Rebel* of Hallettsville are available on microfilm. Very incomplete runs of the *Laborer* (Dallas), the *Ft. Worth Socialist* and its successor, the *Ft. Worth Light*, and the Hallettsville *New Era*, are also available. Single issues of smaller socialist papers are located in various archives and historical societies around the state. Non-socialist papers sometimes contain news of socialists too, especially the *Grand Saline Sun*, the *Houston Chronicle*, and the *Dallas Daily Times Herald*. The most important collection of Texas newspapers is located at the Center for American History (CAH) at the University of Texas at Austin. Begin with their "Guide to Using Newspaper Collections," available online at cah.utexas .edu/documents/using/UsingNewspapers.pdf. There is a small collection of documents relating to the Texas SP in the Socialist Party Papers at Duke University, also available on microfilm. The Thomas Hickey Papers are located at the Southwest Center, Special Collections, Texas Tech University. The CAH and the Labor Library at the University of Texas at Arlington have small collections of papers related to socialism. Ernest William Winkler, ed., "Platforms of Political Parties in Texas," *Bulletin of the University of Texas*, Number 53 (1916), contains all of the party platforms for the SP and SLP to 1916. For election statistics, see Mike Kingston, Sam Attlesey, and Mary G. Crawford, eds., *Political History of Texas* (Austin: Eakin, 1992). In terms of secondary sources, the most complete narrative is James R. Green, *Grass-Roots Socialism: Radical Movements in the Southwest, 1895–1943* (Baton Rouge: Louisiana State University Press, 1978), which, as the title implies, argues that socialism became fully rooted in Oklahoma, Texas, and elsewhere. In *Yeomen, Sharecroppers and Socialists: Plain Folk Protest in Texas, 1870–1914*

(College Station: Texas A&M University Press, 2008), Kyle G. Wilkison argues that the socialist movement attracted culturally based support from among the rural poor in Texas. For a history of the *Appeal to Reason*, see Elliott Shore, *Talkin' Socialism: J. A. Wayland and the Role of the Press in American Radicalism, 1890–1912* (Lawrence: University of Kansas Press, 1988). The millennial culture of socialism is examined in a series of essays, including one on Hickey, the O'Hares, and Wayland in Peter H. Buckingham, ed. *Expectations for the Millennium: American Socialist Visions of the Future* (Westport: Greenwood, 2002). Mainstream politics and government are examined in Lewis L. Gould, *Progressives and Prohibitionists: Texas Democrats in the Wilson Era* (Austin: Texas State Historical Association, 1992). Partial drafts of two essays, "Agrarian Socialism in Texas" and "Thomas A. Hickey and the *Rebel*" are located in the Papers of Ruth Allen, Center for American History, University of Texas, Austin.

2. *Social Democracy Red Book*, 111–12.
3. Winkler, ed., "Platforms of Political Parties in Texas," 420–23.
4. Ibid., 418–20.
5. Ibid., 442–44.
6. Karl Kautsky, "Agitation Among Farmers in America," *International Socialist Review* 3 (September 1902), 155.
7. *Appeal to Reason*, April 4, July 25, 1903, and Green, *Grass-Roots Socialism*, 38, 43.
8. *The Laborer* [Dallas], April 15, 1904, and Peter H. Buckingham, *Rebel against Injustice: The Life of Frank P. O'Hare* (Columbia: University of Missouri Press, 1996), 21–25.
9. Buckingham, *Frank P. O'Hare*, 41–42, 57, and Kyle Grant Wilkison, "The End of Independence: Social and Political Consequences of Economic Change in Texas, 1870–1914" (PhD diss., Vanderbilt University, 1995), 295–98; see also Wilkison, *Yeomen, Sharecroppers and Socialists.*
10. Winkler, "Platforms of Political Parties in Texas," 470–72.
11. *Appeal to Reason*, August 13, 1904. For the national platform, see the *Laborer* [Dallas], July 23, 1904.
12. Newspaper clipping, Hallettsville Public Library, Hallettsville, Texas, and the *New Era* [Hallettsville, Texas], June 12, 1908.
13. *Appeal to Reason*, July 21, 1906.
14. Ibid., October 6 and 20, 1906.
15. *Appeal to Reason*, November 3, 1906; *Laborer* [Dallas], August 18, September 1, 1906; and Winkler, "Platforms of Political Parties in Texas," 483–85.

16. *Appeal to Reason*, March 2, 1907. In 1908, George C. Edwards was appointed as principal of Oak Cliff Central School and fired shortly thereafter for political reasons by the Democratic Party–controlled school board. See the *Laborer* [Dallas], June 6, 1908.

17. Ibid., April 20, 1907. On the Mother Jones tour, see *Appeal to Reason*, March 9, 1907, and the *Laborer* [Dallas], May 4, 1907.

18. *Appeal to Reason*, May 11, 1907, and Jim Bissett, *Agrarian Socialism in America: Marx, Jefferson and Jesus in the Oklahoma Countryside, 1904–1920* (Norman: University of Oklahoma Press, 1999), 6–7, 86–104.

19. *Appeal to Reason*, May 25, 1907.

20. Ibid., June 8, 1907.

21. Ibid., June 29, July 20, 1907.

22. Ibid., December 14, 1907.

23. *Laborer* [Dallas], March 14, 1908. On Debs and manhood, see Nick Salvatore, *Eugene V. Debs: Citizen and Socialist* (Urbana: University of Illinois Press, 1982), 25–26, 63–64, 88–89.

24. Ibid. See also the *Laborer* [Dallas], May 23, 1908.

25. *Appeal to Reason*, June 6, July 11, November 14, 1908; Winkler, "Platforms of Political Parties in Texas," 513–14, and Mike Kingston, Sam Attlesey, and Mary G. Crawford, eds., *Political History of Texas* (Austin: Eakin, 1992), 279. On Andrews, see *Handbook of Texas Online*, "Reddin Andrews, Jr." http://www.tsha.utexas.edu/handbook/online/articles/AA/fan49.html (accessed April 8, 2007).

26. Nat L. Hardy, "The Texas Program," *International Socialist Review* 11 (April 1911), 622–23. See also *Constitution of the Socialist Party of Texas Adopted January 4, 1912* (n.p., 1912).

27. *Appeal to Reason*, August 20, 1910.

28. Ibid.

29. Kingston, et al., *Political History of Texas*, 279.

30. Hickey to William S. U'Ren, April 18, 1916, Papers of Thomas A. Hickey, Southwest Collection, Texas Tech University, Lubbock; *Rebel*, January 10, May 16, July 11, 1914; Ruth Allen, "Agrarian Socialism in Texas" and "Thomas A. Hickey and the *Rebel*" unpublished mss., Papers of Ruth Allen, Center for American History, University of Texas, Austin; Green, *Grass-Roots Socialism*, 117–18; and Kingston, et al., *Political History of Texas*, 283.

31. Hall quoted in Allen, "Thomas A. Hickey and the *Rebel*."

32. Hall quoted in Allen, "Thomas A. Hickey and the *Rebel*"; Hickey quoted in ibid.

33. Ferguson quoted in Lewis L. Gould, *Progressives and Prohibitionists: Texas Democrats in the Wilson Era* (Austin: Texas State Historical

Association, 1992), 128–29. See also James Ferguson, "My Platform," November 13, 1913, Papers of James Ferguson, Center for American History, University of Texas, Austin.

34. U.S., Commission on Industrial Relations, *Final Report and Testimony*, 11 vols. (Washington, D.C.: GPO, 1916) 9:9034.

35. Ibid., 9043.

36. Ibid., 9035–36.

37. Ibid., 9260–89.

38. Allen, "Agrarian Socialism in Texas"; Hickey to J. Friedlander, May 27, 1916, Hickey Papers; *Rebel*, December 23, 1911; Neil Foley, *The White Scourge: Mexicans, Blacks, and Poor Whites in Texas Cotton Culture* (Berkeley: University of California Press, 1997), 945–1000; and Peter H. Buckingham, "Visions from the 'Beautiful Trinity': The Dawning of the Cooperative Commonwealth in the Popular Socialist Press," in Peter H. Buckingham, ed. *Expectations for the Millennium: American Socialist Visions of the Future* (Westport: Greenwood, 2002), 86–87.

39. *Rebel*, February 6, 1915. See also, *Rebel*, September 19, 1914, and July 1, December 16, 1916. See also Frederick C. Luebke, *Bonds of Loyalty: German Americans and World War I* (DeKalb: Northern Illinois University Press, 1974), 83–198.

40. *Rebel*, May 12, 1917. See also March 31, April 7, 14, 21, 28, 1917.

41. Ibid., May 19, 1917; T. A. Hickey, "Kidnapping an Editor," unpublished fragment, Papers of Thomas A. Hickey, Southwest Collection, Special Collections, Texas Tech University, Lubbock; *Rebel*, June 2, 1917; Interview with Mina Lamb and Ilse Wolf, January 30, 1979, cassette tape, Oral History Collection, Southwest Collection, Special Collections, Texas Tech University, Lubbock.

42. *Rebel*, November 25, 1916.

43. Quoted in Robert Wilson, "The Farmers' and Laborers' Protective Association of America, 1915–1917" (master's thesis, Baylor University, 1973), 11. See also pp. 5–10.

44. *Dallas Daily Times-Herald*, May 20, 1917. For the FPLA position, see Z. L. Risley to Hickey, May 23, 1917, Hickey Papers.

45. Ibid, May 26, 1917.

46. *Rebel*, June 2, 1917.

47. Oscar Ameringer, *If You Don't Weaken: The Autobiography of Oscar Ameringer* (New York: Henry Holt, 1940), 320; *Rebel*, April 10, 1915; and Stephen M. Ellis, "The First Amendment on Trial in Texas During World War I: The Espionage Act, Albert Sidney Burleson, and the *Halletsville Rebel*," (master's thesis, Southwest Texas State University, 1997), 41.

48. Lamar quoted in Robert H. Ferrell, *Woodrow Wilson and World War I, 1917–1921* (New York: Harper, 1985), 208. See also Postmaster, Mesa, Texas, to W. H. Lamar, April 30, 1917, U.S. Post Office, Record Group 28, "Case Files: Espionage Act," File 46130, National Archives, Washington, D.C.

49. Lamar to Department of Justice, May 25, 1917, U.S. Department of Justice, Bureau of Investigation, File 46130, National Archives, Washington, D.C.

50. T. W. House to Solicitor, June 1, 1917; Lamar to J. W. Hoopes, June 19, 1917; and "Memorandum for Mr. Ash," June 25, 1917, ibid. and *Rebel*, May 26 and June 2, 1917.

51. Frank P. Walsh to Burleson, July 24, 1917, Hickey Papers.

52. "Dear Comrade," September 1, 1917, Hickey Papers.

53. Ibid.

54. *Aspermont Star*, August 16, 1917. See also Hickey Papers, May 24, 1917, and Interview with Mina Lamb, August 29, 2001, Lubbock, Texas.

55. *Aspermont Star*, July 4, 1918. See also *Austin American-Statesman*, July 16, 1989.

TEXAS … UNIONS … TIME

Unions in Texas from the Time of the Republic through the Great War, 1838–1919

George Norris Green

◀ In the half century between 1870 and 1920 the Texas labor movement and its agrarian allies helped elect reform-minded men to public offices—and even when they failed to do so, their challenges sometimes persuaded the dominant Democratic Party to embrace reform. While labor was under siege both at the beginning and the end of the era, the labor laws passed in the interim, as well as labor's measured success in collective bargaining, helped make Texas a far better place to live in 1920 than it had been in 1870.

The first unions in Texas date back to the Republic, with the founding of the Texas Typographical Association by journeymen printers in Houston on March 28, 1838. They successfully struck for a wage increase that fall. Other locals of Anglo craftsmen, usually inspired by wage and hour grievances, were established before the Civil War. The demand for some of these skills remained high afterward, but labor scarcity in Texas was terminated by the Civil War, which left "thousands of widows and destitute orphans, and others, all over the land," creating "cheap and profitable white labor," not to mention the presence of the freedmen looking for work. Augmented by an immigration surge of hundreds of thousands, the labor force in Texas soon constituted a surplus.[1]

Perhaps the most successful local was the Screwman's Benevolent Association of Galveston (SBA), established in September 1866. Comprising mostly English and Irish immigrants, they were devoted to providing sickness compensation and burial funds for members and their families, but evolved into a union determined to regulate wages and working conditions and keep the craft in the hands of whites. Shipping companies employed screwmen to manipulate huge and dangerous jackscrews to compress the bales by as much as 10–15 percent. For four decades these specialized skills provided screwmen in Galveston and other southern ports more bargaining power and higher wages than other longshoremen.

Inspired by the success of the all-white SBA, black dockworkers in Galveston and Houston attempted to organize in 1871 and 1872. Reconstruction-era whites deeply resented the activism, and blocked the efforts.[2] The 1872 venture was conducted by Karl Marx's International Workingmen's Association, the first hint within labor of leftist ideology in Texas. It was also the first of many occasions in Texas in which potential labor solidarity splintered in the face of racism and fear of radicalism.

The great railroad strikes of 1877 degenerated into violent defeats for labor in much of the United States, perhaps serving as a cautionary lesson to both labor and management by the time they spread into Texas. On July 24 operating hands and shopmen struck at various points on the Texas and Pacific (T&P), the Houston and Texas Central (H&TC), and soon thereafter, on the Missouri, Kansas, Texas (Katy) line. The men, who had suffered a series of wage cuts and were owed back pay of several months, quietly refused to allow freight trains to move, but joined local and railroad police in guarding railroad property against sabotage by tramps. There was also much resentment among the unemployed against the use of convict labor on the railroads. While the *San Antonio Daily Herald* ran one headline entitled "The Commune in Texas," the ensuing story told of the officers of the H&TC amicably inviting the strike committee to a conference, which settled their issues within a day. Railroad pay scales and back wages were restored in Texas without any violence. There was lively agitation among black workers in Galveston, forcing even the hostile Galveston *Daily News* to concede that a laborer could not live on a dollar and a half a day in the city. Black longshoremen used the occasion to successfully strike to raise their pay from thirty to forty cents an hour, equal to the whites.[3]

Given the twelve- and fourteen-hour days, six- and seven-day workweeks, complete lack of benefits, dangerous working conditions in many trades, and subsistence wages for many, in a system that regarded it as a mark of business acumen to cut wages whenever and wherever possible, it is hardly surprising that workers reacted to American industrialization. They not only organized unions, but also took to the streets in protests, strikes, and boycotts, and also plunged into politics. Many workers came to believe that they were the victims of class warfare launched by the corporations.

I agree with Richard Oestreicher that "labor history is still ultimately about workers and what defines people as workers is their economic activity." But I do not agree with him and many others that labor history is primarily about class development. Texas workers seem to have developed, or at least sustained, only a modicum of class consciousness, if that is even the right phrase to describe the more tumultuous labor-management events in Texas. I agree with Lawrence McDonnell that class was a central factor in workers' lives, but that a person's class was established by nothing but his objective place in the hierarchy of ownership relations. Class consciousness does not enter into the definition of one's class position. Workers taking tough stands on economic battlefields, usually desperate and defensive, were not necessarily developing class consciousness, at least not on a basis that would be maintained over a long period of time. Class warfare was waged far better by the capitalists than by the workers, through control of the state or at least powerful influence over it, and the use of naked force, open-shop drives, scientific-management schemes, excess numbers of workers, successful court cases, racial and gender discrimination, and a reluctant, occasional sharing of the rising wealth of the country. I will grant that the process of the struggle itself radicalized some of the labor participants—never a majority—over a sustained period. I also recognize that worker responses to problems varied somewhat due to different cultural backgrounds. Any conflict presents the possibility of violence if the system in which it unfolds does not provide proper mediation to defuse it, and U.S. and Texas capitalism usually did not. The law should have been a mediator, but it too was class-based and often a tool of oppression.

Also, while there is no disagreement that unions wrenched concessions from capitalists, and their strikes and collective bargaining altered capitalism, the capitalists themselves, as well as unions, had a hand in elevating the material well-being of all Americans. I agree with John Diggins that it was factions of workers rather than entire classes that were often moved to protest (frequently expressing individuals' needs collectively), that workers in general were usually motivated by material self-interest, and that despite numerous complaints, they embraced the capitalist system. Labor's considerable identification with the dominant culture of capitalism, as well as the rapidity of economic change, undermined the development of class consciousness. So did ethnic heterogeneity, which in Texas meant a workforce divided among Anglos, blacks, and Latinos. And U.S. workers enjoyed a measure of mobility within the working class. But I disagree that these factors established consensus in American politico-economic culture or that workers completely shared the economic individualism of the middle classes. The spirited and often bitter collective actions of unions through the decades, both economic and political—and marked by occasional deaths—belie any meaningful use of the words "consensus" or "individualism." So do the frequently harsh management practices and tactics. Uneasy coexistence represents neither consensus nor class consciousness.

Moreover, the material self-interest of workers was often supplemented by a genuine striving for political ideals that did not merely cloak economic interests. I concur with Alan Dawley and others that electoral politics operated as a safety valve for worker discontent, just as vital to labor's interests as economic activity, and tended to defuse that discontent over the long haul.[4]

The hard times of the 1870s raised the political awareness of workers and farmers, who blamed tight money and railroad malpractices. Even in agrarian Texas the new Greenback Party had an urban labor component. In Austin the Greenback club and the Workingmen's club, led by skilled workmen, jointly endorsed various independent candidates for local offices in October 1878, and about half the candidates won. The Texas platform pledged to save the working classes from starvation, opposed the use of convicts in competition with free labor, and advocated a national income tax, more money for schools in Texas, and regulation of railroad freight rates. In the Fifth Congressional District in South Central Texas, including Galveston and Austin, G. W. (Wash) Jones defeated the Democratic candidate, 21,101 to 19,721. The district was largely agrarian, but 24 percent urban, and the Protestant labor wards—Galveston's Eighth and Austin's First were populated mostly by black laborers and white clerks and craftsmen—probably constituted Jones's margin of victory, as did black and Republican voters generally. Tensions ran high, and as one independent Texas newspaper noted in 1882, "Greenback men, you must learn to shoot. You must make up your minds to kill." But also by that year dozens of legislative and local defeats pushed the Democrats into bolstering public-school spending and endorsing railroad regulation.[5]

In the 1880s a new national organization, the Knights of Labor, attempted to recruit all workers and farmers. The Knights favored the eight-hour day, industrial-safety laws, child-labor laws, equal pay for women, and the abolition of the southern practice of leasing convict labor. Their 1885 strike against Wall Street tycoon Jay Gould's Southwest system of railroads yielded empty promises of pay restitution and tolerance of unions. Gould did insure that his favorite railroad, the

Missouri Pacific (MP), pioneered guaranteed pay at the middle-class level of about $1,000 per year for what it judged to be its more crucial employees, the engineers, and limited their usual workday to twelve hours. The Knights' "victory" in the Southwest did not even bring recognition of the union, but it prompted national membership to soar from about one hundred thousand to over seven hundred thousand a year later.[6]

Over a third of the workers in the Southwest system—the T&P, Katy, MP, and the International and Great Northern—earned no more than $30 a month, about $360 per year, at a time when just paying board to the railroad section house would take half that amount. These starvation-level wages, along with mismanagement, refusal to discuss such grievances as the promised restoration of wages, and the use of convict and Chinese labor were the underlying causes of the strike, though it was triggered by the firing of C. A. Hall, a Knights leader in the T&P roundhouse in Marshall, Texas. With a highly exaggerated view of their own strength, some five thousand Texas shopmen and trackmen walked out in early March 1886 (and perhaps four thousand elsewhere in the Southwest system), defying the eastern leadership of the Knights and lacking much support from the skilled operators who actually ran the trains. The engineers, firemen, and brakemen were often members of the Knights of Labor, and most were sympathetic to the strike, but they were also members of their own railroad brotherhoods, and were more devoted to the brotherhoods. The leadership of the craft-based brotherhoods feared being subsumed by the all-inclusive Knights, and did not support the walkout. Strike leader Martin Irons secured considerable food from area farmers, many of whom regarded the railroads as the enemies of all producers. Freight traffic was halted for most of the month, and a number of locomotives were "killed" by strikers and sympathizers who drained the water and extinguished the fires in the locomotives. Other railroads, however, served some of the strike-bound communities, and by early April police, militia, and Texas Rangers blocked strikers' access to depots and roundhouses. The strikers were particularly goaded by heavy-drinking, deadbeat Jim Courtright, whose biographer notes, "Incredibly, after hiding from the law for more than a year with a price on his head and still facing unresolved double murder charges, Courtright on his return to Fort Worth was invested with police authority at federal, county, and municipal levels." Soon thereafter four men were severely wounded and one killed in a shootout. The Great Southwest Strike was the first serious defeat for the Knights and seemed to unleash a cascade of losses around the nation that brought about the virtual demise of the order within five years, though not in Texas.[7]

Despite the shattering of the Great Southwest Strike, railroad workers paused only briefly, then continued their efforts to extend their organizations. But now most of the organizing was by the big four brotherhoods (representing the engineers, firemen, brakemen, and conductors), and the machinists in the shops. And, given their growing numbers, these unions and others, those of carpenters and typographers, for example, also turned to politics. Labor played some role in the election of fourteen Farmers' Alliance men, ten Grangers, two Knights of Labor, and two independents to the legislature in 1886. The new Republican solon from San Antonio was also a labor candidate. The Third Ward in Fort Worth, with its railroad workers and the laboring class in general, played a large role in electing the independent candidate H. S. Broiles as mayor, defeating a Democrat. Independents carried various Texas county offices that fall. Democrat Dan Smith, supported by the Knights, narrowly defeated the choice of the business community, the incumbent mayor of Houston. But the budding farm-labor alliance and independent insurgency fizzled after 1886. It was split on the issue of leaving the Democratic Party. And the charismatic C. W. Macune took charge of the Farmers' Alliance and led it away from politics and toward economic strategies. Moreover, the pall of defeat in the great strike had set in—several thousand Texas strikers were never knowingly rehired by the railroads. Most probably dispersed, taking their militancy with them.[8]

One of the great worker movements in the United States and Texas in the late nineteenth century was the drive for shorter hours, widespread efforts to reduce the average workday and workweek. The eight-hour movement triggered the establishment of the first statewide organization of unions, the Texas State Federation of Labor, in 1889. The first delegates, about a fourth of whom were black, came from craft unions, Knights assemblies, and from the Farmers' Alliance.[9] In most Texas cities the carpenters, painters, bricklayers, and stone cutters established the nine-hour day, usually forced to strike in the process. Other reforms were still in play. In Houston, Knights of Labor District Assembly 78 and the city's labor council called for the secret ballot in city elections as early as 1890, and the city council passed the ordinance unanimously in February 1892. The Houston labor platform also included a demand for compulsory education for children.[10]

The sputtering farm-labor insurgency benefited politically because the railroads had earned the ire of the public, and between 1886 and 1891 the battles were fought largely within the Democratic Party. James Hogg took office as attorney general in 1887 and, with the help of irate farmers, the Knights, and undoubtedly the railroad brotherhoods, pushed through a state antitrust law aimed at the monopolistic practices of the railroads, whose pooling agreement was busted. Another 1887 measure held that when a man left the payroll of a railroad, he had to be paid what was owed him within fifteen days. In 1890 Hogg was the first Texas gubernatorial candidate to face vilification as an alleged communist because of his farm-labor support. Railroad construction was slowed in an effort to blame him for it. The *Dallas Morning News* and *Galveston News,* owned by the same company, smeared Hogg's followers as "Union Laborites, Anarchists, and Communists." Hogg was elected anyway and soon established the state railroad commission, with the power to regulate freight rates and fares.[11]

Also at this time—in order to cope with the astounding number of injuries generated by the industrial revolution—the courts, in the service of capitalism, concocted the doctrines of contributory negligence, the fellow-servant rule, and assumption of risk. If the plaintiff was negligent, even slightly, he could not recover from the defendant. This harsh dogma was the favored method by which judges kept tort claims from the deliberations of juries, which tended to sympathize with maimed men suing giant corporations. A plaintiff, whether a railroad employee or the survivor of one of the innumerable railroad crossing accidents, not only had to prove that the railroad was negligent, but also that he was faultless himself. Assumption of risk meant that a worker could not recover if he had put himself willingly in a position of danger, which seems just until one considers that railroad men, miners, and factory hands put themselves in grave danger merely by accepting their jobs. Under the fellow-servant rule an employee (the servant) could not sue his employer (the master) for injuries caused by the negligence of another employee (and, usually, even if the employer was also negligent). Since most accidents came about in this manner, an injured workman frequently could only sue another equally impoverished fellow worker, a meaningless recourse to law. So the cost of industrial accidents had to be borne by the workers themselves and their destitute families rather than the most productive sector of the economy. The common-law doctrines of Texas operated to the prejudice of some 80 percent of all employees injured on the job.[12] Even payments for services rendered were endangered. In 1892 the Texas Court of Appeals tossed out a state law requiring railroads to pay back wages, interest, and damages to men who had left their service. The judge ruled, "Unquestionably, so long as men must earn a living for their families and themselves by labor, there must be, as there always has been, oppression of the working classes."[13] And in 1889 the Texas Supreme Court upheld the notorious blacklist.[14]

Meanwhile, the Populist Party was founded in 1891 because of widespread belief among southern and western farmers and wage hands that the two older parties were hopeless. Jim Hogg did just enough to retain most farm-labor voters, and even upon his retirement in 1894, when the Populists neared their peak strength, neither their farm nor labor support was united. Populists always did best in the countryside, but organized labor and harder times allowed their gubernatorial candidate Tom Nugent to increase his urban vote from 10 percent in 1892 (against Hogg) to 25 percent in 1894 against Attorney General Charles Culberson. In Tarrant County, centered on Fort Worth, the farm-labor alliance (supposedly representing some 1,800 to 2,000 voters out of 5,215 registered) allowed different unions to select Populist candidates for four local offices. But the city's building-trades locals were angered that the Populists challenged preferred, pro-labor Democrats for three other county offices. Nugent apparently carried the working-class Third Ward of Fort Worth, but only with a plurality. Nugent came closest to carrying Austin and Houston in the working-class precincts, losing the First Ward of Houston by only ten votes, and running well in the Fourth Ward north. Texas labor appeared to support the Populists better than previously, in part because Culberson did not agree with Hogg's sympathetic stand on behalf of railroad workers in the American Railway Union (ARU) Pullman Strike that year and because of a new state Democratic plank, a backlash against the ARU strike, that promised penal sanctions against even peaceful persuasion aimed at preventing strikebreakers from taking workers' jobs. (The ARU strike in July had paralyzed Santa Fe freight for about a week in Texas. Large crowds in Galveston, Temple, and Dallas had to be dispersed). But late in the campaign Culberson deftly stemmed labor's desertion of the Democrats by pledging not to sign any bill that abridged labor's right to peacefully ask men not to take strikers' jobs. Democrats generally swept Texas in 1894.[15]

Labor's ranks were still split in 1896. In August the "sound money clubs" made up of railroad workers in Dallas, Houston, Fort Worth, and El Paso denounced the prospect of free silver—pushed by Democrats and Populists—as undermining the wage scale. The sound money club pledge cards had been distributed by the railroad corporations in an effort to control their employees, but the brotherhood members, not necessarily intimidated, may have simply become accustomed to their stabilized wages. Many other craft unions did not oppose free silver, but saw no reason to embrace the Populists either, no doubt in part because the Democratic legislature and governor in 1895 had reconciled their contradictory labor planks by establishing a voluntary arbitration board and promising to exempt unions from the antitrust laws.[16]

Populist Jerome Kearby took 44 percent of the gubernatorial vote in a huge turnout in which the rest of the labor movement helped him carry Austin and Dallas. He carried the working-class Fourth Ward in Houston (947 to 770) and narrowly lost the First and Second wards; he captured the mining towns of Strawn, Mingus, and Gordon. Yet it was the last gasp for the Texas Populist Party, which had alienated many of its own supporters through appeals to blacks and through fusion with other parties in local, state, and federal elections. It was the end of the trail for the Knights of Labor as well. Some fourteen assemblies either closed their doors in 1896 or at least ceased their national affiliations as they faded away.[17] The Knights' goal of organizing all workers and producers would be missed. The successor to the State Federation of Labor, the Texas State Labor Union, did not linger much past the election either, but the craft unions were still intact and the Populist legacy prepared the nation for the Progressive movement in which the renewed farm-labor coalition was vital in Texas. The various strikes, and perhaps the Knights' vision of producer cooperatives, generated accusations of communism and socialism from the state's corporations and conservatives, but in reality workers were mostly using unions to improve their economic and political status.

Another divisive issue of the era, race relations, obviously impacted labor. Longshoring was split between blacks and whites, sometimes harmoniously, sometimes not. In Galveston black longshoremen made a dramatic breakthrough in 1883 on the lily-white docks, by underbidding white stevedores. Other blacks permanently filled white longshoremen's places during the Mallory Strike of 1885. All longshoremen worked in a system based on low wages, long hours, hard and dangerous tasks, and racial competition enforced by the shipping companies and local political leaders. During the strike against the Mallory line by the Colored Protective Labor Union [CPLU] in 1898, Galveston mayor Ashley Fly took personal charge of the police who were guarding black strikebreakers, with the result that one striker and one white bystander were killed and five men wounded. Another bystander was killed later, shortly before the CPLU gave up the strike. Despite Mallory statements that white labor would be preferable to black, the white longshoremen made no effort to take the jobs. Biracial unionism was extremely rare in the South, but the fragile examples of it on the docks of Galveston and New Orleans showed that occasionally whites could rise above racism. It kept hope alive, set precedents for the future, and black organizations—for example, the longshoremen—helped black communities advance.[18]

Mining was another tough industry. By the 1890s several thousand coal miners in the isolated village of Thurber, many of them Italian or

Polish, resided in a fenced-in company town wherein all buildings, including the workers' hovels, were owned by the Texas and Pacific Coal Company. Unable to make it from one monthly payday to the next, they were loaned scrip in lieu of money to keep them going, but it was discounted by the company store by 20 percent. Union sentiments could bring beatings. Suddenly, in early August 1903, a Mexican United Mine Workers (UMW) organizer disappeared, and the body of a murdered Mexican was soon discovered. Smoldering resentment broke into the open, and Thurber miners spontaneously marched out of town and joined the UMW. The company vainly tried to import strikebreakers, but agreed to a UMW contract that secured a substantial increase in wages, an eight-hour day, and two paydays per month. The entire town unionized![19] Tejano miners in Webb and Maverick counties also unionized, overcoming the firings of union activists, the beating of at least one of them, and the importation of nonunion Mexican workers.[20]

The Texas State Federation of Labor (TSFL) was organized in 1900, composed strictly of craft unions, and its convention of 1903 affiliated the federation with the AFL and set forth specific political objectives. Texas labor wanted the initiative and referendum as state laws, a compulsory school attendance law for a nine-month school term, and free textbooks for the public schools. Convict labor, child labor under fourteen, and the poll tax should be abolished, labor believed. Women should receive equal pay for equal work and all workers should receive the eight-hour day. Presidents, vice presidents, and U.S. senators should be elected by direct vote of the people. A graduated state income tax was favored. The platform heralded the Progressive movement in Texas. The TSFL and the railroad brotherhoods organized the Joint Labor Legislative Board to lobby in Austin. A political alliance was soon established with the Farmers' Union, established in 1902. Many Farmers' Union leaders were former Populists, but now determined to work within the Democratic Party. Their first statewide electoral success was helping Tom Campbell, who opposed corporate control of the state and the convict-lease system, win the governor's office in 1906.[21]

In 1905 four of the bills preferred by the Joint Labor Legislative Board passed, the most important being an amendment of the "assumed risk" law, stating that railroad employees were not forced to assume responsibility for defective equipment. The state's first child-labor laws were adopted between 1903 and 1917, but various loopholes and sporadic enforcement rendered them inadequate. Most labor bills were adopted during the gubernatorial administrations of Thomas Campbell, 1907–1911 (with twenty-four labor measures passed), and Oscar Colquitt, 1911–1915, though the former was more openly sympathetic to unions. Anti-blacklisting and mine-safety codes were adopted in 1907, though the former still proved impossible to enforce. Safety laws were also passed for railroad operators, machine shop hands, and stevedores. Between 1903 and 1909 several laws granted hours of rest to railroad workers, culminating in eight hours of rest required after sixteen hours of duty during a twenty-four-hour period. The state Bureau of Labor Statistics was founded in 1909, supposedly to enforce protective labor legislation. The phased abolition of the convict-lease system commenced in 1910.[22]

A heroine of the labor movement was Emma Goldsmith, described as a "noble little working girl," who, in the legislature in 1913, seemed to single-handedly rescue the stalled maximum-hour bill for women. After her dramatic testimony about the effect of long hours of labor upon the moral, mental, and physical condition of the female workers in the state's textile and cotton-mill industries, women were limited to fifty-four hours and six days per week.[23]

By this time the lumber industry emerged as perhaps the most dangerous in the state. At the snake-infested, malarial logging sites, hot and humid conditions in the summer and freezing weeks in the winter contributed to the killing environment. Foremen with whips and knives would force crews to compete against each other. The sawmills were so loud that workers' skulls vibrated, and the pace of work was set by machinery speeded up to the limit of human endurance, with daylong (ten-to-twelve-hour), continuous repetition of the same motion at top speed. Casualties were high, but men making a dollar and a half or two dollars per day, whose only other option was usually tenant farming, were less likely to sue than were railroad workers.[24]

Rebellions and spontaneous strikes without benefit of union leadership wracked the camps and mills beginning in the 1880s. After a futile attempt to cope with the "virtual chattel slavery conditions" of the largely black workforce at Groveton's Trinity Lumber Company, who struck in 1904, the TSFL made no effort to organize the industry. It was the independent Brotherhood of Timber Workers (BTW) that signed up some twenty thousand workers in East Texas and Louisiana during 1911 and 1912. Like the Knights of Labor, the BTW organized across craft lines, attempted ritualistic secrecy, welcomed minorities and women members, tapped into antimonopoly sentiment, and backed antiestablishment political candidates. Unlike the Knights, and even more unlike the AFL, the BTW—by integrating its locals, embracing sabotage, and finding its political outlet in the Socialist Party—was rejecting capitalism. Eugene Debs polled over 20 percent of the vote in four Texas lumber counties in 1912. Joining the Industrial Workers of the World (IWW) in May 1912, the union was soon broken by lockouts, blacklists, spies, some impenetrable company towns in Texas, heavily guarded black strikebreakers from outside the area, and finally companies' thugs who did not hesitate to commit violence, which drove the union to respond in kind.[25]

Texas socialists' most notable spokesman within the TSFL, where they were tolerated, was George Edwards, editor of the *Dallas Laborer*. For a time, he was a schoolteacher, and chose to live in the city's worst slum, the cotton-mill district. He went door to door, seeking out those who wanted to learn to read. Then he taught school day and night, and lobbied successfully to have night school incorporated into the public school system. His public efforts to abolish child labor and place the kids in schools prompted the *Dallas Morning News* to write editorials in defense of child labor—it kept those twelve-year-olds off the streets, out of the reformatory, and taught them how to work.[26]

The TSFL finally hired a woman organizer, Myrtle Berry, who was in the field during part of 1918. In that brief time she organized the needle trades and laundry workers, retail and shipyard clerks, and cooks, among others.[27] But it would be difficult to sustain these gains once managements resumed union-busting and the temporary wartime labor shortages disappeared, especially since the TSFL did not keep organizers in the field.

During the war the AFL adopted a policy of organizing Mexican Americans, and sent Laredo native Clemente Idar to the Southwest to take charge of the campaign. With the exception of the United Mine Workers and some craft locals along the border, Texas unionists in this era would only tolerate separate locals for Tejanos. Even this limited acceptance was undermined by employer policies of deliberately importing large numbers of workers from Mexico to keep wages low and discourage unionization. State federation president Ed Cunningham believed that the majority of labor-management disputes in Texas during the war involved employers' refusals to recognize Mexican and black workers' unions.[28] There was also a minorities dimension in labor's ongoing battle to establish free textbooks in the public schools. Alma Bartlett of the carpenters' Woman's Auxiliary, "made an impassioned talk on the textbook matter, citing 4,000 Mexican children in El Paso, who were eager to learn in school."[29]

After the war employers remained determined to keep minorities in their place. Some twelve hundred black sawmill laborers in Orange struck their two mills in January 1919, demanding higher pay and lowering the workday from ten or eleven to eight hours. The central trades council of Orange brought in federal conciliators, who arranged a small pay raise and a nine-hour day, but over the weekend the sawmill operators reneged and soon blasted unionism, blacks, and the IWW in vile language.[30] In El Paso in October 1919, local and state AFL organizers established a local of the International Laundry Workers' Union. Two veteran Tejana workers who were recruiting new members were quickly fired by Acme Laundry. Within days nearly five hundred laundrywomen had walked out of the city's six laundries, demanding reinstatement of the two workers as well as wages higher than their average of six dollars per week. It was one of the earliest displays of union and ethnic solidarity among Mexican American female workers in the United States, and symbolized their acculturation to an industrial-urban culture, but their timing was wretched. The strike failed in December, deluged by anti-Mexican sentiments, the notion that it was a radical Industrial Workers of the World strike, and the usual excessive number of workers available to take the strikers' jobs.[31]

Indeed, most of the industrial and unskilled workers in Texas were unable to utilize their supposed wartime leverage. Ten thousand Texas and Louisiana workers on the oil rigs, victimized by rising prices, static wages, and primitive working and living conditions, struck in 1917 when producers refused to discuss grievances, and spurned federal mediators. Denounced by employers as anarchists and German agents, the strikers were beaten when the Texas National Guard was summoned to protect strikebreaking farm boys and lumberjacks.[32] The Amalgamated Butcher Workmen in the Fort Worth packinghouses—during the war—had won the eight-hour day, overtime rates on holidays, a pay raise, and equal pay for women, but they were largely unskilled and overly dependent on federal wartime controls which were about to disappear. The bituminous coal miners around Thurber were better established, but had not yet realized that low-grade Texas coal was rapidly losing its market, doomed by the discovery of oil.[33] Skilled hands predictably fared better during the war, but were blindsided afterward.[34]

In the immediate postwar period in 1919, many unions demanded higher wages to cope with soaring prices, but many businessmen in Texas responded by establishing open-shop associations, often backed by local chambers of commerce. The building trades unions were targeted by local contractors in Texas, beginning May 1, 1919, when electricians bolted off a dairy company construction site in San Antonio because a nonunion handyman had been sent in to string a temporary electrical wire. Other strikes and lockouts followed, strikebreakers were imported, and some unions lost their contracts. An open-shop association was established in October in Beaumont, where employers wrecked a strike by building trades and other crafts. A strong union town turned almost completely open shop in two or three months.[35] In response to a building trades strike in Dallas in October, the chamber of commerce established an open-shop association, which soon imported some fifteen hundred craftsmen from across the United States as strikebreakers.[36]

Among white-collar workers, many public school teachers were still being paid prewar salaries, and were fed up with "gentle requests met by soothing promises." An AFL organizer helped establish locals in San Antonio, Denison, Austin, Dallas, Fort Worth, Houston, and Galveston in April 1919. They were defended by the *Houston Post* because they had stayed in their positions during the war, but gone unrewarded because they were not organized and because they were women. They too were done in by the climate of the time as well as the usual promises. The San Antonio Rotarians, for instance, endorsed higher salaries for teachers, in February 1920, provided teachers disaffiliate with the AFL.[37]

In 1919 the state federation engaged in a final, brief burst of reformism. Organized labor, women's suffrage lobbyists, and other progressives persuaded the legislature to adopt free textbooks for the public schools, minimum-wage provisos for women and children, and the Nineteenth Amendment to the U.S. Constitution, granting women's suffrage. But amidst the defeats and the open-shop drives, labor itself became increasingly conservative in politics, in organizing the unorganized, and in reaching out (however tentatively) to minorities and women. The federation voted down a resolution against discrimination by race, color, or creed, and voted Ed Cunningham out of the presidency.[38] Also, enforcing reform laws had been an ongoing problem, and in 1919 enforcement of the minimum wage awaited determination of different scales in different parts of the state (an impractical notion that soon served as a pretext for repealing the law).[39] In another ominous sign of the times, some El Paso labor leaders who had backed the laundry strike withdrew into a local alliance with the Ku Klux Klan.[40]

Many of the petitions, demonstrations, boycotts, strikes, and court cases over the decades were labor defeats. The railroad strikes of the late nineteenth century accomplished nothing tangible, but certainly inspired the farm-labor movement. That movement itself crashed in 1896, but arose from the ashes six years later. All of these events, even the defeats, seem to have had a cumulative effect in Texas, and did set the stage for much Progressive-era labor legislation in Texas. Perhaps the reforms were as much illusion as reality, given their general lack of enforcement and given the pervasive racism that undermined social justice, but they marked a change in attitudes toward the powers of government and against localism, attitudes that could never be completely undone. Much of this structure was shattered during and after World War I, typified by debilitating losses by some of the most progressive unions, but then the movement was reborn in the late 1930s. It was all part of the rhythm of progressive and conservative cycles typical in democracies. Organized labor's most basic task in all free societies is to push corporations into sharing more of their wealth, but labor often promotes reforms that go beyond that bread-and-butter approach. Corporations and conservatives considered this push to emanate from the far left, but that was only occasionally true from within the ranks of labor. A movement that for some four decades pushed the eight-hour day, the secret ballot, a progressive income tax, equal wages for women, women's suffrage, free textbooks for public schools, the abolition of the convict-lease system, the eradication of adult illiteracy, the abolition of child labor and the poll tax, the creation of a rational system of accident compensation, and—on the waterfront and in the mines and timberlands, at least—a measure of racial toleration, helped bring civilization to Texas and should be remembered for these accomplishments.

NOTES

1. *Telegraph and Texas Register* [Houston], May 2, 1838; William Hogan, *The Texas Republic* (Norman: University of Oklahoma Press, 1947), 105; Samuel Hamlett, "Labor Legislation in Texas, 1836–1876," (master's thesis, University of Texas at Austin, 1949), 10–11, 59; Ruth Allen, *Chapters in the History of Organized Labor in Texas* (Austin: University of Texas, 1941), 136–37; James Reese, "The Early History of Labor Organizations in Texas, 1838–1876," *Southwestern Historical Quarterly* 72 (July 1968), 1–10; James Reese, "The Worker in Texas, 1821–1876" (PhD diss., University of Texas at Austin, 1964), 201–202; S. S. Munger, article in *Texas Almanac for 1868* (Galveston: Richardson and Company, c.1869), 98–102 (quote); John Spratt, *The Road to Spindletop* (Austin: Texas State Historical Association, 1970), 228–32; Harold Shapiro, "The Labor Movement in San Antonio, Texas, 1865–1915," *Southwestern Social Science Quarterly* 36 (September 1955), 160; Robert Zeigler, "The Workingman in Houston, Texas, 1865–1914" (PhD diss., Texas Tech University, 1972), 75; F. Ray Marshall, *Labor in the South* (Cambridge: Harvard University Press, 1967), 43.
2. Reese, "Early History of Labor Organizations in Texas," 11–13.
3. *Marshall Messenger,* July 24, 26, 31, 1877; *San Antonio Express,* July 28, 31, 1877; *San Antonio Daily Herald,* July 27, 28, 1877; *Aus-*

tin Statesman, July 27, 29, 1877; *Denison Daily Cresset,* July 27, 28, 1877; *Galveston Daily News,* July 28, 31, August 1, 1877; *Dallas Weekly Herald,* July 28, August 4, 1877; *Waco Daily Examiner,* July 31, 1877.

4. See Richard Oestreicher, "Separate Tribes? Working Class and Women's History," *Reviews in American History* 19 (1991), 228–31; Lawrence McDonnell, "You Are Too Sentimental": Problems and Suggestions for a New Labor History," *Journal of Social History* (Summer 1984), John Diggins, "Comrades and Citizens: New Mythologies in American Historiography," *American Historical Review* 90 (June 1985), 614–38; John Diggins, *Rise and Fall of the American Left* (New York: Harcourt Brace, 1973), 68; and Alan Dawley, *Class and Community* (Cambridge: Harvard University Press, 1976), 219, 238–39.

5. Alwyn Barr, *Reconstruction to Reform: Texas Politics, 1876–1906* (Austin: University of Texas Press, 1971), 43–56; quote in Ray Ginger, *The Age of Excess* (Prospect Heights, Ill.: Waveland Press, 1975), 110. Elizabeth Sanders, *Roots of Reform: Farmers, Workers, and the American State* (Chicago: University of Chicago Press, 1999), 36, identifies the urbanization level of the Texas Fifth Congressional District.

    Alwyn Barr helpfully notified me that the 1878 election information on Waco comes from the *Waco Daily Examiner,* November 7, 1878, and from John Sleeper and J. C. Hutchins, *Waco and McLennan County, Texas, Containing a City Directory of Waco* (Waco, 1876; reprinted, 1966). And the voting ward and gubernatorial information comes from the 1880 censuses for Travis County and Galveston County, and from the Austin *Weekly Democratic Statesman,* November 14, 1878, and the *Galveston Daily News,* November 19, 1878.

6. Foster Dulles and Melvyn Dubofsky, *Labor in America* (Wheeling, Ill.: Harlan Davidson, 2004), 128–30; Norman Ware, *The Labor Movement in the United States, 1860–1895* (New York: Vintage, 1929), 139–45; Reed Richardson, *The Locomotive Engineers, 1863–1963* (Ann Arbor: University of Michigan Bureau of Industrial Relations, 1963), 223–25.

7. On wages issues, see *Temple Times,* April 25, 1886 and *Waco Daily Examiner,* March 11, 1886 (the monthly and yearly totals are based on the reports of the T&P to the Texas Railroad Commission in the 1890s, of 313 workdays per year); *San Antonio Light,* March 6, 1886, on causes of the strike; Ruth Allen, *The Great Southwest Strike* (Austin: University of Texas Bureau of Research in the Social Sciences, 1942), 44–50, 73, 86–87, 96, 129; Theresa Case, "Free Labor on

the Southwestern Railroads: The 1885–1886 Gould System Strikes,"
(PhD diss., University of Texas at Austin, 2002), 235–80; Robert
DeArment, *Jim Courtright of Fort Worth* (Fort Worth: Texas Chris-
tian University Press, 2004), 194–202 (quote on 194), 221; Dulles and
Dubofsky, *Labor in America*, 133–36.

8.   Roscoe Martin, *The People's Party in Texas* (Austin: University of
Texas Bulletin #3308, 1933), 32; Barr, *Reconstruction to Reform*, 98–
99; *San Antonio Light*, November 5, 1886; *Dallas Morning News*,
September 16, October 16, November 3, 5, 7, 1886; *Austin Daily
Statesman*, November 4, 5, 1886; Donna Barnes, *Farmers in Rebel-
lion* (Austin: University of Texas Press, 1984), 70–79; Allen, *The
Great Southwest Strike*, 90–91; *Houston Post*, April 3, 4, 10, 1886;
Oliver Knight, *Outpost on the Trinity* (Norman: University of Okla-
homa Press, 1953), 146–47. See Terry Jordan, "The German Settle-
ment of Texas After 1865," *Southwestern Historical Quarterly* 73
(October 1969), 198, on footloose nature of those who settled Texas.

9.   *Dallas Morning News*, July 4, 1889.

10.   Charles Gibson, "Organized Labor in Texas From 1890 to 1900,"
(master's. thesis, Texas Tech University, 1973), 86–97.

11.   Robert C. Cotner, *James Stephen Hogg: A Biography* (Austin: University of Texas Press, 1959), 163, 166–67, 170–74, 201–206 (quote
on 206); *Texas Railway Journal*, January 1907. The *Galveston Daily
News*, June 8, 1890, believed the railroad commission would mark
the state government as "an engine of communism."

12.   Lawrence Friedman, *A History of American Law* (New York: Simon
and Schuster, 1985), 467–87; John Peace, *Selected Cases and Materials on Texas Workmen's Compensations Law* (San Antonio: St.
Mary's University Book Store, 1950), 11–12, on the 80 percent figure.

13.   *San Antonio and Aransas Pass Ry. Co. v. Wilson*, 19 S. W. 910–14
(1892).

14.   *Missouri Pacific Railway v. Richmond*, 11 S. W. 555–58 (1889).

15.   Martin, *People's Party*, 137–39, 184–85; Barr, *Reconstruction to Reform*, 150–51, 157–58; Zeigler, "Workingmen in Houston," 180;
Gibson, "Organized Labor in Texas," 147–57; *Fort Worth Gazette*,
October 2, November 6, 1894; *Dallas Morning News*, August 24, 28,
September 25, 1894; Lawrence Goodwyn, *Democratic Promise: The
Populist Moment in America* (New York: Oxford University Press,
1976), 332–33.
        In Fort Worth's Third Ward, Culberson received 214 votes, Nu-
gent "2_5," and other candidates 108. There is a 90 percent chance
that the missing integer in Nugent's total is higher than zero, meaning that he probably carried the ward, but only with a plurality. See
the *Fort Worth Gazette*, November 9, 1894.

Of the nine relatively modest Texas labor demands put forward in 1894, three directly concerned railroad workers—the passage of an anti-blacklist law, a better fellow-servant statute, and the abolition of child labor among railroad telegraphers. See *Dallas Morning News*, September 21, 1894.

16. Nathan Fine, *Labor and Farmer Parties in the United States, 1828–1928* (New York: Rand School of Social Science, 1928), 85; Milton Garner, "The Application of the Anti-Trust Laws of Texas to Labor Unions," *Southwestern Law Journal* 2 (Spring 1948), 112; Gibson, "Organized Labor in Texas From 1890 to 1900," 157–58, 169–70.

17. Barr, *Reconstruction to Reform*, 171; Zeigler, "Workingmen in Houston," 180–81; Jonathan Garlock, *Guide to the Local Assemblies of the Knights of Labor* (Westport, Ct.: Greenwood Press, 1982), 491–513; *Stephenville Empire*, November 13, 1896, for mining town votes.

    The Populists may have done better than the figures suggest, of course, since they continued to be routinely defrauded by Democrats, who arranged votes for dead people, droves of mules, and Jefferson Davis, among others—see Martin, *The People's Party*, 184–85.

18. Edward Ayers, *The Promise of the New South* (Oxford: Oxford University Press, 1992), 430–31; David Roediger, *The Wages of Whiteness*, rev. ed. (New York: Verso, 1999), 168–80; see Cliff Farrington, "The Galveston Waterfront and Organized Labor, 1866–1900," (master's thesis, University of Texas at Austin, 1997).

19. Allen, *Chapters in the History of Organized Labor*, p91–97; Gibson, "Organized Labor in Texas," 167–68; John Miller Morris, *A Private in the Texas Rangers* (College Station: Texas A&M Press, 2001), 263, 271, 274, 276–78, 310; *United Mine Worker Journal*, September 24, 1903.

20. Roberto Calderon, *Mexican Coal Mining Labor in Texas and Coahuila, 1880–1930* (College Station: Texas A&M Press, 2000), 184–88, 196.

21. Grady Mullennix, "A History of the Texas State Federation of Labor," (PhD diss., University of Texas at Austin, 1955), 14; Allen, *Chapters in the History of Organized Labor in Texas*, 125; Barr, *Reconstruction to Reform*, 237; Lewis Gould, *Progressives and Prohibitionists* (Austin: University of Texas Press, 1973), 39.

22. Marshall, *Labor in the South*, 37; James Tinsley, "The Progressive Movement in Texas" (PhD diss., University of Wisconsin, 1953), 136, 139–145, 227. See chapter 2 in Maroney, "Organized Labor in Texas, 1900–1929," for a thorough discussion of labor's legislative efforts.

23. *Proceedings of the Texas State Federation of Labor, 1913* (Austin: Texas State Federation of Labor, 1913), 20.

24. Steven Reich, "The Making of a Southern Sawmill World: Race, Class, and Rural Transformation in the Piney Woods of East Texas,

1830–1930," (PhD diss., Northwestern University, 1998), 117–24, 130, 133–34.

25. Ruth Allen, *East Texas Lumber Workers* (Austin: University of Texas Press, 1961), 166–73; *Dallas Morning News*, April 14, 22, 24, 1904; James Green, "The Brotherhood of Timber Workers 1910–1913: A Radical Response to Industrial Capitalism in the Southern U. S. A.," *Past and Present* 60 (August 1973): 161–200.

26. Tinsley, "The Progressive Movement in Texas," 139–41; George Edwards, *Pioneer at Law* (New York: W. W. Norton, 1974), pp. 20–23; *Dallas Laborer*, November 20, 1909; *Dallas Morning News*, January 18, 1902, July 14, 16, August 25–28, 1907; Patricia Hill, *Dallas: the Making of a Modern City* (Austin: University of Texas Press, 1996), 49.

27. Mullennix, "A History of the Texas State Federation of Labor," 168–72.

28. Emilio Zamora, *The World of the Mexican Worker in Texas* (College Station: Texas A&M University Press, 1993), 69–70, 162–79; Lisa Berry, "Cooperation and Segregation: A History of North Central Texas Coal Mining Towns, Organized Labor, and the Mexican Workforce," (master's thesis, University of Texas at Arlington, 2004), 16, 85–86; *Proceedings of the Texas State Federation of Labor, 1919* (Austin: Texas State Federation of Labor, 1919), 46. See letters to and from A. P. Hall, Superintendent of the Gulf, Colorado, and Santa Fe Railroad, April 1918, Box 82, Santa Fe Railroad Collection (Houston Metropolitan Research Center).

29. *Weekly Dispatch* [San Antonio], May 19, 1917.

30. Maroney, "Organized Labor in Texas," 204–206.

31. Irene Ledesma, "Texas Newspapers and Chicana Workers' Activism, 1919–1974," *Western Historical Quarterly* 26 (Fall 1995): 311–16; *El Paso City and County Labor Advocate*, October 31, November 7, 14, 1919; Mario T. Garcia, *Desert Immigrants: The Mexicans of El Paso, 1880–1920* (New Haven: Yale University Press, 1981), 46–51, 64, 85–88, 100–105; Mario T. Garcia, "The Chicana in American History: The Mexican Women of El Paso, 1880–1920—A Case Study," *Pacific Historical Review* 49 (May 1980): 330–37. Despite defeat, the workers' own American Union Laundry was reportedly still thriving in the fall of 1922—see *El Paso City and County Labor Advocate*, September 22, 1922.

32. Harvey O'Connor, *History of the Oil Workers International Union* (Denver: Oil Workers International Union, 1950), 5–7; William Greer, "The Texas Gulf Coast Oil Strike of 1917," (master's thesis, University of Houston, 1974), 21–26, 38–39; James Maroney, "The Texas-Louisiana Oil Field Strike of 1917," in *Essays in Southern Labor History*, ed. Gary Fink and Merl Reed (Westport, Ct.: Greenwood Press, 1976), 163–65; Henrietta Larson and Kenneth Porter,

History of Humble Oil and Refining Company (New York: Harper, 1959), 67.

33. See Barry Sandlin, "The 1921 Butcher Workmen Strike in Fort Worth, Texas," (master's thesis, University of Texas at Arlington, 1988); Reinhardt, *A Way of Work and a Way of Life,* 107–10.

34. Michael Botson, "The Labor Aristocracy of Houston's Hughes Tool Company, 1901–1964: From Autocracy and Jim Crow to Industry Democracy and Civil Rights," (PhD diss., University of Houston, 1999), 36–57, notes the company union fate of machinists, blacksmiths, and others.

35. W. S. Mosher, "Open Shop in the Southwest," *Open Shop Review* 18 (March 1921): 115–17; *San Antonio Weekly Dispatch,* June 7, June 28, September 13, October 18, October 25, 1919, April 3, May 15, 1920; *Proceedings of the Texas State Federation of Labor, 1920* (Austin: Texas State Federation of Labor, 1920), 52; Allen Wakstein, "The Origins of the Open Shop Movement, 1919–1920," *Journal of American History* 51 (December 1964), 463; Mullennix, "A History of the Texas State Federation of Labor," 248.

36. *Electrical Workers Journal,* February, July, 1919; *Dallas Craftsman,* June 27, July 4, September 5, October 14, October 31, November 21, 1919; *Dallas Morning News,* October 14, November 19, 1919; Mosher, "Open Shop in the Southwest," 117–20; Jay Todes, "Organized Employer Opposition to Unionism in Texas," (master's thesis, University of Texas at Austin, 1949), 68–73.

37. *The Weekly Dispatch* [San Antonio], April 12, April 26, May 3, 1919, February 14 (quote), February 28, 1920; *El Paso Labor Advocate,* April 18, 25 (citing *Houston Post*), 1919; Helburn, "The American Federation of Teachers in Texas," 207.

38. *San Antonio Weekly Dispatch,* May 31, 1919; *Proceedings of the Texas State Federation of Labor, 1919,* 106, 107, 117, 121.

39. Lewis Gould, *Progressives and Prohibitionists,* 251–52; James Maroney, "Organized Labor in Texas," 15–16. H. J. Buest, secretary of the Houston Building and Trades Council and secretary-treasurer of the state Building and Trades Council, told traveling investigator P. A. Speek, October 1914, that the Joint Labor Legislative Board was "quite powerful in getting labor laws enacted, but it is entirely powerless in getting labor laws enforced." See Speek SC 299, "Notes on Migrant Labor in Texas," 9–10, RG 174, Department of Labor (National Archives).

40. Shawn Lay, *War, Revolution, and the Ku Klux Klan: A Study of Intolerance in a Border City* (Urbana: University of Illinois Press, 1992), 95–103, 155–56.

LOOKING FOR LEFTY
Liberal/Left Activism and
Texas Labor, 1920s–1960s

George Norris Green with Michael R. Botson Jr.

◀ In the spring of 1985, at Houston's University of St. Thomas, the late Texas historian Joe B. Frantz presented a paper entitled "The Mind of Texas." Professor Frantz's wit and wisdom enthralled the audience, especially his cogent observations on Texas ideology. He remarked that Texans tend to be more conservative than other Americans and what passes as liberal in Texas would at best be considered moderate in the rest of the country.[1] Similarly the Texas State Federation of Labor appeared to display less liberal or left-wing influence after 1919 than most other state federations. Nevertheless, despite the historically conservative nature of Texas, including some of its working class, beginning in the 1920s and continuing through the 1960s there were strains of liberal activism in the Texas labor movement that periodically flared up.

These outbursts occurred in times of economic stress or social upheaval, such as the Great Depression and the civil rights movement of the 1960s, manifesting themselves into full-blown popular movements that challenged Texas's conservative economic, political, and social establishment as well as the race-relations status quo. The conservative establishment as well as conservative unionists responded with ferocious opposition to these episodes of labor activism, and ultimately crushed them. Nonetheless, liberal/left labor activism between the 1920s and 1960s made its mark on the overall Texas labor movement. It popularized labor unions to a level previously unseen and contributed to the steady membership growth and stability of organized labor. Perhaps most importantly, liberalism and left-wing activism helped secure organized labor a place in conservative Texas.

In the two decades preceding 1920 the Texas labor movement enjoyed considerable success in advancing the cause of working people through the efforts of the Texas State Federation of Labor (TSFL), founded in Cleburne in 1900. By 1920 TSFL membership stood at fifty thousand. During this period the Joint Labor Legislative Board—a political alliance of the TSFL, the railroad brotherhoods and Farmers' Union—successfully lobbied to enact labor-friendly legislation. As mentioned in chapter 6, most major labor bills were adopted during the gubernatorial administrations of Thomas Campbell, 1907–1911 (with twenty-four labor measures passed), and Oscar Colquitt, 1911–1915. By 1920 Texas boasted an array of labor laws to the left of center of the ideological spectrum. They included laws that established a minimum wage and eight-hour workdays for some workers, outlawed blacklisting, and provided for mine-safety codes, the regulation of child labor, railroad safety laws, workers' accident compensation, and the establishment of the state Bureau of Labor Statistics to enforce labor legislation. By 1920 Texas workers were protected by laws that rivaled or surpassed those in more industrialized states. But this turned out to be labor's high-water mark. Beginning in 1919, labor's opponents, conservative/reactionary politicians and businessmen, launched a full-scale assault against labor's gains, seeking to roll them back. They regarded unions as dangerous threats to the free-enterprise system and private property rights, and mobilized under the banner of the newly formed Texas Open Shop Association (TOSA) to destroy them.[2]

"Open shop," a euphemism for a union-free work environment, became a powerful national movement of employers bent on destroying organized labor. Various employer trade associations such as the National Association of Manufacturers, Citizen's Industrial Association, National Metal Trades Council, and others recruited, organized, and mobilized businessmen and industrialists in a reactionary juggernaut that crippled the labor movement in Texas and nationally.[3] The first TOSA chapter appeared in San Antonio in 1919. Its leader George Armstrong bluntly summarized the organization's goal: "We are for the Open Shop and are against the basic eight-hour day, the minimum wage and the right to picket, to strike, and to boycott." In fact TOSA was against the right of unions to exist. TOSA intended to break the power of organized labor by intimidating employers willing to recognize and negotiate with unions, engaging in race-baiting, and manipulating public opinion.[4]

TOSA intimidated employers that were willing to recognize unions, by threatening economic boycotts against them. Since any business relies on a network of other businesses to survive, an employer targeted by a TOSA boycott faced potential economic ruin. TOSA demanded compliance to its anti-unionism from all employers, whether TOSA member or not, and ruthlessly wielded the boycott threat. In just one example, the TOSA chapter in Sherman compiled and distributed a buyer's guide that listed merchants, professional men, and manufacturers appropriate to patronize. It also placed a full-page ad in the local newspaper warning about the dangers of black sharecroppers unionizing. In racially charged rhetoric the ad stated, "If you want your farm Unionized that is your business. If you want to take orders from a Negro business agent of the Cotton Choppers Union that is your business."[5] On a more positive note, TOSA asserted that a union-free environment benefited everyone, by stimulating greater economic development through higher productivity that would result in higher wages and lower prices. TOSA never candidly expressed the actual goal of the open-shop campaign, which was lower wages and higher profits.

The Texas open-shop campaign also enjoyed the support of political leaders in Austin, and the political climate had turned hostile toward organized labor. Governors William Hobby and Pat Neff called out the Texas National Guard and Texas Rangers on several occasions to break strikes.

The most spectacular victory for open-shop proponents came during the strike by some sixteen hundred coastwise longshoremen in Galveston, beginning in March 1920. It was fought not only along the usual class line between labor and management over the usual wage and hour issues, but also along the local class line between labor and the business community over political control of the city. Members of the economic elite, especially from the Wharf Company and the Galveston Cotton Exchange, ruled the city after 1900, but were voted out in 1919 by a coalition of labor, blacks, and small businessmen. Companies and wealthy individuals' resentment arose when a tax-equalization program shifted some of the burden from homes and small stores to them. Local corporate interests—spurning arbitration, which could have settled the actual strike issue of wages—used the strike as a lever to discredit labor and the city government, and take the city back. Race riots appeared imminent when the Mallory steamship line, which had previously employed only blacks, hired white strikebreakers, with the reverse true of the Morgan line. But the tactic failed to provoke the violence that the companies, several Texas chambers of commerce, and the open-shop agitators believed they needed so that they could ask for martial law. Nevertheless on June

2, 1920, a committee representing corporate interests asked Governor Will Hobby to declare martial law, and send the National Guard to enforce open shop policies.[6]

The mayor and city council informed the governor that there was no need for such a drastic step, and General John Hulen, commander of the Texas National Guard, agreed with them. Hulen was set aside and replaced by Jacob Wolters, a lobbyist for the Southern Pacific Company, which owned the Morgan line and the Morgan docks in Galveston. On June 7, Wolters—and eventually a thousand National Guardsmen, with three machine gun companies—moved into Galveston to protect the strikebreakers and get cargoes moving faster. Mallory then imported large numbers of Mexican strikebreakers. Wolters suspended the police department, deprived all city officials of their power to enforce penal laws, and did away with freedom of assembly and freedom of the press. The soldiers, who had little to do, were not needed to keep the peace, but they guaranteed the eventual implementation of the open shop policy, as the companies eventually hired enough men who would stay and work. The weakened International Longshoremen's Association locals lost their charters, and the men straggled back to work as individuals. By 1925 the local aristocracy had reasserted political control. Meanwhile the newly elected governor, Pat Neff, had called a special session of the legislature and pushed through the Open Port Law, which made illegal any interference with the free passage of commerce in the state. The Texas Court of Criminal Appeals struck it down in 1926 as an unconstitutional invasion of local rights.[7]

The Non-Partisan Political Conference had been organized in 1922, representing two new farmers' organizations, the TSFL, and the four railroad brotherhoods, but the TSFL was weakened by its membership losses of 1920 and 1921. The coalition backed Fred Rogers for governor in the primary, who lambasted incumbent Pat Neff as a sympathizer of the Ku Klux Klan, and called for state credit to allow farmers and laborers to buy land and homes. During the primary the nationwide railroad shopmen's strike broke out, and violence flared at several Texas sites when the railroads hired strikebreakers. Some of them were kidnapped and flogged at Denison, where every city official was a member of the farm-labor coalition. Wary of the labor vote, Neff took no action beyond dispatching Texas Rangers to various places, who appeared to have the situations under control, but he faced corporate and newspaper demands that he enforce the open-port law by calling out the National Guard. In the primary, Rogers garnered the votes of a third of those who turned out, but Neff won a majority. As soon as the primary was over in July, Neff, under extreme federal pressure, sent guardsmen to Denison and sixteen other Texas towns, declaring martial law in many of them, imposing it on six towns until the end of the year. Labor's strength ebbed even more in this lost strike, with many shop-craft locals wrecked.[8]

The "farm-labor bloc" could count on about fifty members of the House and Senate in 1923, and they and Governor Neff hoped to shift the tax burden away from property and sales taxes, which hit farmers and workers hardest, and levy taxes on crude oil, minerals, corporate income, and large inheritances. But they were overwhelmed by hundreds of lobbyists. The last hurrah of the old coalition aided the passage of only two significant laws. One was the only important tax bill adopted, a 2 percent gross-receipts tax on oil and sulfur. The other favorably amended workers' accident compensation.[9]

In 1924 the coalition campaigned for a constitutional amendment to abolish the property tax and replace it with a mix of income, luxury, franchise, and inheritance taxes. The coalition would repeal the open-port law and the poll tax, pump more money into the public schools, and extend state credit for the purchase of homes. It was a progressive agenda, and eight of their eleven endorsed candidates won in the primary—but not those at the top of the ticket, for governor and U.S. senator. The coalition had to fend off charges of socialism (just as a candidate embracing those taxes would today), and its ranks were split by the Ku Klux Klan, dissension over some candidates, and by the old issue of railroad workers' demands for higher wages versus farmers' demands for lower freight rates. None of their demands were seriously considered by the legislature, and the progressive farm-labor movement dissolved.[10]

The agrarian Left vanished, and labor's allies in the legislature, confronted by TOSA, bought into the business mind-set of the 1920s. Labor laws died from lack of enforcement. The TSFL found itself in full retreat, its membership dropping from fifty thousand in 1920 to half that by 1927.[11]

The Great Depression changed everything. Elected president during the depth of the hard times, Franklin Roosevelt pledged many reforms. Spurred by two of them, the National Industrial Recovery Act and the National Labor Relations Act (Wagner Act), the TSFL grew from some twenty-five thousand in 1933 to about forty thousand in 1940, with another sixty thousand affiliated with the AFL but not the TSFL. Liberal impulses were resurrected. New president Wallace Reilly revived the old alliance with the railroad brotherhoods, the Joint Labor Legislative Board. The TSFL helped write the Texas Democratic Party platform in 1934 and 1936, working with Governor Jimmie Allred. Labor pushed through a prevailing-wage law, an amendment that made the new eight-hour law more effective, a boiler inspection law, and a law creating the Unemployment Compensation Committee. There was also legislation that expanded employment services to all parts of the state, a teacher retirement act, a law preventing the sale of prison-made goods that were not clearly marked, and a minimum wage of $150 a month for firemen. Labor tickets were swept into office in Port Arthur, Beaumont, and Fort Worth.[12]

Yet TSFL progressivism seemed bound by the same limits of Anglo craft primacy that had hindered it twenty years earlier. No effort was made to organize industrial workers, though some organized themselves. A few oil-worker locals sprang up and affiliated. The Sheep Shearers' Union, whose Tejano members averaged less than $700 per year, appealed to the TSFL during their strike against many ranches in 1934. The federation, which had abandoned efforts to organize Tejanos in the 1920s, passed friendly resolutions, but granted no money, no legal assistance, and no organizers. Onion and cotton pickers attempted to work with the TSFL, from 1935 to 1937, but also became disenchanted with lack of concrete support. Admittedly, it appeared hopeless. Even when some five or six hundred better-paid and higher-skilled packing-shed workers in the Rio Grande valley were organized in 1937, and wages standardized in many sheds, the great surplus of nonunion labor overwhelmed the local in fourteen months.[13]

The Wagner Act, which empowered workers to join unions of their own choosing, and provided punishments for employers violating that right, was an open invitation for workers to unionize. Most members of the unorganized workforce, however, were industrial workers, and the craft-oriented AFL was not much interested in them. Along with a few other industrial unionists, John L. Lewis broke with the AFL and founded the Congress of Industrial Organizations (CIO). He broke with traditional organizing methods by employing radicals such as communists as organizers, and recruiting workers regardless of their race or ethnicity, or whether they were skilled or unskilled.[14] Such tactics clearly identified it as radical left-wing in Texas.[15] The CIO in Texas was much more aggressive than the TSFL in the late 1930s in organizing the unorganized. J. P. Thompson, an employee of Houston's Hughes Tool Company, reflected the new militancy of workers at his company and Texas in general when he declared in testimony before the National Labor Relations Board in 1939, "All the talk out there at the plant, at the time, was unionism. Has been ever since."[16]

Over a hundred delegates from ten international unions formed the Texas branch of the CIO, the Texas State Industrial Unions Council (TSIUC) on July 31 and August 1, 1937. At the Beaumont convention the delegates established various committees charged with assisting the constituent local unions of the TSIUC in a number of ways. In addition to assisting in organizing campaigns, the committees served the local unions as an educational and informational clearinghouse, maintained public relations through various community endeavors, lobbied for favorable legislation and against unfavorable bills in the state legislature, and campaigned on behalf of local, state, and national candidates for office who were perceived to be pro-labor.[17] The campaigning and lobbying were usually fruitless, since the split from the TSFL and the election of the antilabor W. Lee O'Daniel as governor in 1938 destroyed labor's unity and legislative success. From its founding in 1937 through 1944, the TSIUC suffered internal warfare between left-wing pro-communist and moderate, anticommunist factions vying for control of the organization.

The pro-communist faction seized control in 1938, holding it until the summer of 1941, when anticommunist opposition took over and spent the next several years purging the TSIUC of communist influence. The battle between the pro- and anticommunist factions in the TSIUC transcended labor issues and was fought over the issue of whether the United States should get involved in World War II. When Germany invaded Poland in September 1939, the pro-communist faction supported U.S. isolationism and opposed taking sides in the conflict. The pro-communist faction hewed to this line due to the Nazi-Soviet nonaggression pact of August 1939. The anticommunists favored Roosevelt's internationalism that called for supporting England and France in their struggle against Hitler's Germany. Hitler's massive invasion of the Soviet Union in June 1941 shattered the nonaggression pact and validated the anticommunist position of the TSIUC while discrediting and weakening the pro-communist position. The anticommunist faction of the TSIUC exploited the moment and seized the initiative. The entry of the United States into World War II after Japan's sneak attack on Pearl Harbor strengthened the anticommunists' hand and they used their growing power within the TSIUC to purge pro-communist influence by 1944.[18]

The communist influence over the TSIUC was short-lived, but noteworthy when one considers the conservative nature of Texas. It is also instructive regarding the depth of resentment among working-class Texans caused by the economic suffering of the Great Depression, that many who opposed communism in principle would join unions with a communist connection. A pent-up class antagonism was unleashed among Texas workers, that had not been seen since the rise of the Populist Party in the 1890s. Against this backdrop the Texas Communist Party enjoyed a measure of toleration for championing such liberal/left causes as a minimum wage, an eight-hour day, an old-age pension system, low interest state loans to landless farmers and agricultural workers, protection of farm workers under the Wagner Act, a state income tax, abolition of the poll tax and the white primary, and civil rights for blacks and Mexican Americans.[19]

When the CIO organizers came to the Lone Star State in 1937 to organize refinery, steel, smelter, and agricultural workers, as well as seamen and others, they shocked the Texas caste system by organizing African Americans in the same unions with whites. It was too strong a jolt for many Anglo unionists, who resisted even to the point of abandoning the CIO. Moreover, integration challenged the southern plantation mentality of the state's corporate and political leaders, threatening to deprive them of using race as an effective weapon in undermining union solidarity. Given the racial egalitarianism and the fact that a few CIO organizers were communists, the state's economic elite regarded this new unionism as the radical Left.[20]

In 1935 Texas communists on the Upper Gulf Coast began publishing the *Red Trade Unionist*, a monthly newsletter. Printed or mimeographed, the monthly organ ran to an average of ten pages, and included local organizing issues and articles from the *Daily Worker*, the national newspaper of the Communist Party USA. Homer Brooks served as publisher and editor of the *Red Trade Unionist*. Brooks was one of only half a dozen professional communists in Texas at the time. Brooks and his wife, San Antonio communist and labor activist Emma Tenayuca, were the Lone Star State's most visible communists. Homer Brooks served as the executive secretary of the Texas Communist Party from 1936 until 1938 when Houstonian P. F. Kennedy replaced him. Kennedy served in that capacity until 1942.[21]

Kennedy's career as a labor activist began at Houston's Hughes Tool Company in the mid 1930s. According to available sources it seems likely that Kennedy, though never formally a card-carrying member of the Communist Party nonetheless embraced its ideology. He published a short lived newsletter in Houston, the *Fighting Hughes Workers*, while actively participating in the organizing campaign of the CIO at Hughes in the late 1930s. Overall, though, rank-and-file membership in the Texas Communist Party remained small. The Texas Communist Party never topped one thousand members, with the Houston chapter's two hundred members making it the state's largest branch.[22]

Houston served as the headquarters of communist operations in Texas in the 1930s. The Bayou City's large manufacturing base and refining operations were targets of CIO organizing campaigns. That plus the vigorous labor activism and the growth of Houston's unions made it the logical base of operations for the Texas Communist Party.

Waco native Elizabeth Benson joined Brooks and Kennedy in Houston to help in the CIO organizing campaigns. Benson regarded Houston as ripe for communist recruiting, owing to the city's numerous industrial plants and what she perceived as growing dissatisfaction with capitalism among Houston's proletariat, due to the suffering of the Great Depression.[23]

Communist influence also overshadowed labor activism in the Texas maritime industry during the 1930s. Sailors and longshoremen on the Texas Gulf Coast suffered abominable working and living conditions. Sailors aboard U.S.-flag vessels suffered cramped, unventilated, vermin-infested quarters, rotten food, and harsh discipline. Even while in port, sailors still on duty were not provided with fresh milk, fruit, or vegetables, and could not wash their clothes. Tuberculosis and other diseases and illnesses were widespread. In each port, prominent boardinghouse keepers were also the shipping agents who victimized the lowly paid sailors with their rackets, along with prostitutes, bootleggers, and other hustlers. The International Seaman's Union (ISU) failed to protect sailors from the abuses they suffered at the hands of shippers, due to internal corruption.[24] The deplorable working conditions and corrupt union leadership made the maritime industry the target of communist organizers on the Texas Gulf Coast. The friction between communists and ineffective ISU leadership resulted in wildcat strikes in 1936 and 1937 that led to the establishment of the National Maritime Union (NMU). The communist NMU offered a militant alternative to the ineffective ISU.

The strikes pitted ISU loyalists against the insurgent NMU in Texas coastal cities. During the strikes, NMU seaman who had sailed the world experienced such widespread violent repression that some of them believed "there wasn't much difference between Port Arthur under the oil companies and Hamburg under the Nazis." ISU members resorting to violence against the NMU strikers included toughs such as business agent Wilbur Dickey, who shot and killed NMU insurgent John Kane during the strike in Houston. During the same month, December 1936, ISU tanker seaman Peter Banfield died after a brawl with strikers in Galveston. On Christmas Eve, on the Houston docks, approximately fifty policemen wielding blackjacks attacked NMU pickets and seamen's haunts, beating up about 150 strikers and some local bystanders, sending eighteen to the hospital. But it was Gulf Coast strikes and strikes along the Atlantic coast that had led to the formation of the NMU.[25]

The 1936 and 1937 strikes were accompanied by violence at the hands of ISU members and the police, but NMU perseverance led to success in overthrowing the semi-feudal hierarchy that governed sailors' lives. The NMU brought about a quick and dramatic transformation that improved seamen's living and working conditions. The most significant established the union hiring hall, which was fully established by 1939 and set up hiring guidelines in the nation's maritime fleet, except for the ships of oil companies. NMU communists led the way in forcing these changes, and though a tiny minority in the union, they had more energy and direction than any other faction, allowing them to succeed in improving conditions where others had failed. Communists, along with some members of the old Industrial Workers of the World, led the Houston NMU during and after the 1936 and 1937 strikes. But their influence was short-lived. Between 1937 and 1939, members who opposed communist efforts to enroll blacks in the union mobilized and seized control of the local. Additionally, during World War II communist NMU leaders failed in their efforts to force shippers and the government to abolish Jim Crow hiring practices in Texas ports. Racial discrimination and legalized segregation remained insoluble problems, even in Texas's left-leaning unions.[26]

Oil refineries were the first goal of the CIO in Texas, and the Oil Workers International Union (OWIU) began its organizing drive at the Texas Gulf Coast refineries in 1937. Not until 1942 did the OWIU, which had some communists in one or two locals, begin to overcome the smears of the House Un-American Activities Committee and the hostility of the refiners, especially Standard Oil. In the spring of 1943 the big Gulf Oil Company refinery in Port Arthur voted for the OWIU, defying the police chief's terrorist and red-baiting tactics, completely unionizing the nation's greatest refinery center, and making Local 23 the second-largest local in the international union (the United States and Canada). By 1944 the OWIU was the fastest-growing union in the CIO.[27]

During World War II, left-wing influence continued to play a role in Texas through the Fair Employment Practices Committee and National War Labor Board, though both of these federal agencies also served to reign in left-wing power in the Texas labor movement by institutionalizing it and throttling its radical tendencies. Postwar labor enjoyed an institutionalized presence in Texas thanks in part to left-wing labor activism promoted by the CIO, but its momentum was spent. During the war and especially in the postwar period, the CIO moved away from its radical policies of the 1930s. In Texas the CIO sometimes bowed to white racists, who threatened to abandon the CIO over its stated goal of organizing blacks and whites in egalitarian, biracial unions.[28]

During and shortly after the war, the United Cannery and Agricultural Workers totaled a few thousand in Texas, mostly Tejano pecan shellers in San Antonio, and Tejano and black compress workers in Houston. The Packinghouse Workers had organized the Armour plant in Fort Worth, where the workforce of over a thousand was split between Anglos, Tejanos, and blacks, and wracked by ethnic schisms. In El Paso local Tejano activists and the Mine, Mill, and Smelter Workers had organized some eleven hundred hands at the city's two copper smelters. Some of the organizers and national leaders of all three unions were communists, and, in fact, communist organizers were often the only ones who would work with minorities. Their locals, especially in San Antonio and El Paso, were red-baited by local sheriffs and media, part of the employer smokescreen to cloak hideous working conditions and abysmal pay. There were few communists, however, among the workers themselves, and their unions—with the help of the wartime labor boards—greatly enhanced the pay scales. The agricultural workers' union faded from Texas in the 1950s, while the other two—after the communist issue had vanished in the 1960s—were absorbed by larger international unions.[29]

By 1944 the TSIUC represented thirty-eight locals with thirty thousand members, the great majority of whom were in Houston, Beaumont–Port Arthur, and Dallas. By then the oil, steel, and auto unions were the biggest. Through 1948 most CIO locals and members were unaffiliated with the TSIUC, usually due to lack of finances and apathy. The affiliation of the Communications Workers of America in 1950 created a fourth large union. Many smaller unions also made inroads in Texas, including the Amalgamated Clothing Workers, in several plants; the Brewery Workers, in San Antonio and Galveston; and the Transport Workers Union in Houston. None of these unions in Texas, representing roughly 90 percent of the membership and leadership, had any significant communist presence.[30]

Even before the war, reactionary forces had taken over Texas. Governor O'Daniel was the first of two generations of state officials who constituted a plutocracy of Anglo businessmen dedicated to a regressive tax structure, extreme reluctance to expand state services, continued oppression of minorities, and the passage of antilabor laws. In March 1941, O'Daniel delivered a highly emotional diatribe about "labor leader racketeers" to a joint session of the legislature. A resulting law forbade force in preventing someone from working. If a picketer used violence to prevent a strikebreaker from entering a plant, it was a felony. If a strikebreaker slugged a picketer, it remained a misdemeanor. In 1941 antilabor politics became the mainstay of the state's conservative hegemony. After the passage of another antilabor law in 1943, the TSIUC, the TSFL, the railroad brotherhoods, the rebuilding Farmers' Union, and old-age pension groups organized the Texas Social and Legislative Conference (TSLC). It was the beginning of the modern liberal-farm-labor coalition in Texas, except that there was not yet much connection with minority groups. The immediate purpose of the TSLC was to reelect Franklin Roosevelt on a liberal platform, but it was also looking to the future.[31]

Texas newspapers played a significant role in promoting antilabor sentiment that created a public atmosphere hostile to unions. A four-month study in late 1945 of Texas newspapers revealed that of 381 labor editorials, 295 were hostile, 82 took no positions and only 4 were sympathetic. The National Association of Manufacturers provided a weekly newsletter, laced with antilabor columns and cartoons, to many Texas newspapers, and these newsletters were used verbatim without acknowledging that they came from the conservative, anti-union, special-interest group.[32]

As the war ended, the Texas establishment, conservative businessmen who supported pro-business government, state's rights, and segregation, stepped up its assault on labor, and the unions barely staved off oppressive legislation in 1945. Meanwhile thousands of Texas workers, like those elsewhere, bolted off their jobs in an attempt to keep up with the rising cost of living. In the 1946 elections, candidates supported by labor lost all over the state, many of them in bitter campaigns against "left-wing political terrorists of the CIO." The state legislature in 1947 passed a right-to-work bill by a large majority, preventing compulsory unionization even in unionized plants where the unions were required by the Wagner Act to represent all workers, and Governor Beauford Jester signed it into law. An array of antiunion laws followed during the same session, which included a law banning the paying of union dues through payroll deduction, a law requiring union members to give written consent before dues could be collected, an anti-mass-picketing law (that defined mass picketing as two pickets either within fifty feet of a plant entrance or within fifty feet of another picket), a secondary boycott law that outlawed boycotts, and an antitrust law against unions. In response to the draconian measures imposed on labor unions, a pro-labor legislator offered an amendment to one of the antilabor laws, suggesting tongue in cheek that unions should be abolished, union members' property confiscated, union members all lined up against a wall and shot, and their families put in concentration camps. The Texas House of Representatives voted down this particular bill 63 to 8, but nine antilabor measures became law in 1947.[33]

Vance Muse, the leader of the Christian Americans, a right-wing extremist group based in Houston, lobbied hard for antilabor legislation, and jubilantly distributed a leaflet with photos of legislators who voted against repressive labor laws, identifying them as "Communists in the Texas Legislature."[34] Muse had been at it for years. When the CIO began organizing Houston workers in 1937, Muse viciously race- and red-baited the union. He charged that the CIO would force "white men and women into organizations with black African apes whom they shall have to call brother or lose their jobs."[35] Though Muse and the right-wing politicians he aligned himself with provided the meanest and most sensationalized race- and red-baiting against real and perceived radical left-wing influence in unions, they merely served as useful pawns in rallying public support for the antilabor agenda of the business establishment. Rather than sullying their hands with the vicious and outrageous race- and red-baiting useful to its ends, the establishment left the dirty work to extremists like Muse and an assortment of right-wing ideologues in the legislature while they preferred a more benign approach in their attacks.

The Texas Manufacturers Association (TMA) and the state's regional chambers of commerce waged their own propaganda campaign against labor unions. The TMA and regional chambers asserted that unions had acquired uncontrollable, monolithic power that threatened the very freedom of workers who they claimed to protect. They argued that the closed shop, where union membership is required to hold one's job, undermined the country's basic value system of independence and rugged individualism. While reactionary extremists like Muse hoped that legislation would destroy Texas unions, the conservative business elements represented by the TMA and chambers of commerce wanted them legislated into insignificance.[36]

The CIO organizational drive called Operation Dixie foundered in 1946, the year it began. As labor historian Barbara Griffith notes, most of the southern victories came in tobacco or in southern branches of highly organized northern industries—for example, the auto, steel, packinghouse, and oil industries. The struggles came in the lumber, furniture, paper, pulp, woodworking, and textiles industries. This was certainly the pattern in Texas. Griffith believes that the traditional reasons cited for the failures are inadequate—paternalism, low class mobility, low wages, sharp imbalances of power, and segregation—because most of these features were present in the North too. Southern imbalances of power may have been more gargantuan, however; indeed, as an example Griffith cites the $3,500 mustered by the CIO's Political Action Committee in Texas in 1946, as compared to the $3,400,000 raised by the Texas Manufacturers Association. Texas did defy the national pattern at first: between May 1946 and February 1947 the Texas CIO enjoyed sixty-four election victories and signed up 14,500 new members, making it the most successful affiliate in the South at the time. But Griffith also notes the relatively heavy-handed criminal-justice system in the South and expensive litigation as a ready weapon of employers, and Texas was certainly an example. At the 1951 TSIUC convention, the Highland Park decision of the U.S. Supreme Court was lamented. It knocked out four of the most important unfair-practice charges in Texas when all these cases had been won at lower levels. The Carter Lumber Company, for instance, had had CIO organizers thrown in jail, including the regional director, and consequently the company had been found guilty in all the lower courts of virtually every unfair labor practice imaginable.[37]

The combination of the antilabor laws enacted primarily in 1947, the collapse of Operation Dixie, the CIO internal purge of communists and left-wing unions in 1949 and 1950, effective race- and red-baiting against the supporters of integrated unions, and a view held among a growing number of Texans that organized labor had become too powerful, all worked together to mute left-wing influence over Texas labor. Though these forces purged left-wing influence from Texas labor, the labor movement in the state nonetheless enjoyed steady growth in the ten years following World War II. This strongly suggests that although efforts by foes of labor succeeded in imposing restrictions on unions and silenced the labor Left, many working Texans regarded unions as a legitimate voice to protect the rights of working-class people.

The growth was significant, reaching three hundred seventy-five thousand in the TSFL and the TSIUC by the mid-1950s, corresponding roughly to 17 percent of the Texas workforce. About half the state's union members were found in the Beaumont-Houston area and roughly a third in Dallas–Fort Worth. Even in heavy industry outside the biggest cities, such as steel in Daingerfield, autos in Arlington and Greenville, rubber in Bryan, and oil in Tyler, Borger, and Dumas, there were unions. The purging of left-wing elements, negative publicity, and restrictive labor laws did not destroy the Texas CIO. Perhaps the suppression of left-wing elements encouraged more conservative workers who favored labor unions, but opposed radicalism, to join CIO unions. By 1954 the TSIUC counted 188 locals, with eighty-six thousand members out of some one hundred eight thousand CIO members in the state.[38] Just in terms of membership, both the AFL and the CIO in Texas were stronger in the 1950s than at any previous time, and consequently remained the foremost target of the Texas corporate establishment.

In 1954 Governor Jester's successor, Allan Shivers, was in political trouble due to insurance company scandals and the governor's dubious real estate transactions in the Rio Grande valley, but Shivers nevertheless declared for an unprecedented third term. Organized labor endorsed liberal challenger Ralph Yarborough. Eight months before the primary, the Distributive, Processing and Office Workers called a recognition strike against twenty-two retail businesses in Port Arthur, but the DPOW had not quite purged all the communists in its ranks. Two of the original DPOW strike leaders were communists or ex-communists, but they were quickly replaced with noncommunist CIO organizers. The supposedly tainted connection enabled Shivers to rail about a communist conspiracy that threatened to consume Texas, and Yarborough, he said, was in bed with them. Port Arthur was depicted in a famous televised film as a ghost town, shut down by communist picketing; the town did look deserted, but the film was made at 5:00 A.M. The desperation tactic allowed Shivers to beat Yarborough. This was the last campaign in which labor-baiting was the decisive issue in a statewide election, but it served as the most dependable tactic employed by conservative Democrats against progressive Democrats in virtually every contested primary for governor and senator from 1941 through 1956.[39]

The AFL and CIO merged in 1955 in the United States, and in 1957 in Texas, just in time to boost Ralph Yarborough, who ran in the special senatorial election in 1957 and won it, taking advantage of two conservatives splitting their votes in an election that had no runoff. Yarborough served as a liberal Democratic U.S. senator for over thirteen years. Liberal congressmen, for example, Bob Eckhardt and Henry Gonzales were elected, as were many legislators who gradually repealed some of the obnoxious state laws of the 1940s and 1950s. Texas never became a promised land for organized labor, but labor and its allies did at least restore pluralism to a state that had been missing it for fifteen years, and they did so after the supposed weakening effects of the Taft-Hartley Act, right-to-work laws, and the purging of communists.

Texas politics shifted toward the center in the late 1950s, traceable to the election (and reelection in 1958) of Yarborough, the collapse of the white-hot phase of the resistance to integration, and the election of Governor Price Daniel, whose instincts were more moderate than those of his four predecessors. Also, of course, since antilabor and segregation laws had reached their zenith in Texas, no more needed to be passed. Daniel and his successor John Connally had limited relationships with organized labor. Governor Connally was unconcerned that Texas ranked last in weekly compensation for injured workers or that Texas was the last of the ten largest states without a minimum-wage law, but in 1967 a weak bill on general job safety was allowed to pass. The Texas AFL-CIO favored it in order to at least get something on the books that might enhance the safety of its members, while the Texas

Manufacturers Association thought it might delay passage of a federal law.[40]

The most spectacular labor events of the decade—with a civil rights dimension—revolved around the efforts of the National Farm Workers Association to organize Tejano and Mexican field hands in the Rio Grande valley, which came to the public's attention with a strike against eight major growers on June 1, 1966. Farm workers are not covered by the National Labor Relations Act, which means that they live in the law of the jungle in attempting to win collective bargaining rights. If employers won't talk with them, strikes and boycotts are labor's only weapons. The union sought recognition, an eight-hour day, and a raise in wages—some of which were as low as a quarter to fifty cents an hour—to a dollar and a quarter. Backed by the Catholic Church, Mexican American organizations, and the Texas AFL-CIO, the strike was highlighted by a 490-mile march on Austin—though the marchers were intercepted on the highway near New Braunfels by Governor Connally and his party in a cavalcade of Lincoln Continentals. The governor went considerably out of his way to inform the marchers that he was not going to meet them in Austin and was not going to call the legislature into special session to enact a minimum wage of a dollar and a quarter. (The strike, in fact, was driving wages upward). Another facet of the strike was the arrest and beating of strike leaders by Texas Rangers in 1967, which provoked one lawsuit, *Allee et al. v. Medrano et al.*, that was heard by the U.S. Supreme Court. Although the strike failed in 1967, on May 20, 1974, the Supreme Court upheld the injunction that had restrained the Rangers from their acts of intimidation. The Court also struck down five Texas antilabor laws, including parts of statutes that dealt with mass picketing, secondary picketing and boycotts, and unlawful assembly. Had these Rio Grande valley events occurred ten, twenty, or thirty years earlier, they would have surely been labeled as communistic, but the Red Scare was over. The strike tactic and the union itself had long since failed by 1974 because of the intimidation and the excessive number of available workers. But the minimum wage march helped to politically unify Mexican Americans in Texas and contributed to their alliance with organized labor and their growing sense of self-identity.[41]

Governors Preston Smith and Dolph Briscoe, 1969–1979, brought labor into the governing coalition of Democrats, more or less. Governor Smith signed the state's first minimum-wage law in 1969, requiring a dollar and a quarter per hour. Another victory that year was the deluge of letters and telegrams known as the "housewives' revolt," largely orchestrated by labor, that prevented the House from concurring with the Senate and the governor that the regressive state sales tax should be extended to groceries. The federal Occupational Safety and Health Act of 1970 marked real gains for workers. Among other requirements, it meant that after a century of industrialization, Texas employers were now required to keep records of work-related injuries, diseases, and deaths.[42] Democrats Mark White (1983–1987) and Ann Richards (1991–1995) worked closely with labor on issues of the day. Republican governors—Bill Clements (1979–1983, 1987–1991), George W. Bush (1995–2000), and Rick Perry (2000–present)—heavily funded by corporations and wealthy individuals, have spurned any significant relationship with organized labor.

NOTES

1.   Joe B. Frantz, "The Mind of Texas," Smith Lecture in History, University of St. Thomas, Houston, Texas, March 1985, cassette recording in author's possession.

2.   Thomas B. Brewer, "State Anti-Labor Legislation: Texas—A Case Study," *Labor History* Vol. II (Winter 1970) 1:58–62; Grady Lee Mullennix, "A History of the Texas State Federation of Labor" (PhD diss., University of Texas, 1955), 12–72; Jay Littman Todes, "Organized Employer Opposition to Unionism in Texas, 1900–1930," (master's thesis, University of Texas, 1949), 19–49.

3.   Todes, "Organized Employer Opposition to Unionism in Texas," 19–49; Mullennix, "A History of the Texas State Federation of Labor," 243–52; Brewer, "State Anti-Labor Legislation," 62–63; Allen M. Wakstein, "Origins of the Open Shop Movement, 1919–1920," *Journal of American History* 51 (December1964): 460–70; Joseph McCartin, *Labor's Great War: The Struggle for Industrial Democracy and the Origins of Modern American Labor Relations* (Chapel Hill: University of North Carolina Press, 1997), 90–93.

4.   *Texas State Federation of Labor Proceedings,* 1919, 132; George Armstrong to J. A. Arnold, May 28, 1920, George Armstrong Papers, 1920 "A" File, Special Collections, University of Texas at Arlington Library.

5.   *Sherman Daily Democrat,* May 28, 1920; Brewer, "State Anti-Labor Legislation," 63–65.

6.   Hulen Knox, "Galveston: An Exercise in Aristocratic Control, 1838–1921," (master's thesis, University of Houston at Clear Lake City, 1983), 60–98.

7.   James Maroney, "Organized Labor in Texas, 1900–1929" (PhD diss., University of Houston, 1975), 210–221; Knox, "Galveston," 102–84.

8. *El Paso Labor Advocate,* May 28, 1920, April 14, 1922; Robert Anderson, "History of the Farm Labor Union of Texas," (master's thesis, University of Texas at Austin, 1928), 1, 7, 10–15, 18–19, 51, 55,
59; Robert Hunt, *A History of Farmer Movements in the Southwest,
1873–1925* (College Station: Texas A&M Press, 1935), 145–48, 185–
86; Norman Brown, *Hood, Bonnet, and Little Brown Jug* (College
Station: Texas A&M University Press, 1984), 81–86; S. S. McKay,
Texas Politics, 1906–1944 (Lubbock: Texas Tech University Press,
1952), 107–108; Mullennix, "A History of the Texas State Federation
of Labor," 280.

9. Anderson, "History of the Farm Labor Union," 67–73; *Texas State
Federation of Labor Proceedings, 1923,* 95–96; Brown, *Hood, Bonnet,
and Little Brown* Jug, 153–55; *Dallas Morning News,* May 15, 29,
1923.

10. *Dallas Morning News,* May 25, November 19, 1923, January 24,
April 13, 19, June 23, 30, July 6, 16, 1924; Hunt, *A History of Farmer
Movements in the Southwest,* 186–90; McKay, *Texas Politics,* 143.

11. Brewer, "State Anti-Labor Legislation," 64–65; Mullennix, "A History of the Texas State Federation of Labor," 255.

12. Mullennix, "A History of the Texas State Federation of Labor," 325–
28; Robert Christopher, "Rebirth and Lost Opportunities: The Texas
AFL and the New Deal, 1933–1939," (master's thesis, University of
Texas at Arlington, 1977), 22–23, 31–34.

13. Stuart Jamieson, *Labor Unionism in American Agriculture,* Bulletin No. 836, U. S. Bureau of Labor Statistics (Washington, D.C.: U. S.
Government Printing Office, 1945), 225–29, 271–77; *Proceedings of
the Texas State Federation of Labor, 1934,* 26, 30; Christopher, "Rebirth and Lost Opportunities," 99–104.

14. Art Preis, *Labor's Giant Step: The First Twenty Years of the
CIO,1936–55,* 2nd ed. (New York: Pathfinder, 1972), 489–90; Melvyn
Dubovsky, *The State and Labor in Modern America* (Chapel Hill:
The University of North Carolina Press, 1994), 124–51; Steve Ross-
wurm, "Introduction: An Overview and Preliminary Assessment
of the CIO's Expelled Unions," in *The CIO's Left-Led Unions,* ed.
Steve Rosswurm, (New Brunswick: Rutgers University Press, 1992),
1–3: Robert Zieger, *The CIO, 1935–1955* (Chapel Hill: University of
North Carolina Press, 1995), 82–83.

15. See Murray E. Polakoff, "The Development of the Texas State Congress of Industrial Organizations Council," (PhD, diss., University of
Texas, 1955), 141–71; Zieger, *The CIO,* 83–85.

16. National Archives and Records Administration, College Park, Mary-
land, RG25, Case File 1661, "Official Report of Proceedings Before

the National Labor Relations Board in the Matter of Hughes Tool Company and Steel Workers Organizing Company, Lodge 1742 and Employees Welfare Organization of Hughes Tool Company and H.T.C. Club of Hughes Tool Company," 922.

17. Polakoff, "The Development of the Texas State Congress of Industrial Organizations Council," 3, 7, 8.

18. Ibid., 141–60.

19. Don E. Carleton, *Red Scare! Right-wing Hysteria, Fifties Fanaticism and Their Legacy in Texas* (Dallas: Texas Monthly Press, 1985), 19–24, 28.

20. Polakoff, "The Development of the Texas State Congress of Industrial Organizations Council," 160–171.

21. *Red Trade Unionist* 1, nos. 2–4, Center for American History, University of Texas at Austin, Box 2E 307, File 4; Carleton, *Red Scare,* 27–32; Zaragosa Vargas, "Tejana Radical: Emma Tenayuca and the San Antonio Labor Movement During the Great Depression," *Pacific Historical Review* 66, no. 4 (1997), 553–80; Polakoff, "The Development of the Texas State Congress of Industrial Organizations Council" (see chapter 6, notes 22, 23).

22. Michael R. Botson Jr., *Labor, Civil Rights, and the Hughes Tool Company* (College Station: Texas A&M University Press, 2005), 63, 72, 86–87; Polakoff, "The Development of the Texas State Congress of Industrial Organizations Council" (see chapter 6, notes 22, 23); "Red Charge is Denied by C.I.O. Worker," *Houston Chronicle,* July 21, 1939, 8.

23. Carleton, *Red Scare,* 30–34.

24. Bruce Nelson, *Workers on the Waterfront* (Urbana: University of Illinois Press, 1988), 15–19; *Report on the Status and Working Conditions of Seaman in the American Merchant Marine* (New York: International Juridical Association, 1936), 12–17; William LaFollette interviewed by George Green, Angleton, Texas, August 14, 1987, Oral History Project, Texas Labor Archives, University of Texas at Arlington.

25. Nelson, *Workers on the Waterfront,* 21 (quote), 257–58, 268; Joseph Goldberg, *The Maritime Story* (Boston: Harvard University Press, 1958), 164; Max Kampleman, *The Communist Party vs. the C.I.O.* (New York: Praeger, 1957), 83–84.

26. Nelson, *Workers on the Waterfront,* 242–44, 259; Goldberg, *Maritime Story,* 212–14, 258; Bert Cochran, *Labor and Communism* (Princeton University Press, 1977), 255, 324; *Galveston Daily News,* December 14 and 16, 1936; Gilbert Mers, *Working the Waterfront* (Austin: University of Texas Press, 1988), 168, 150–76.

27. *Houston Chronicle,* April 5, 1938; Ray Marshall, *Labor in the South,*

(Cambridge: Harvard University Press, 1967), 196, 227, 231–33; Harvey O'Connor, *History of Oil Workers International Union-CIO* (Denver: OWIU, 1950), 32–50, 314–15.

28. Zieger, *The CIO*, 277–93.

29. *Handbook of Texas Online*, s.v. "Texas State Industrial Union Council," http://www.tshaonline.org/handbook/online/articles/TT/octbg .html (accessed May 6, 2009).

30. Polakoff, "The Development of the Texas State Congress of Industrial Organizations Council," 128–33.

31. Ibid., 356–60, 368–69, 385–86, 400–415; George Green, "Anti-Labor Politics in Texas," in *American Labor in the Southwest*, ed. James Foster (Tucson: University of Arizona Press, 1982), 217–18.

32. George Green, *The Establishment in Texas Politics: the Primitive Years, 1938–1975* (Norman: University of Oklahoma Press, 1979), 103–104.

33. Green, "Anti-Labor Politics in Texas," 220–21; Polakoff, "The Development of the Texas State Congress of Industrial Organizations Council," 266–271.

34. Green, *The Establishment in Texas Politics*, 106.

35. Michael R. Botson Jr., "Jim Crow Wearing Steel-Toed Shoes and Safety Glasses: Dual Unionism at the Hughes Tool Company, 1918–1942," *Houston Review* 16 (1994): 113–14; Polakoff, "The Development of the Texas State Congress of Industrial Organizations Council," 240–46.

36. Green, *The Establishment in Texas Politics*, 106–107.

37. Barbara Griffith, *The Crisis of American Labor: Operation Dixie and the Defeat of the CIO* (Philadelphia: Temple University Press, 1988), 33, 89, 90, 95, 112–14; *Minutes, Fifteenth Annual Convention, Texas State Industrial Union Council—CIO, 1951*, 10; Green, *The Establishment in Texas Politics*, 103.

38. *Handbook of Texas Online*, s.v. "Texas State Industrial Union Council," http://www.tshaonline.org/handbook/online/articles/TT/octbg .html (accessed May 6, 2009); David Botter, "Labor Looks at Texas," *Southwest Review* 31 (Spring 1946), 112–115; Polakoff, "The Development of the Texas State Congress of Industrial Organizations Council," 128, 136.

39. Green, "Anti-Labor Politics in Texas," 222–224; Polakoff, "The Development of the Texas State Congress of Industrial Organizations Council," 88.

40. Green, *The Establishment in Texas Politics*, 201–204.

41. Julian Samora, Joe Bernal, and Albert Pena, *Gunpowder Justice* (Notre Dame: Notre Dame Press, 1979), 131–56; *Dallas Morning News*, June 15, 1967; Marilyn Rhinehart and Thomas Kreneck, "The

Minimum Wage March of 1966: A Case Study in Mexican-American Politics, Labor, and Identity," *Houston Review* 11 (1989), 27–44.

42. Green, *The Establishment in Texas Politics*, 203–204; Roy Evans, *Tragedy at Work* (Houston: Institute of Labor and Industrial Relations, University of Houston, 1979), 16.

NOT WHISTLING DIXIE
Women's Movements
and Feminist Politics

Judith N. McArthur and Harold L. Smith

Texas being such a big state, "it actually contains several different cultures. They are all rotten for women," the late Molly Ivins once deadpanned in an article for *Ms.* magazine. Throughout most of the twentieth century the culture that progressive women struggled against was the southern one that Texas shared with the other states of the former Confederacy. That culture denied black women civil rights and threatened their lives if they resisted white repression. It held white women "hostage to the lost Cause," in Marjorie Spruill Wheeler's phrase, disfranchising black men in the name of protecting white womanhood. Conservative southern men grounded their politics in patriarchal dominance, rejecting the concept of female moral authority that northern Republican women used to claim a role in public affairs, and resisting extensions of government power—especially federal power—as encroachments on white men's rights and authority over their households.[1]

The removal of black men from politics left black women without even the "indirect influence" on the ballot that white women supposedly could exert in private on their men. At the same time, by making public space "safe" for white women, black disfranchisement opened the way for them to assume public roles and pursue social reforms and the vote, although not without trailing their skirts in the racial mud. The force and bitterness of the opposition that progressive women encountered shaped their tactics and rhetoric in ways that made them appear complicit in maintaining white supremacy—and indeed the majority shared the racial attitudes of their white opponents. But as Suzanne Lebsock has pointed out in a seminal study of Virginia suffragists, historians need to examine southern women's behavior bifocally. Viewed through the lens of the egalitarian present, they are undeniably flawed, but getting an accurate image also requires "a second lens for distance" that locates them "on a political spectrum that would have been meaningful to white southerners at the time."[2] Examined through this second lens, the definition of the political Left is situational and regional. Where conservatism is pervasive and powerful, moving to the center is perceived—and decried—as a leftward tilt. Attitudes and activities that northerners would have judged moderate were denounced as radicalism in the patriarchal and racially polarized South. Accordingly, we define the female Left in Texas as those women who stood in opposition to the dominant culture and its supporting pillars: restricted democracy and white male supremacy; cheap, limited government; unfettered, low-wage capitalism; and traditional gender and racial norms.

Race and class markers shaped feminist practice. Women who were white and middle-class saw their struggle in straightforward gender terms. While they contended against male privilege, they also benefited from access to the influence and financial resources of powerful men. For women of color, who lived and worked with men who were also exploited, campaigns for gender equality were intertwined with the pursuit of racial justice. Among African American women, female assertiveness has been termed "womanism," a pursuit of empowerment for the race, female and male alike.[3] Wage-earning women had still another perspective: "labor feminists" sought economic independence and union recognition in alliance with blue-collar men, as well as demanding an equitable share of leadership positions alongside them. Organized women were early and skilled practitioners of interest-group politics, and they challenged power structures through a variety of means—female voluntary associations, gender-integrated reform organizations, radical minority parties, and the left wing of the Democratic Party—in pursuit of expanded democracy and a more just and inclusive state.

SUFFRAGE

Woman suffrage got a late and fitful start in the hostile South; in Texas no state organization existed until the Texas Equal Rights Association (TERA) formed in 1893. Many of the organizers were members of the Woman's Christian Temperance Union (WCTU), which had endorsed suffrage as a "home protection" ballot in 1888. The TERA failed to thrive, and was defunct by 1896. Annette Finnigan of Houston next

took up the cause and founded the Texas Woman Suffrage Association, which functioned from 1903 to 1905 and lapsed into inactivity
when Finnigan moved to New York City. Revived in 1913 by Eleanor Brackenridge, and conjoined with the Progressive-era women's social reform movement, it finally took root and flourished. Finnigan
returned and began the process of organizing the state during another
term as president. Minnie Fisher Cunningham, who succeeded her
in 1915, completed the process and ramped up the lobbying effort in
Austin for a suffrage amendment. Progressive women significantly expanded the framework of the suffrage debate and altered its rhetoric.
While they never abandoned the nineteenth-century natural rights argument, they forged a broad coalition by emphasizing gender difference: women needed the ballot because as housekeepers and mothers
they had a perspective that men lacked. By stressing these municipal
housekeeping and social-motherhood arguments for the ballot, Cunningham attracted non-politicized women and built one of the largest
organizations in the South. Renamed the Texas Equal Suffrage Association (TESA), it ultimately claimed nearly ten thousand members, all of
them white because admitting African American women would have
been political suicide.[4]

Although the TESA members failed to stand up for black women's
rights, they and other southern suffragists mounted a more radical assault on male dominance than their northern counterparts. Outside
the South the woman suffrage campaign was simply the final phase of
the steady push for universal suffrage underway since the early nineteenth century. In the southern states, by contrast, conservative white
males had deliberately constricted the electorate in order to eliminate
challenges to their power. As a consequence of the poll tax (which
eliminated many poor white men who had supported the Populist insurgency, as well as blacks) and a de facto white primary, more than
two-thirds of Texas men were disfranchised. Voter turnout by 1910
had dropped to 29 percent for whites and 2 percent for blacks.[5] Thus
while northern suffragists had only to finish pushing open a door already partly ajar—a hard enough task that took three generations of
women seventy-two years—the TESA proposed to force open one that
had been deliberately closed and padlocked. In the process suffragists
publicly rejected the concept of "protection" for white womanhood.
Even more disquieting to white male supremacists, they refused to toe
the states' rights line and kept steady pressure on their congressmen
and senators to vote for the federal suffrage amendment.

The conservatives countered with ferocious race-baiting, accus-
ing suffragists of betraying white supremacy and, by their support for
a federal amendment, inviting Washington to intervene in Texas elec-

tions to enforce the Fifteenth Amendment. And while the suffragists denied that their movement challenged the racial status quo, they were not worried about adding some black women to the electorate. TESA president Minnie Fisher Cunningham came as close as was politically possible to defending black voting rights. In reply to the accusation that woman suffrage would guarantee the Republicans one hundred sixty thousand black female votes, she wrote a letter to the *Galveston Daily News* pointing out that denying the ballot on such grounds was contrary to American democracy.[6] All too aware that enfranchised women might side with the Constitution, the legislature ignored suffragists' petitions and repeatedly rejected their bills. The TESA won limited suffrage—the right to vote in party primaries—in 1918 only because it was an election year and a factional split in the Democratic Party unexpectedly gave Cunningham the opportunity to strike a political deal. In return for a primary suffrage bill, she promised to turn out the female vote for the incumbent governor, William P. Hobby.[7] In the registration drive that followed the signing of the bill, black women, who had been excluded from the suffrage campaign, refused to be pushed aside without protest, forcing county officials to make on-the-spot decisions. In some places they succeeded in registering; where they were refused, in more than one case they brought or threatened legal action.[8]

To help insure a heavy turnout of female voters, the suffrage leadership persuaded Annie Webb Blanton, a professor of education at North Texas State College, to run for state superintendent of education. Hobby and Blanton won by large margins, but the landslide victory did not change enough men's minds. In the general election the following year male voters refused to ratify a state constitutional amendment extending full suffrage to women. Finally made full voters by the Nineteenth Amendment in 1920, the former suffragists formed a Texas branch of the League of Women Voters (TLWV), under president Jessie Daniel Ames, and immediately confirmed the conservatives' fear that they would trouble the political system. The TLWV's twin goals of expanding and educating the electorate positioned it in direct opposition to conservative Democratic Party leaders who had worked for decades to shrink the voter pool. Lorraine Gates Schuyler has pointed out that in the South the LWV's Get Out the Vote campaigns were "white women's most persistent and effective challenge to disfranchisement." The state and local League of Women Voters chapters publicized the deadline for poll tax payment and mounted innovative public awareness campaigns as part of voter mobilization drives: Dallas LWV members, for example, gave three-minute talks every evening at movie theaters. To lessen the possibility that election officials could disqualify ballots—Texas required voters to scratch through the names of the candidates they *didn't* support—local League of Women Voters chapters held ballot-marking classes for the general public.[9]

In addition to advocating that everyone should vote and that every vote should be counted, the LWV preached the heresy of nonpartisanship. The male model of politics relied on urban machines and courthouse "rings" to control and deliver the vote; the female model wanted thoughtful voters rather than loyal ones. The LWV distributed questionnaires to candidates (an innovation many greatly resented) and used the answers to compile voter information guides, urging both sexes to choose the best-qualified office seekers, regardless of party. As a result, Schuyler found, Republicans "increased their voting strength in nearly every county in the South."[10]

FROM PROGRESSIVISM TO LEFT FEMINISM

Texas, in effect, had two Progressive movements, arising from separate male and female political cultures and divergent values. Women's political culture developed through a network of voluntary associations, state branches of national organizations such as the WCTU, the General Federation of Women's Clubs, and the National Congress of Mothers and Parent-Teacher Associations. Membership in federated voluntary associations pulled middle-class Texas women into a national network of suffragists and social feminists, and introduced them to a reform agenda shaped by women such as Jane Addams and Florence Kelley. Federating with northern women turned Texas clubwomen into social investigators and critics of their cheap, minimalist state government that resisted spending money on social services. Voluntary association politics positioned female progressives well to the left of male "business progressivism," which aimed to systematize and streamline corporate capitalism. While business progressives in the legislature focused on measures to facilitate market competition and attract industry and investment, such as antitrust laws and a banking and insurance commission, female reformers pressed for restraints on the power of business and industry to exploit consumers, workers, and children.

Women dominated the social welfare side of progressivism. Embracing Jane Addams's concept of municipal housekeeping, they challenged men for the role of family protector. Women progressives redefined the community as an extended household, and asserted a female claim to shared governance based on their expertise as housewives and mothers. Vocal critics of the priorities of male-controlled government, they insisted that child mortality and consumer protection merited as much legislative attention as boll weevil eradication and hog cholera. "It wouldn't have taken a Congress of mothers seventeen years to pass pure food laws," *Dallas Morning News* columnist Isadore Callaway ("Pauline Periwinkle") observed tartly after the passage of the federal Meat Inspection Act and Pure Food and Drug Act.[11] She and other members of the Dallas Woman's Forum pressured the city council into adopting the first municipal food ordinance in Texas, while the Texas Federation of Women's Clubs and the wctu lobbied the Pure Food Act of 1907 through the legislature. The Housewives' League in Houston and the Women's Health Protective Association in Galveston spearheaded city milk-inspection campaigns. The Dallas Federation of Women's Clubs devoted five years to a public relations and lobbying campaign that finally led to a bond issue to build a water filtration plant. In every major Texas city, organized women attacked the problems of urban growth and industrial development, founding settlement houses, free public kindergartens, clean milk stations, and day nurseries for wage-earning mothers.[12]

In marked contrast to the boosters of development and the proponents of the New South creed of industrial progress, voluntarist women advocated a proactive state with expanded power to protect the vulnerable. They lobbied for minimum wage and maximum hours laws for women workers, and restrictions on child labor—the Texas Federation of Women's Clubs created its own child labor committee and lobbied a bill through the legislature in 1911. Regarding government as an ally rather than an enemy, progressive women wanted it not only to restrain the rapacious but to spend at a level that would elevate Texas out of the bottom decile of states on social welfare and bring it closer to northern standards. The Texas Federation of Women's Clubs and the Texas Congress of Mothers crusaded for years for a public school system on the (expensive) northern model, with terms that lasted more than a few months. They were on record for compulsory education years before the male-dominated reform group, the Conference for Education in Texas, and their public relations campaign and forceful lobbying pried a compulsory education law out of the legislature in 1915.[13]

After women won the vote, the Texas Federation of Women's Clubs, Texas Congress of Mothers, wctu, and Texas Business and Professional Women's Clubs formed the Women's Joint Legislative Council (jlc) in 1922, led by executive secretary Jane McCallum, to continue left/liberal pressure on the legislature. (The Graduate Nurses' Association joined in 1924). The jlc secured, among other things, supplemental appropriations for the public schools, a bill to strengthen the child labor law, and, over strenuous opposition, the state's participation in the federal Sheppard-Towner Protection of Maternity and Infancy Act. The first federal social welfare program, Sheppard-Towner offered grants-in-aid to the states to set up prenatal and infant-care education programs to combat high maternal and infant mortality rates. To participate, a state had to appropriate matching funds and submit a plan of work to the U.S. Children's Bureau (administered by women). JLC lobbyists did battle for Sheppard-Towner against legislators who denounced the bill as "Bolshevism," and "pernicious federal snooping," an insult to southern racial mores because "the Federal Government would send 'Nigger' women down here to run over our white women."[14]

A decade after the JLC disbanded, the Roosevelt administration's *Report on Economic Conditions in the South* spurred former TESA president Minnie Fisher Cunningham to set up the Women's Committee on Economic Policy in 1938 to address poverty issues. Chaired by Lillian Collier, with Margaret Reading as secretary, it drew attention to discriminatory railroad rates as a key factor in keeping southern families poor and their children in fields and factories. In 1941 pressure on the legislature from the Women's Committee on Economic Policy helped secure full funding for a state Teacher Retirement System (80 percent of Texas teachers were women) and financing of pensions for the destitute elderly (also disproportionately women) by an increase in the oil and gas tax, despite the industry's opposition.[15]

Enfranchised women met continuing difficulty in translating their new status into political authority; winning elective office above the local level proved elusive and party bosses refused to share power. Instead, during the 1940s and 1950s a women's movement developed on the left flank of the Democratic Party, committed to undermining the interrelated oppressions of gender, class, and race. Strengthening liberalism was crucial to improving opportunities for women, Minnie Fisher Cunningham stressed, because liberals, unlike conservatives, genuinely believed in democracy, "and it is only in a democracy that women are regarded as people at all." Left feminist grassroots activists allied with labor and small producers against big corporate interests, which bankrolled the conservative white elites who controlled state government and politics. Cunningham was the motivating force behind the founding of both the Texas Social and Legislative Conference, a farm-labor organization financed largely by the CIO, in 1944, and the People's Legislative Committee in 1946. Both groups advocated abolishing the poll tax and eliminating racial discrimination in education and employment. The TSLC functioned as the Left's political action committee and paid the rent on an Austin office, overseen by Cunningham and Marion Storm, which was the unofficial left/liberal headquarters. Cunningham, Margaret Reading, and Storm served on the TSLC executive committee, and Storm subsequently became the secretary and research director. In the 1950s Cunningham and Frankie Randolph, a leader of the liberal Harris County Democrats, founded the *Texas Observer* as a voice for the left/liberal minority. Randolph provided the financial backing for Cunningham's idea and chose the first editor.[16]

LABOR FEMINISM

Dorothy Cobble has termed labor feminism "the other women's movement": working-class women lobbying, striking, and demonstrating for first-class economic citizenship.[17] Houston telephone operators were the vanguard of Texas labor feminism in 1900 when they joined the International Brotherhood of Electrical Workers Local 66 to get the sickness and death benefits that Southwestern Telephone and Telegraph (STT) offered to its male line and ground crews. STT fired some of the operators and threatened others with dismissal; the women retaliated with a strike and were eventually rehired. San Antonio operators who wanted their eleven- and thirteen–hour shifts reduced also struck that year; the strike spread to other cities but ultimately failed. The first reduction in hours for working women resulted from the legislative lobbying of Eva Goldsmith, president of the Texas District Council of United Garment Workers and the first female member of the legislative committee of the Texas State Federation of Labor, who successfully argued in 1913 for a bill restricting women's hours to nine a day or fifty-four a week. The low-wage, anti-union New South industrialists who opposed it, however, wrangled an exception for cotton mills and commercial laundries, the largest employers of female labor.[18]

Wage justice was the principal goal of labor feminists and their middle-class allies; sex discrimination concentrated women in low-wage service and manufacturing jobs where they were paid half what men were paid, or less. Eva Goldsmith lobbied without success in 1915 for a minimum wage bill, backed by the Texas Federation of Women's Clubs, the WCTU, and the YWCA. In 1919 the Tejana laundry workers of El Paso, who earned less than subsistence ("Mexican" wages being less than half of "American" wages) organized a union, which led to firings and a walkout. One of the earliest strikes by Hispanic women in the United States, it failed because of the oversupply of needy, unskilled women willing to be strikebreakers. That year labor and voluntarist women got a minimum wage law through the legislature, which repealed it in 1921 before the provisions went into effect. A decade later the U.S. Women's Bureau reported that Texas women were paid the lowest wages in the nation, and that women of color earned less than white women. A Dallas garment manufacturer told a complaining employee that a "girl" should be able to live on a five-dollar-a-week wage, and if not, she could supplement it by prostitution.[19]

During the 1930s, employers' evasion of National Recovery Administration (NRA) codes that established minimum wages and maximum hours prompted a succession of strikes in low-wage, female-dominated industries. Charlotte Duncan (Graham) and a dozen Dallas garment-industry workers formed a local and requested affiliation with the International Ladies' Garment Workers' Union (ILGWU), which sent help in organizing additional locals. In 1935 the ILGWU struck all fifteen plants of the Texas Dress Manufacturers' Association. The women endured a barrage of verbal abuse from the virulently open-shop Dallas business community and press. Like the opponents of suffrage two decades earlier, the manufacturers blamed northern agitators and contended that white southern women would never have picketed on their own. The strike failed when the union ran out of funds, and the strikers were blacklisted. Subsequent ILGWU strikes in Houston (1935) and San Antonio (1936, 1937) brought union recognition and, in Houston, contracts for the NRA-recommended twelve-dollar, forty-hour week. In 1933, 1934, and 1935, Tejana cigar rollers at Finck Cigar Company in San Antonio walked out to protest wages far below the NRA minimum, harsh rules, and unhealthful working conditions. Pecan shellers, not covered by the NRA codes because they were considered agricultural employees, struck in San Antonio in 1938. In this abysmal seasonal industry, which had been mechanized until Mexican immigrants made hand labor cheaper, women were not the only workers but they had the worst job. They were paid by the pound for picking nuts out of the broken shells, and a reduction in this piecework prompted the walkout.[20]

The pecan shellers asked Emma Tenayuca, a young labor activist who had walked the picket line with the Finck cigar strikers, to be their spokesperson, and women dominated the strike leadership and membership. Tenayuca and Minnie Rendon, secretary of the International Pecan Shellers Union, spent time in jail, as did female picketers, whose children were incarcerated with them. Tenayuca, known as La Pasionaria for her union organizing in San Antonio's impoverished West Side barrio, was the voice of Tejano labor protest in the 1930s. She led the San Antonio locals of the Workers' Alliance of America, which championed the interests of the unemployed, and also served on its national executive council. At the time of the strike she belonged to the Communist Party, which was a boon for red-baiters, and she ultimately yielded to CIO pressure to step down as strike chairwoman. The pecan shellers won their major demand, a recision of the pay cut, but the industry re-mechanized soon afterward, and thousands of workers lost their jobs.[21]

In the postwar decades labor feminists sought not only wage justice but contract provisions such as maternity leave that protected female employment rights. Texas telephone operators joined the Southwestern Telephone Workers Union, an affiliate of the National Federation of Telephone Workers (NFTW), and took part in its 1947 nationwide strike for higher wages, the largest walkout of women in U.S. history. Nelle Wooding, president of the Dallas local and chair of traffic (operators) for the northeastern division of Texas, led the strike in Dallas, where nearly one thousand women stayed out for six weeks. Wooding spent most of the remainder of her working years as a field representative for the Communication Workers of America, which superseded the NFTW.[22] In the meatpacking industry, where women were 20 percent of the labor force and represented by the United Packinghouse Workers of America (UPWA), women workers began convening biennial national conferences—in effect, a women's caucus—to discuss gender issues. Pressure from activists at contract meetings secured maternity leave and by 1956 eliminated the wage differential between men and women. Mary Salinas, elected president of the UPWA local at Fort Worth's Armour plant in 1954, took an unequivocal stand for civil rights when the national union negotiated a contract with Armour that required desegregation of all plant facilities, including those in the South. Racist whites formed a "local rights committee," but Salinas contended that if whites and blacks were going to heaven and hell together they could certainly work and eat together. She refused to back a department of white women who staged a sit-down protest rather than accept a black coworker, and after Armour removed the partition that had divided the cafeteria into white and black sections, she helped break down the remaining self-segregation by leading other union officers to sit on the former "Negro" side. "We were called a lot of names due to that," she recalled, "but we didn't care."[23]

Garment workers staged two of the most prolonged and bitter postwar strikes. The ILGWU struck (unsuccessfully) Tex-Son Company, a San Antonio children's wear firm, from 1959 to 1961. Led by Gregoria Montalba and Sophie Gonzales, it was one of the first protests against the practice of subcontracting work to an out-of-state, nonunion facility, which reduced workers' hours and take-home pay. In 1972–1974 a strike against Farah Manufacturing Company in El Paso prompted a national boycott of Farah pants. Nearly four thousand Hispanic garment workers, 85 percent of them women, went out over the demand for union representation, but the workers were also motivated by gender grievances. One woman recalled working up to her eighth month of pregnancy. "It was pretty bad, because they take no consideration; even if you're pregnant you still have to do the same thing, the same quota. They don't even take you down (from the machine) to rest your legs. If you're standing up you have to stand all day. Then after the baby is born you just take a month off, and that's it. . . . If you didn't go back to work exactly a month later, you would just lose your whole seniority." Interviews conducted three years after the Farah strike's successful conclusion found that the two years of picketing and struggling transformed some women in unexpected ways, even to the point of questioning subservience to husbands at home. One strike veteran articulated the essence of labor feminism when she told an interviewer, "I don't believe in burning your bra, but I do believe in having our rights."[24]

CIVIL RIGHTS

African American women challenged discrimination and segregation in the courts, on picket lines, at lunch counters, and, largely invisibly to history, in stores. It was as consumers being denied the right to try on shoes, hats, and dresses that they most regularly experienced the humiliation of Jim Crow, and they responded by refusing to buy the desired merchandise or with defiance. Although "try ons," as such one-on-one confrontations between black customers and white salesclerks might be called, received no publicity, they were as much acts of defiance as the lunch counter sit-ins. Lulu B. White, executive secretary of the Houston NAACP, went into department stores in the 1940s and tried on hats before the clerks could stop her. Told that she couldn't do that, White would reply, "I have," and walk out; other women would follow her example the next day. Christia Adair, White's successor in the 1950s, left a memorable account of buying a girdle she didn't need as a civil rights protest. When the saleswoman refused to show her to a fitting room, Adair demanded to see the department manager, who capitulated—stores did not want to provoke African Americans into staging a boycott. Once inside the room, Adair escalated the confrontation by insisting on the same assistance in getting a correct fit that the saleswoman extended to white shoppers, "and so she had to stand there and touch my Negro hide."[25]

African American women have been described as the foot soldiers of the civil rights movement, and as womanist race leaders they worked with men to build the Texas State Conference of Branches, NAACP. Lulu B. White's close ties with national NAACP leaders made her second in influence only to the state executive secretary, Maceo Smith. When she became secretary of the Houston branch in 1943, White launched a membership drive that more than doubled membership in two years; by 1945 she had built enrollment to twelve thousand, making the Houston branch the largest in the South. In Dallas, Juanita Craft emulated White's methods and led a membership campaign that boosted membership to seven thousand by 1946. White and Craft were "the two most successful field workers" of the Texas Conference of Branches, according to its historian. In 1946 White became director of branches and Craft was named state organizer; they traveled the state organizing new branches, revitalizing old ones, and raising money. Craft accepted the additional task of advisor to the NAACP Dallas Youth Council; she led it in picketing the State Fair of Texas in 1955 to protest the segregated admission policy.[26]

Young white women came to the civil rights movement through religious conviction. At the University of Texas in the late 1950s, participation in the Christian Faith-and-Life Community (CFLC), a religious study center, and in the University YMCA-YWCA shaped the radicalism of Sandra "Casey" Hayden, Dorothy Burlage, and Vivien Franklin. As members of the CFCL they pursued an existentialist search for meaning in the only integrated housing on campus and came to see activism as the route to authenticity. At interracial Y committee meetings and study groups they absorbed Christian liberalism and made the connection between religion and social justice. New Left historian Doug Rossinow judges Casey Hayden "the most important Y activist in helping move a group of white UT students into civil rights action between 1958 and 1961." Hayden chaired the Y's Race Relations Committee, and taught at a church school in Harlem the summer after her graduation in 1959. Returning to the University of Texas (UT) as a graduate student, she coauthored civil rights pamphlets for the National Student Association and attended its annual conference at the University of Minnesota in the summer of 1960. There she challenged the white members to endorse the sit-ins of African American students in the South. At UT that fall she helped found Students for Direct Action (SDA), which organized a yearlong series of interracial desegregation protests at movie theaters near campus.[27]

Hayden also joined Students for a Democratic Society (SDS) and the Student Nonviolent Coordinating Committee, as did Vivien Franklin, who was also an SDA activist. Franklin was part of the SDA group that protested dormitory segregation and the barring of blacks from athletic teams. She cofounded the Southwest Student Action Coordinating Committee, which in 1963 orchestrated theater desegregation protests in downtown Austin, Dallas, Houston, Fort Worth, and Denton. Franklin also organized a civil rights conference in Dallas for SDS. She was arrested multiple times and was jailed in Tyler, with three male UT students, for "vagrancy," and then warned out of town.[28]

White women who made common cause with black civil rights activists defied rigid social taboos and unspoken sexual ones—the justification for Jim Crow was keeping black men far removed from white women. Dorothy Burlage always felt that she was violating the norms of southern womanhood, and shaming her family by speaking out, but she also had to face down the southern lady's personal racial demons. Driving from the women's dormitory at the Christian Faith-and-Life-Community to the men's residence, where the lectures were held, she offered a ride to a white male student, who then invited two black men to join them. One of the black men got in the front seat beside Burlage. "In a split second, I felt my world turn upside down," she writes in her memoir. "For the first time in my life, I experienced being in a situation of apparent social intimacy with a black man." For a moment she felt physically ill at this breach of racial separation, and then her rational mind took over. "I did not want white children to be raised the way I had been. From that moment on, I was even more determined to fight segregation."[29]

SECOND WAVE FEMINISM

The revival of feminism in the 1960s and 1970s is sparsely documented; only the Austin movement has been written about, and not in depth. Women's liberation in Austin grew out of New Left activism at the University of Texas, as young women came to resent male authoritarianism in organizations such as Students for a Democratic Society (of which Austin had one of the largest chapters in the nation). Early in 1969 a handful of coeds, several of them former members of the by-then-defunct SDS, began meeting in a discussion or "rap" group at the University Y for consciousness raising. Sharing personal experiences, they worked toward an understanding of how social norms devalued women and suppressed their potential, confining them in sexualized roles as "good mothers and loving wives, charming lays," in the words of one participant. Some of their earliest activities were agitprop demonstrations against consumer capitalism's use of sexualized female images in advertising—the display of women as commodities. They picketed a fashion show jointly staged by the university's home economics department and Neiman Marcus, wearing paper dresses made from advertisements for beauty products and theater makeup applied to make garish, doll-like faces. To protest a campus visit by Miss America, they dressed up as lipstick tubes, permanent wave boxes, "and all the other products Miss America use[d] her body to sell."[30]

In the fall of 1969, University Women's Liberation began operating a birth control counseling service at the University Y; the following year it established a Women's Center in a house near campus. On August 26, 1970, more than two hundred Austin feminists observed National Women's Strike Day with a demonstration on the Capitol grounds. Called by the National Organization for Women to commemorate the fiftieth anniversary of winning woman suffrage, it was taken up by feminists in ninety cities across the country under the slogan "Don't Iron while the Strike is Hot!" The Austin gathering, at which women discussed job discrimination, day care, and abortion, concluded with an evening of music, skits, and rap sessions. Subsequently women not affiliated with the New Left who worked at the University of Texas Press began weekly consciousness-raising sessions that grew into another feminist group, the Austin Women's Organization; in 1972 it opened the Austin Women's Center.[31]

Hispanic women shaped a separate feminism within the Chicano movement of the 1970s and its political arm, La Raza Unida Party (LRUP), which functioned from 1970 to 1978. Challenging sexism along with racism, they founded a women's caucus, Mujeres por la Raza, and Maria Elena Martinez, one of the organizers, rose to become state chair of LRUP in 1976. Despite criticism that feminism was a borrowed Anglo ideology that undercut Chicano solidarity, Mujures por la Raza stressed female political education and organizing strategies. Martha P. Cotera of Austin, a prominent member of Mujeres, emerged as the voice of Tejana feminism with *Diosa y Hembra: The History and Heritage of Chicanas in the U.S.* (1976) and *The Chicana Feminist* (1977). In Crystal City, where LRUP was most successful in winning electoral office, Chicanas were initially relegated to a women's auxiliary within Ciudadanos Unidos (United Citizens), which had been organized to support the successful 1969 school boycott and became the base and political machine of LRUP. They protested by invading a meeting and demanding equal recognition, which they won on a close vote.[32]

Tejana feminists hosted their first interstate conference, La Conferencia de Mujeres por la Raza, also called the National Chicana Conference, in Houston in May 1971. In three days of workshops, six hundred participants debated issues of sex, marriage, contraception, education, employment, and religion. "I have been told that the Chicana's struggle is not the same as the white woman's struggle," conference organizer Elma Barrera announced. "I have been told that the problems are different and that ... fighting for our rights as women and as human beings is anti-Chicano and anti-male. But let me tell you what being a Chicana means in Houston, Texas. It means learning how to best please the men in the Church and the men at home, not in that order." The conference resolutions pointedly linked women's subordinate status to patriarchal religion, labeling the Catholic Church "an oppressive institution," and pointing out that "religious writing was done by *men* and interpreted by *men*"; women, therefore, should interpret the Bible according to their own lights and have their marriages performed outside church. One resolution urged Chicana mothers to teach their sons to respect women as equals and asserted that "marriages must change: [t]raditional roles for Chicanas are not acceptable or applicable." About one-half of the participants felt that the conference was giving short shrift to racism and walked out.[33]

After Vilma Martinez became president and general counsel of the Mexican American Legal Defense and Educational Fund (MALDEF) late in 1973 she launched the Chicana Rights Project (CRP), which lasted until MALDEF ran out of funds to support it a decade later. Patricia M. Vasquez directed the Texas office of the CRP (there was also one in San Francisco), which mounted successful legal challenges to employment discrimination by the major San Antonio banks and against the city itself for discriminating against women in its administration of the federal Comprehensive Employment and Training Act. The CRP also went to court over sterilization of Hispanic women. Its education component published guides to health issues, employment rights, and legal rights for Chicanas.[34]

The most radical demand of second-wave feminism was for sexual liberation and control of reproduction, including the right to abortion, which in Texas was illegal except when the pregnancy was life-threatening. The anti-abortion statute was a denial of personal autonomy and discriminated against poor women who could not afford to travel to a state where abortion was legal; it also spawned a dangerous underground of unregulated abortion providers. The roots of *Roe v. Wade,* the 1973 Supreme Court case that struck down state anti-abortion laws, reach back to the counseling service, the Women's Liberation Birth Control Center, that UT graduate students Judy Smith, Victoria Foe, and other members of Austin Women's Liberation established in a tiny office at the University Y in 1969. Staffed by volunteers, the center also quietly gave referrals to safe abortion clinics in Mexico. Smith received assistance from the Austin chapter of the New York–based Clergy Consultation Service on Abortion, which screened clinics and doctors in Mexico.[35]

The volunteers at the center did not know what kind of legal trouble they might be courting with abortion referrals or if they could

be prosecuted as accomplices to an illegal act. Neither did Sarah Weddington, who was fresh out of UT law school and doing volunteer legal
research for the counselors. After a bill to reform the state's abortion
law failed, she agreed to challenge its constitutionality in court. Weddington solicited assistance from former classmate Linda Coffee in
Dallas; Coffee located a pregnant plaintiff, Norma McCorvey, who
was listed as Jane Roe in the lawsuit that Weddington and Coffee filed
in federal court. The decision handed down on June 17, 1970, was a
technical victory but a practical defeat. The three-judge panel agreed
that the Texas abortion law was an unconstitutional violation of a
woman's right to privacy under the Ninth Amendment, but declined
to issue an injunction ordering the state to cease enforcing it.[36]

At the same time, grassroots organizations promoting abortion reform were forming around the state. Virginia Whitehill took the initiative in founding the Dallas Committee to Study Abortion in 1969; she
gave speeches and the committee mailed out literature and lobbied in
Austin. After the *Roe* verdict, pro-choice groups emerged in Houston,
Galveston, and Austin, and an umbrella group, the Texas Abortion
Coalition (TAC), formed at the end of 1970, with Sarah Weddington as
acting chair. Adopting the slogan "Abortion is a Personal Decision,"
the TAC planned a statewide campaign for a repeal law. Weddington
drafted a model bill, which failed in the 1971 legislative session, and
she argued the appeal of *Roe v. Wade* before the U.S. Supreme Court.
The high court ruling on January 22, 1973, upheld a pregnant woman's
constitutional right to privacy and provoked a backlash that has not
abated. The Texas Abortion Rights Action League formed in 1978 to
counter attempts to undermine *Roe*.[37]

While young women's liberationists challenged cultural oppression, professional women formed local chapters of the National Organization for Women (NOW) and, in 1973, a state organization. Modeled
on the NAACP, NOW focused on economic equality and legal rights, and
its version of female empowerment diverged significantly from the
gender-difference ideology and emphasis on distinctive female values
of the Progressive-era women's movement. Second-wave feminists asserted that women should not have to choose between family and career; they demanded both support for childrearing (child care centers,
pregnancy leave) and an end to sex discrimination in the workplace.
The Texas locals adhered to national policy but chose their own projects. The Houston NOW chapter, for example, formed an equal opportunity task force early in 1972 to confront sex-segregated "help
wanted" newspaper ads and government contractors who failed to
meet equal–opportunity guidelines. Three years later it filed a class action complaint with the Equal Opportunity Employment Commission

against the Houston Police Department for discrimination in hiring.[38]
The Texas State NOW worked through task forces that created rape
crisis centers and shelters for battered women, pressed the Texas Education Agency to reject textbooks that included sexist portrayals of
women, and lobbied the legislature for stronger child support enforcement and for the Displaced Homemaker Act of 1977, which set up
two pilot centers to provide services for widowed and divorced women
without workplace experience or skills.[39]

The rallying point for second-wave feminism was equal rights
legislation, over which Progressive-era feminists had divided. Texas
suffragists had opposed Alice Paul's Equal Rights Amendment (ERA),
first introduced in Congress in 1923 and annually thereafter; they
feared it would invalidate state laws protecting women factory workers. Minnie Fisher Cunningham, Jane McCallum, and others in the
old Progressive women's coalition maintained their opposition to the
ERA through the 1950s, when Dallas attorney Hermine Tobolowsky
and the Texas Federation of Business and Professional Women's Clubs
(BPW), an affluent, relatively conservative group, began lobbying for a
Texas ERA. Tobolowsky and the BPW finally succeeded in getting the
Texas Equal Legal Rights Amendment (ELRA) through the legislature
in 1971. The following year Congress at last passed the ERA and sent
it to the states for ratification. By then, nearly one-half of American
women were in the labor force, and the increasing number of women
in white-collar jobs found protective legislation based on gender-
difference ideology an impediment rather than a benefit. Some union
women, having discovered that protective legislation kept them from
earning overtime pay and promotions, were beginning to challenge the
laws in court. To the many feminists who had absorbed the language
of the civil rights movement, gender equality was the logical corollary
of racial equality. By 1972 left/liberal women regarded the federal ERA
as essential legislation, and the Texas legislature ratified it in special
session; voters ratified the state ELRA in the general election that same
year.[40]

Second-wave feminism peaked at the National Women's Conference held in Houston in November 1977. Funded by Congress as a
follow-up to International Women's Year in 1975, it was the first national women's meeting since the Seneca Falls Convention in 1848.
Delegates were elected at fifty preliminary statewide conventions.
More than twenty-nine hundred Texas women met for three days
at the University of Texas in Austin to choose a delegation and hold
workshops. The convention passed twenty-seven resolutions, including demands for the appointment of a governor's commission on the
status of women, an end to credit and insurance discrimination against

women, more minority appointments to state offices, civil rights protection for lesbians, and support for the ERA. Fifty-eight delegates were chosen, including Sarah Weddington, Martha Cotera, future governor Ann Richards, state representative Irma Rangel, and future congresswoman Eddie Bernice Johnson. Only six were ERA opponents, which prompted a Dallas participant to complain that "the militant libbers and lesbians were in control."[41]

When the Houston conference convened, International Women's Year (IWY) Commissioner Liz Carpenter and keynote speaker Barbara Jordan likened the women's rights movement to the human rights initiative that President Jimmy Carter was pursuing in foreign policy. The IWY Commission had submitted twenty-six resolutions, called the National Plan of Action, to be voted on, and some 20 percent of the delegates opposed it. The three most controversial resolutions were support for the ERA (Ann Richards gave the seconding speech), abortion (Sarah Weddington gave the seconding speech), and lesbian rights. The anti-Plan faction, however, was not strong enough to drag out debate and keep them from coming to a vote. (Prudence Mackintosh, who reported for *Texas Monthly,* credited Richards and the other Texas delegates seated near the microphone for keeping the agenda moving; one of them moved the previous question whenever the momentum was in danger of stalling.) All of the resolutions passed except one calling for the creation of a cabinet-level Women's Department in the federal government.[42]

The promise of the Houston conference, however, went unfilled. While it was in progress, a larger gathering of right-wing women, headed by Phyllis Schlafly of Stop ERA met across town to condemn feminism as a threat to family, God, and nation. Although the Plan of Action was submitted to President Carter, the recommendations were never implemented. The backlash against feminism helped propel the rise of the politically powerful New Right and stopped the ERA, which fell short of ratification even though Congress extended the deadline until 1982 and Liz Carpenter, as codirector of ERAmerica, stumped the country for it.

On the surface, there are obvious parallels between first- and second-wave feminism. Both expended enormous effort in pursuit of state and federal constitutional amendments to remove gender discrimination. With the success of the woman suffrage amendment and the failure of the ERA, both feminist movements supposedly went into decline. A close look at the evidence, however, points to a different conclusion. In the more than four decades between the disbanding of the Joint Legislative Council in 1927 and the founding of the Texas State NOW in 1973, multiple feminisms flourished as groups of women on the Left pursued economic and racial justice and political influence. Their agendas helped shape second-wave feminism, and their diversity contributed to its strength. Similarly, the "post-feminist" label attached to the 1980s and '90s overlooks the continuing erosion of gender barriers. While social conservatives fought the ERA to a standstill and entrenched against reproductive freedom, women steadily gained traction in electoral politics. When the Texas Women's Political Caucus formed in 1971, with the goal of getting more feminist women elected to office and promoting women's issues within the parties, two women sat in the legislature. Two decades later there were twenty-four, black and Latina as well as white, and the state had a liberal woman governor, Ann Richards.[43]

In their pursuit of a more just and equitable society, feminist movements have challenged and eliminated the most obvious legal discriminations against women. Decades of pressure slowly yielded the right to vote, to sit on a jury, and to attend an all-male or all-white university, as well as equal pay for equal work, and independent credit. Deeply embedded cultural assumptions about gender roles that have produced an antifeminist backlash are more intractable. The concept of "woman's sphere" has been retired from the language, but the reconceptualization of what constitutes fairness for women remains a subject of debate for the twenty-first century.

NOTES

1. Molly Ivins, "There Will Always Be a Texas," *Ms.*, July/August, 1987, 82–84; Marjorie Spruill Wheeler, *New Women of the New South: The Leaders of the Woman Suffrage Movement in the South* (New York: Oxford University Press, 1993), chap. 1; Rebecca Edwards, *Angels in the Machinery: Gender in American Party Politics from the Civil War to the Progressive Era* (New York: Oxford University Press, 1997), 5–27.

2. Suzanne Lebsock, "Woman Suffrage and White Supremacy: A Virginia Case Study," in *Visible Women: New Essays on American Activism*, ed. Nancy Hewitt and Suzanne Lebsock (Urbana: University of Illinois Press, 1993), 65.

3. Elsa Barkley Brown, "Womanist Consciousness: Maggie Lena Walker and the Independent Order of Saint Luke," *Signs* 14 (Spring 1989): 610–33.

4. A. Elizabeth Taylor, "The Woman Suffrage Movement in Texas," in *Citizens at Last: The Woman Suffrage Movement in Texas*, ed. Ruthe Winegarten and Judith N. McArthur (Austin: Ellen C. Temple Publishing, 1987); Judith N. McArthur and Harold L Smith, *Min-*

nie Fisher Cunningham: A Suffragist's Life in Politics (New York: Oxford University Press, 2003), chap. 3. For analyses of local movements, see Elizabeth York Enstam, "The Dallas Equal Suffrage Association, Political Style, and Popular Culture: Grassroots Strategies of the Woman Suffrage Movement, 1913–1919," *Journal of Southern History* 68, no. 4 (November 2002), and Elizabeth Hayes Turner, "'White-Gloved Ladies' and 'New Women' in the Texas Woman Suffrage Movement," in *Southern Women: Histories and Identities*, ed. Virginia Bernhard, et al. (Columbia: University of Missouri Press, 1992).

5. Michael Perman, *Struggle for Mastery: Disfranchisement in the South, 1888–1908* (Chapel Hill: University of North Carolina Press, 2001), 61.

6. *Galveston Daily News*, November 20, 1916.

7. Judith N. McArthur, "Minnie Fisher Cunningham's Back Door Lobby in Texas: Political Maneuvering in a One-Party State," in *One Woman, One Vote: Rediscovering the Woman Suffrage Movement*, ed. Marjorie Spruill Wheeler (Troutdale: Ore.: NewSage Press, 1995), 315–31.

8. Ruthe Winegarten, *Black Texas Women: 150 Years of Trial and Triumph* (Austin: University of Texas Press, 1995), 210; Judith N. McArthur, *Creating the New Woman: The Rise of Southern Women's Progressive Culture in Texas, 1893–1918* (Urbana: University of Illinois Press, 1998), 141–42.

9. Lorraine Gates Schuyler, *The Weight of their Votes: Southern Women and Political Leverage in the 1920s* (Chapel Hill: University of North Carolina Press, 2006), 192 (quotation), 64, 58.

10. Ibid., 97.

11. *Dallas Morning News*, February 11, 1907.

12. For a full account of women and Progressive-era reform, see McArthur, *Creating the New Woman*; Megan Seaholm, "Earnest Women: The White Women's Club Movement in Progressive Era Texas" (PhD diss., Rice University, 1988); Elizabeth Hayes Turner, *Women, Culture, and Community: Religion and Reform in Galveston, 1880–1920* (New York: Oxford University Press, 1997); Jacquelyn Masur McElhaney, *Pauline Periwinkle and Progressive Reform in Dallas* (College Station: Texas A&M University Press, 1998); Elizabeth York Enstam, *Women and the Creation of Urban Life: Dallas, Texas, 1843–1920* (College Station: Texas A&M University Press, 1998); and Elizabeth York Enstam, "They Called it 'Motherhood': Dallas Women and Public Life, 1895–1918," in *Hidden Histories of Women in the New South*, ed. Virginia Bernhard, et al. (Columbia: University of Missouri Press, 1994).

13. Judith N. McArthur, "Saving the Children: The Clubwomen's Crusade Against Child Labor, 1902–1918" in *Women and Texas History: Selected Essays*, ed. Fane Downs and Nancy Baker Jones (Austin: Texas State Historical Association, 1993); McArthur, *Creating the New Woman*, chap. 3.

14. Jane Y. McCallum, "Activities of Women in Texas Politics," in Winegarten and McArthur eds., *Citizens at Last*, 222–26 (quotation on 222); McCallum to Mrs. Abe Blum, February 8, 1923, box 5, McCallum Family Papers, Austin History Center–Austin Public Library. See Emma Louise Moyer Jackson, "'Petticoat Politics': Political Activism Among Texas Women in the 1920's" (PhD diss., University of Texas at Austin, 1980), for a full account of the Joint Legislative Council.

15. McArthur and Smith, *Minnie Fisher Cunningham*, 155–56.

16. Ibid., 166–68, 186 (quotation), 187–89, 193–94, 197.

17. Dorothy Sue Cobble, *The Other Women's Movement: Workplace Justice and Social Rights in Modern America* (Princeton: Princeton University Press, 2004), 3. See also Dennis A. Deslippe, *"Rights, Not Roses": Unions and the Rise of Working-Class Feminism, 1945–1980* (Urbana: University of Illinois Press, 2000).

18. McArthur, *Creating the New Woman*, 90–91, 95.

19. Irene Ledesma, "Unlikely Strikers: Mexican-American Women and Strike Activity in Texas, 1919–1974" (PhD diss., Ohio State University, 1992), 83–91; Mary Loretta Sullivan and Bertha Blair, *Women in Texas Industries: Hours, Wages, Working Conditions, and Home Work* (Washington, D.C.: U.S. Government Printing Office, 1936), 7, 14, 71–78, 80–81; Patricia Everidge Hill, "Real Women and True Womanhood: Grassroots Organizing among Dallas Dressmakers in 1935," *Labor's Heritage* 5 (Spring 1994): 6.

20. Hill, "Real Women and True Womanhood"; Melissa Hield and Richard Croxdale, eds., *Women in the Texas Workforce: Yesterday and Today* (Austin: People's History in Texas, 1979), 5–12; Ledesma. "Unlikely Strikers," 92–105; Julia Kirk Blackwelder, *Women of the Depression: Caste and Culture in San Antonio, 1929–1939* (College Station: Texas A&M University Press, 1984), 104–106, 132–35.

21. On Emma Tenayuca, see Gabriela Gonzalez, "Two Flags Entwined: Transborder Activists and the Politics of Race, Ethnicity, Class, and Gender in South Texas, 1900–1950" (PhD diss., Stanford University, 2004), chap. 7; Zaragosa Vargas, "Tejana Radical: Emma Tenayuca and the San Antonio Labor Movement during the Great Depression," *Pacific Historical Review* 66 (1997): 553–80; Julia Kirk Blackwelder, "Emma Tenayuca: Vision and Courage," in *The Human Tradition in Texas*, ed. Ty Cashion and Jesus F. de la Teja (Wilmington, Del.:

Scholarly Resources, 2001), 191–208; and "Living History: Emma Tenayuca Tells Her Story," *Texas Observer*, October 28, 1983.

22. John Schacht, Oral History Interview with Nelle Wooding, 1970, University of Iowa Oral History Project (copy at University of Texas at Arlington). On the strike, see John N. Schacht, *The Making of Telephone Unionism, 1920–1947* (New Brunswick, N.J.: Rutgers University Press, 1985).

23. Roger Horowitz, *"Negro and White, Unite and Fight!": A Social History of Industrial Unionism in Meatpacking, 1930–1990* (Urbana: University of Illinois Press, 1997), 227–31; Rick Halpern, "Interracial Unionism in the Southwest: Fort Worth's Packinghouse Workers, 1937–1954," in *Organized Labor in the Twentieth-Century South*, ed. Robert Zieger (Knoxville: University of Tennessee Press, 1991), 158–82; interview with Mary Salinas, United Packinghouse Workers of America Oral History Project, State Historical Society of Wisconsin.

24. George L. Green, "ILGWU in Texas, 1930–1970," *Journal of Mexican American History* 1 (1971): 147–49; Toni Marie Nelson Herrera, "Constructed and Contested Meanings of the Tex-Son Strike in San Antonio, Texas, 1959: Representing Mexican Women Workers" (master's thesis, University of Texas at Austin, 1997); Emily Honig, "Women at Farah Revisited: Political Mobilization and its Aftermath Among Chicana Workers at El Paso," *Feminist Studies* 22, no. 2 (Summer 1996): 425–441; Laurie Coyle, Gail Hershatter, and Emily Honig, *Women at Farah: An Unfinished Story* (El Paso: REFORMA, 1979), 10 (first quotation), 45 (second quotation).

25. Merline Pitre, *In Struggle Against Jim Crow: Lulu B. White and the NAACP, 1900–1957* (College Station: Texas A&M University Press, 1999), 134–35; interview with Christia Adair, April 25, 1977, Black Women Oral History Project, Arthur and Elizabeth Schlesinger Library, Radcliffe College, 71–72.

26. Michael Lowery Gillette, "The NAACP in Texas, 1937–1957" (PhD diss., University of Texas at Austin, 1984), 10, 25–26, 28 (quotation), 29; Rachel Northington Burrow, "Juanita Craft: Desegregating the State Fair of Texas," *Legacies* 16, no. 1 (Spring 2005): 19–26; Stefanie Decker, "African American Women in the Civil Rights Era," in *Black Women in Texas History*, ed. Bruce A. Glasrud and Merline Pitre (College Station: Texas A&M University Press, 2008), 159–76.

27. Doug Rossinow, *The Politics of Authenticity: Liberalism, Christianity, and the New Left in America* (New York: Columbia University Press, 1998), 54–57, 76–92, 102 (quotation), 103–106, 122–34; Casey Hayden, "Fields of Blue," in *Deep in Our Hearts: Nine White Women in the Freedom Movement*, ed. Constance Curry, et al. (Athens: University of Georgia Press, 2000), 338–41.

28. Rossinow, *The Politics of Authenticity*, 136–37.

29. Dorothy Burlage, "Truths of the Heart," in Curry et al., *Deep in Our Hearts*, 95–96 (quotation).

30. Rossinow, *The Politics of Authenticity*, 285, 294–96; Barbara Wuensch, "Women's Liberation," *The Rag*, September 15, 1969, 3 (first quotation); "Women's Liberation in Austin," *Second Coming*, December 1, 1970, 6–7 (second quotation); Bea [Vogel], "Women's Liberation in Austin," *The Rag*, June 26, 1969.

31. Frieda L. Werden, "Adventures of a Texas Feminist," in *No Apologies: Texas Radicals Celebrate the '60s*, ed. Daryl Janes (Austin: Eakin Press, 1992), 199–202; "Sisters Strike," *The Rag*, September 8, 1970.

32. Teresa Paloma Acosta and Ruthe Winegarten: *Las Tejanas: 300 Years of History* (Austin: University of Texas Press, 2003), 234–38; Vicki L. Ruiz, *From Out of the Shadows: Mexican Women in Twentieth-Century America* (New York: Oxford University Press, 1998), 115–16; Mirta Vidal, *Chicanas Speak Out: Women, New Voice of La Raza* (New York: Pathfinder Press, 1971), 5.

33. Vidal, *Chicanas Speak Out*, 12–14.

34. Acosta and Winegarten, *Las Tejanas*, 245–46.

35. Sarah Weddington, *A Question of Choice* (New York: Penguin Books, 1992), 26–33; Werden, "Adventures of a Texas Feminist," 199–201; David J. Garrow, *Liberty and Sexuality: The Right to Privacy and the Making of Roe v. Wade* (Berkeley: University of California Press, 1998), 390–93.

36. Weddington, *A Question of Choice*, 36–38, 44–70.

37. Marian Faux, *Roe v. Wade: The Untold Story of the Landmark Supreme Court Decision that Made Abortion Legal* (New York: Macmillan, 1988), 108–29, 215–22. The Texas Abortion Rights Action League is now called NARAL Pro-Choice Texas.

38. *The Broadside*, May 1972 and August 1975, both in box 1, folder 20, Peggy Hall NOW Collection, University of Houston Libraries. See also Judie Karen Walton Gammage, "Quest for Equality: An Historical Overview of Women's Rights Activism in Texas, 1890–1975" (PhD diss., University of North Texas, 1982).

39. *Texas State NOW Newsletter*, February 1977, August 1977; *Austin NOW Times*, March–April 1983, October 1983.

40. Ann Kennedy, "ERA's Texas History," *Houston Breakthrough*, May 1977; McArthur and Smith, *Minnie Fisher Cunningham*, 184–85; Rob Fink, "Hermine Tobolowsky, the Texas ELRA, and the Political Struggle for Women's Equal Rights," *Journal of the West* 42, no. 3 (Summer 2003), 52–57. On sex discrimination in employment, see Alice Kessler-Harris, *In Pursuit of Equity: Women, Men, and the*

Quest for Economic Citizenship in 20th-century America (New York: Oxford University Press, 2001), 234–41.

41. "Texas Women's Meeting: A Mini Report," box 1, folder 1, Marjorie Randal NOW Collection, University of Houston Libraries; "Anti-ERA Forces Demand Probe of Balloting at Austin Women's Meeting," *Houston Post*, July 2, 1977 (quotation).

42. "First Woman," *Daily Breakthrough*, November 20, 1977, 20; Cheryl Knott, "Gavel-to-Gavel," *Houston Breakthrough*, December 1977–January 1978, 4; Prudence Mackintosh, "The Good Old Girls," *Texas Monthly* 6, no. 1 (January 1978): 88–93, 149–55; Carol Barnes, "Local Delegates to Women's Conference Support Resolutions," *Houston Post*, November 4, 1977, 1B.

43. Nancy Baker Jones and Ruthe Winegarten, *Capitol Women: Texas Female Legislators, 1923–1999* (Austin: University of Texas Press, 2000), 279–80.

CONFRONTING WHITE SUPREMACY
The African American Left
in Texas, 1874–1974

Bruce A. Glasrud and Gregg Andrews

Oh, how can we forget
Our human rights denied?
Oh, how can we forget
Our manhood crucified?
When Justice is profaned
And plea with curse is met,
When Freedom's gates are barred,
Oh, how can we forget?

—Melvin B. Tolson

On July 7, 1912, a gun battle broke out in the small mill town of Grabow, Louisiana, during a "lumber war" between members of the Brotherhood of Timber Workers (BTW), a biracial union in western Louisiana and East Texas, and forces representing the Southern Lumber Operators' Association, an owner's group set up not only to prevent workers from unionizing in the timber industry, but also to enforce the southern racial order by keeping blacks subordinate. During this class conflict, when Association guards fired into the workers, union members retaliated. Three individuals were killed immediately, one died later, and forty were wounded. Although most shots were fired from Association weapons, authorities arrested the leadership and sixty-four members of the BTW who, while in jail awaiting trial, formed a Socialist Party local. They were found not guilty; unfortunately their legal expenses broke the union and over the next few years the BTW faltered and ended.[1]

Before that battle, the BTW had become a unified biracial force. As James R. Green asserts, it was "a radical, collective response to industrial capitalism." African Americans in East Texas comprised nearly 40 percent of the timber workers as well as a significant percentage of the union leadership, and neither white nor black wanted the other to be used as strikebreakers. The BTW emerged from owner-worker disputes and owner mistreatment of workers in the early years of the twentieth century. In 1904, for example, black mill hands in Groveton conducted a strike against the virtual slavery in which they were held, and served notice that they were to be included in any major movement against industrial capitalism in East Texas. By December 1910, timber workers, led by Arthur Lee Emerson and Jay Smith, organized the first local. Additional locals organized in East Texas and western Louisiana in 1911, leading to the formation of the BTW, an industrial union of black and white, men and women members. Early in 1912 the BTW affiliated with the Industrial Workers of the World (IWW), presented a set of grievances to the owners, and the Operator's Association retaliated with a lockout. Ultimately the union was busted.[2]

The broad appeal of the BTW showed that biracial unionism could succeed in East Texas. But the combined forces of wealthy southern industrialists, bent on preventing and destroying labor union activity, together with a strong conservative element of white Texans opposed to any form of black economic strength, proved too much to overcome so early in the twentieth century. To a certain extent, also, the BTW was an anomaly. African Americans in Texas[3] generally did not associate with leftist activities, since the Left in an organized framework such as the Industrial Workers of the World or the Socialist or the Communist parties, too often did not solicit black participation.[4] Partially this was the case since Left leaders also were Texans, and it was Texas whites who set up the racial parameters of Texas society. White Texans viewed blacks as inferior beings who should be separated from white society, should obey white demands, should willingly work in underpaid positions for whites, and should generally acquiesce to whites' dominance. Blacks fought back with practical and reform-minded alliances. Afro-Texans resisted restrictive, violent white behavior, they were part of the mass of underpaid workers, and they sought freedom, equality, and opportunity. Many wished to overthrow or radically transform an entire southern way of life. White Texans saw the resistance of black Texans to their mandated status as radical, often taking steps to break up black associations; for example, white officials sought membership rolls of black militant organizations such as the NAACP.

To define what is meant by the Left in the Texas black community let us start by stating what it is not. It is not composed of Afro-Texans who acquiesced or accommodated to white society. Rather, it is those black Texans who with their ideas and actions resisted white beliefs and practices designed to subordinate African Texans, those who pursued collective action against the white power structure both economically and politically, who allied themselves with the lower classes, who joined left-leaning organizations, and who sought radical change in the status of black Texans vis-à-vis white domination. Those numbers included black nationalists, radical labor unionists, tenant and small farm owner alliances, and individuals who stood up to white supremacy. This definition takes account of political and civil rights advocates, women reform activists, supporters of overt resistance, champions of the lower class, and especially "race men" and their adherents. Some black Texans were Populists or Socialists, a few affiliated with Communists. Individuals such as Lulu B. White, Matthew Gaines, R. D. Evans, Heman Marion Sweatt, and Christia Adair fought for Afro-Texan liberty and rights. To do so placed them on the "left" of African Americans in the Lone Star State.

This chapter covers the years from 1874, which marked the end of efforts to aid black Texans during Reconstruction and the takeover of the state government by racist whites determined to retain blacks in subordinate roles, to 1974, when initial fruits of the civil rights movement could be seen, as black Texas political leader Barbara Jordan argued persuasively and successfully to impeach and remove Richard M. Nixon for unconstitutional behavior as president of the United States. This significant development was brought about in large measure by actions of "left-leaning" black Texans during the previous one hundred years. The cost of that changeover can be seen in the titles of works examining the efforts of those years. Lamar L. Kirven titled his dissertation on black Texans "A Century of Warfare"; Melvin James Banks, in his dissertation on the struggle for first-class citizenship, emphasized "The Pursuit of Equality"; and Gregg Cantrell's biography of John B. Rayner is called *Feeding the Wolf*. That black Texans sometimes succeeded is indicated by Darlene Clark Hine's book, *Black Victory*.[5]

The point from which African Americans resisted white oppression, struggled for freedom to work, advanced their interests, and utilized collective action goes back to the first presence of blacks in Texas. Slavery existed when the Spanish brought Africans to the region that became Texas; slavery increased with the influx of Anglos, and by 1850 slavery was a firmly entrenched institution, dubbed "the peculiar institution." Prior to Juneteenth (June 19, 1865), black slaves revealed in their actions their feelings about their deplorable situation in slavery, running away, striking, organizing rebellions, standing up to their masters, and in a few instances physically challenging white owners or owners' white employees. Occasionally murder resulted. Paul D. Lack's informative article "Dave: A Rebellious Slave" provides us with an example of a recalcitrant black slave from Galveston. Dave (no last name known) benefited from the urban environment, from the Civil War, and from the "hiring out" system. What these circumstances meant to Dave was that increased opportunity was not enough; he continually challenged white society.[6]

The end of the Civil War brought legal freedom for black Texans, and with their freedom, they assumed, came opportunity and choices. Blacks expected education, land, and the vote. They established families, churches (without white interference), and social networks. However, beset by often vicious white antagonism, bereft of legal redress, and desirous of maintaining their dignity and freedom, black Texans fought to protect their communities. At first helped by the Freedmen's Bureau, state police, U.S. Army, and Republican control nationally, blacks asserted their rights. However, the state government sided with whites over blacks, and too few Bureau agents or military men were available to accomplish as much as might have been done on behalf of black Texans. Later, from 1870 to 1873, Republicans controlled Texas and provided additional support for Afro-Texans during the final bitter years of Reconstruction. Overall, given the circumstances, black Texans managed remarkable achievements. They were able, as Randolph B. Campbell states so well in *Grass-Roots Reconstruction in Texas, 1865–1880*, to "make freedom mean something more than inequality, intimidation, and violence."[7] They pursued collective action against the dominant white power structure.

An example of the problems faced by blacks during Reconstruction and their efforts to control their destiny and to resist white aggression with courageous leadership and collective action took place in 1868 in Millican, a community in Brazos County. Essentially a small civil and class war broke out. Trouble began when the local Ku Klux Klan began harassing and intimidating blacks. Bent on protecting their community, armed blacks retaliated by firing at the Klansmen. The Klansmen retreated. Local black leader George E. Brooks, a Methodist minister, schoolteacher, and Union League head, organized a black militia with the support of Harry Thomas, a black Millican leader. Only a few years earlier, blacks were forbidden to bear arms; now they marched, armed and militant. Such organized Afro-Texan resistance frightened and angered whites. When a black man went missing, allegedly killed by unknown whites, Brooks asked his militia to investigate. Whites from Millican and the surrounding area confronted the black militia, and in the ensuing melee no whites but twenty-five blacks, including Thomas, were killed. Whites killed unarmed blacks, including Brooks who was discovered hanged a few days later.[8] The power of white supremacy would be exceedingly difficult to break.

After conservative white Democrats overthrew the state Republican officeholders in 1873, African Americans in Texas were left without protection and support; they depended even more on their own resources. Strong leaders continued during the late nineteenth century, including Republican politician and union leader Norris Wright Cuney and black Populist leaders John B. Rayner and Melvin Wade. However, two men—George T. Ruby and Matthew Gaines—whose leadership had been important during Republican Reconstruction, faded from public view in Texas after 1873. Known as an aggressive black leader, Ruby organized the short-lived Labor Union of Colored Men in Galveston and encouraged rights for black Texans. Elected to the Texas Senate, Ruby was the most important and powerful black Texas political leader, but moved to Louisiana in 1873.[9] Matt Gaines, referred to as "The Militant," by Merline Pitre in *Through Many Dangers Toils and Snares,* settled in Washington County after Emancipation and soon emerged as a strong, vigorous black leader. Also elected to the Texas Senate, Gaines was the guardian of the rights and interests of black Texans. He supported the black masses and strove for adequate protections for black tenants. Gaines lost his Senate seat in 1873, but remained somewhat active in public affairs until his death in 1900.[10]

Following Reconstruction, efforts calling for black cooperation, leadership ability, and collective action from the Left continued. In 1883, black men led by Norris Wright Cuney, a prominent Republican political leader from Galveston, formed a longshoremen's association that worked loading and unloading ships at Galveston. African Americans had established themselves on the Galveston docks before the Civil War but by the mid-seventies whites tried to exclude black labor on the waterfront, abetted by the white unions that refused black membership. George Ruby had started a union as early as 1870, but he saw it more as a tool for political recruiting than as an aid for black workers. In the mid-seventies, Cuney, who followed Ruby as Republican leader in Galveston and eventually the state, set up the Cotton Jammers and Longshoremen's Association, a union for black workers, probably for some of the same motives as Ruby. That group applied for a state charter in 1879, and in 1883, led by Cuney, received a contract for work on the Galveston wharf, thus establishing a regular position for black workers on the waterfront that led to sharing work with the white union and workers. Although Cuney succeeded in securing work on the Galveston waterfront for black laborers, that success did not occur readily. Many white union members fought for white- only employment on the wharf, and most ship company owners preferred white workers. Some union leaders though realized that it was better to fight white capitalist owners with a unified biracial front, and Cuney clamored for that approach. By the time of his death in 1898, however, he had lost control of the Republican Party in Texas to "lily whites," and Galveston's black community lost its most powerful voice. As Maud Cuney Hare, Cuney's talented daughter, noted in the subtitle to her father's biography, he was "a tribune of the black people."[11]

During the late nineteenth century, black and white Texas farmers and workers established the People's Party—the Populists—which endeavored, among other things, to develop an egalitarian and racially unified movement to topple the state's conservative white governing monopoly. From the beginning the Populists realized that their fortunes could best be accomplished by a biracial movement. Led by their primary organizer and representative, John B. Rayner, together with Dallas carpenter and labor leader Melvin Wade, many blacks, dissatisfied with race-baiting Democrats on the one hand and the "lily white" Republicans on the other, turned to the Populists. Born in North Carolina, Rayner arrived in Texas in 1880, settled in Robertson County, and by 1887 became politically involved while speaking in favor of prohibition. A hard-working individual and an excellent orator, Rayner saw the Populists as saviors for black Texans, and became a leading recruiter and speaker for Texas Populism. Wade arrived in Texas from Tennessee, and was important to black recruitment efforts because he represented the black working class from a large city.[12]

Although disappointed with a poor showing in 1892, Texas Populist support increased in 1894. Their biracial coalition held together. They enthusiastically turned to the election of 1896. However, on the national level the Populists pursued fusion with the Democratic Party, a position that was anathema to Texas and other southern Populists since southern white Democrats controlled state politics. Texas Populists worked out an arrangement with the Republicans. Although the black Republicans upheld their end of the bargain by voting for Populists on the state and local level, white southerners—farmers, laborers, and small businessmen—could not bring themselves to vote for the Republican Party ticket, that is the party of Abraham Lincoln and of African Americans. Instead they voted racial tickets, and cast their ballots for the Democrats. The biracial effort in Texas shattered. Whites soon joined together and virtually eliminated blacks from the political process (by 1910 only 2 percent of the black population voted). As Gregg Cantrell emphasizes, "Radicalism failed in Texas because it underestimated the power of white supremacy."[13]

In 1899, Texas-born minister and author Sutton E. Griggs offered a different and more radical challenge to white supremacy in Texas. Griggs published a novel entitled *Imperium in Imperio*; this black-nationalist novel called for blacks, either with force or by the ballot and numbers, to take over Texas. Griggs asserted what a number of black Texans had already perceived, that a strong nationalist stance was called for in the Lone Star State. Black nationalists realized that they must depend upon self-reliance and racial pride, through separation from whites and through working within their community by pursuing collective action. Although varied schemes emerged, in general three types of black nationalist objectives developed—to establish separate black communities within or outside Texas, to create a separate state or nation for blacks (such as that suggested by Griggs), and colonization in Mexico or Africa.[14]

Black Texans were involved in numerous efforts for racial advancement and political change via black-nationalist proposals. They migrated to Kansas and Oklahoma to set up all-black communities or at least to establish themselves in states that seemed to have less white racial antagonism. As Thad Sitton and James H. Conrad note in *Freedom Colonies: Independent Black Texans in the Time of Jim Crow*, blacks also established many separate, nearly all-black communities in Texas. Other individuals attempted, as Griggs suggested, to transform Texas from a white-dominated state to an all-black state. As far back as 1863, U. S. Senator James Henry Lane, a Kansas Republican, introduced legislation to divide Texas in two, and make one half a separate state for blacks. The law was endorsed by a Senate committee, but failed in the Senate at large. By the twentieth century, similar efforts emerged. In 1910, the Texas Purchase Movement called upon the federal government to purchase the state of Texas from landowners, sell it to African Americans, and give them one hundred years to repay the debt. A later proposal, in 1919, called for the creation of a separate state on the border between Texas and Mexico that would have the same relation to the United States as Canada had to England. Others suggested establishing black colonies in the western United States or in Mexico.[15] These efforts, though supported by black Texans, had the disadvantage of needing white support. That support was not forthcoming.

Black nationalists pursued black-only, self-help strategies, including the back-to-Africa movement of Chief Alfred Charles Sam. From Oklahoma, Chief Sam purchased a ship to transport blacks to the Gold Coast of Africa. Most followers came from Oklahoma, but Texas blacks followed his progress enthusiastically and some sailed with Sam. Local Texas leaders of Chief Sam's movement included O. L. Parker and R. A. Burt, who acted as Sam's agents in Galveston. The ship sailed from Galveston on August 21, 1914. Parker best explained the reason for leaving: "We wanted to go to a place where we could have similar privileges and not have to take our orders from a dominant and unfriendly race." Whites became worried due to the massive outpouring of support for black-nationalist proposals. Conservative, capitalist whites fretted over the potential loss of cheap labor.[16]

Black males were not alone in the struggle against Texas racial mores and economic and political exploitation. As noted in the story of the Brotherhood of Timber Workers, black women[17] actively fought white power and capitalism in Texas. Early in the twentieth century, black women refused to accept new Jim Crow laws, and resisted their implementation in cities such as Houston and Austin. They knew that the right to vote was a vital aspect of achieving power, and they became suffragists. This was a revolutionary step. Black women reformers not only challenged the disadvantaged status of women, but also of African Americans. Black women were not admitted to the Texas Equal Suffrage Association (TESA), the progressive organization that white women established to seek the right to vote. Even worse, some white women (and men) opposed women's suffrage because it would give black women the vote. Nevertheless black women struggled, organized, and worked for the vote. When finally they were eligible to register for the 1918 primary, they attempted to register. One of the black suffragists, Christia Adair of Kingsville, encouraged black women to seek the vote, and to participate in the Democratic primary. Though in general black women were unable to register to vote, some succeeded, a few voted, and in 1920, after ratification of the Nineteenth Amendment, in a radical departure from the past, black women not only registered and voted, they ran for office.[18]

During World War I and its immediate aftermath, black activists in Texas mobilized against lynching, vigilante violence, political disenfranchisement, discrimination, low wages, and Jim Crow practices and customs. The conscription of black soldiers, along with the exodus of large numbers of African Americans to fill wartime labor shortages in northern factories, and the inclusion of local black leaders on government wartime committees, contributed to a heightened sense of self-awareness and political assertiveness. Many middle-class activists, energized by the wartime and postwar militancy of black farmers and workers, seized the moment to launch an organized civil rights campaign in the state.

After the wartime organization of numerous local chapters of the NAACP, branches in Dallas, Corsicana, and other towns led important voter-registration drives. The emergence of strong "lily-white" factions in the Republican Party and the ever-tightening restrictions of the Democratic Party's white primary threatened black political empowerment, but in early 1919 a new racial assertiveness led the Forum, a black political and civic organization in Waco, to challenge the primary in Waco's nonpartisan municipal elections. In *Sublett v. Duke*, Richard D. Evans, a black civil rights attorney in Waco, engineered a temporary legal victory when district court judge Erwin J. Clark, who later became chief counsel of the Ku Klux Klan in the state, ruled that the white primary violated the Fifteenth Amendment. In 1922, however, another judge reversed Judge Clark's ruling after three years of stepped-up KKK activities had inflamed race relations in the area.[19]

In some local NAACP branches, particularly those along the Texas Upper Gulf Coast, where strong, if segregated, black International Longshoremen's Association (ILA) locals affiliated with the American Federation of Labor (AFL) existed, militant leaders tried to forge an alliance with black trade unionists. Clifton Richardson Sr., a self-described radical who cofounded the *Houston Observer* and then established the *Houston Informer* in 1919, tried to recruit black unionists into the Houston NAACP. A rival group of Houston activists offered an alternative to Richardson's more militant pro-labor group, which applied for a charter in 1918. Despite the appearance of competing factions, the rival groups soon closed ranks for the sake of broader common goals.[20]

It was in Galveston, though, that strong, labor-based civil rights activism emerged during the war, due largely to the important role of black ILA unionists in the local branch of the NAACP. Federal intelligence agents attributed the militancy of the city's black longshoremen to their association with white ILA unionists. A progressive interracial coalition of unionists and middle-class activists captured control of Galveston's commission government in the municipal election of 1919. White officials headed the victorious City Party but drew heavily on the organizational, planning, and voting support of reform-minded, pro-labor activists such as Edward M. Henderson, John T. Maxey, Luther Graves, and others at the grassroots level in the city's black community. The reform coalition, despite martial law and occupation of the island by the state militia during the longshoremen's strike of 1920, remained strong enough to win reelection in 1921. In large part, the supportive role of black social reform activists such as

Anna Bradley and Laura Pinkney, who headed the Women's Progressive Club in Galveston, contributed to the victory. Many black and white longshoremen in Galveston, alienated from the Republican as well as the Democratic Party, spearheaded a class-based attempt to form an independent, if short-lived, Labor Party in 1920.[21]

In response to the statewide growth of racial assertiveness, state authorities moved swiftly against the NAACP, which subsequently was nearly wiped out. There is no evidence to indicate that IWW, Communist, or Socialist elements played a meaningful role in Galveston's activism, but Governor William Hobby claimed that Bolshevik influences were at the root of black political mobilization. He received help from federal intelligence agents, local authorities, and vigilante groups in a campaign of terror, surveillance, and repression against the newly formed NAACP chapters. Federal authorities harassed militant black newspapers such as the Galveston *New Idea*.[22]

The militancy of black workers and their middle-class supporters in Texas also led to challenges to the Jim Crow practices inside the Texas State Federation of Labor (TSFL). By 1921, however, those efforts had lost steam due to stiff resistance by the officers who controlled the federation's convention machinery. Wartime and postwar cooperation between black and white trade unionists soon gave way to a period of cultural retrenchment. In the face of the state's increasingly repressive policies toward organized labor in the 1920s, trade unionists struggled merely to survive. Not until President Franklin D. Roosevelt's New Deal did black unionists again revive their militant activities with the support of middle-class activists.[23]

The repressive racial and anti-labor climate in Texas, which fed a surging Ku Klux Klan and encouraged lynching, discouraged black left-wing activism in the 1920s, but Marcus Garvey's Universal Negro Improvement Association (UNIA) attracted a significant following in the state in the wake of the NAACP's collapse. Garvey's militant nationalism and message of racial pride and separatism resonated with a lot of black Texans despite the NAACP's opposition to his separatist philosophy. The consul general of the UNIA and a trusted associate of Garvey's, Wilfred H. Smith was a former resident of Galveston. Garvey visited Texas in 1922, and local branches of the UNIA sprang up, particularly in Northeast Texas. Garvey's movement provoked harassment and intimidation from white vigilantes, who often operated in collusion with law enforcement authorities. In 1922, for example, when Robert B. Moseley, a black chef in Dallas who was the UNIA commissioner to Texas, went on a speaking tour through Jacksonville, Rusk, and other East Texas towns, he was dragged off a train, arrested on vagrancy charges, and fined, without having access to a lawyer. After he paid the fine and headed for the train station, a group of white men intercepted him, took him out in the woods, and whipped him.[24]

As a result of state and federal wartime agricultural policies, the activism of black agrarian reformers such as Joseph E. Clayton, who sought to secure better services for rural Afro-Texans, continued into the 1920s, laying the groundwork for later political mobilization during the Great Depression. Clayton, a graduate of Guadalupe College in Seguin, and principal of Travis County's Manor Colored School, worked as a volunteer organizer for the Texas Department of Agriculture (TDA) in 1917, helping to establish hundreds of black farmers' institutes. A member of the NAACP and disciple of Booker T. Washington's philosophy of self-help, he downplayed political activism in an effort to convince Texas officials to authorize his activities promoting canning, cash-crop production, better food preservation techniques, and efforts to combat soil exhaustion. Although Clayton's activism at this time did not challenge the fundamental structure of race and class relations in the countryside, his work put him in touch with the plight of black farmers, in particular, and prepared the way for his political metamorphosis in the 1930s.[25]

Some black activists left Texas after World War I, feeding the wartime stream of black migrants to northern industrial cities. To cite a few examples, Thyra J. Edwards, a feminist teacher, social worker, and member of the Houston chapter of the NAACP who was further radicalized by the outbreak of race riots in Longview and other cities in the "Red Summer" of 1919, moved to Gary, Indiana. In Gary, she continued as a social worker and civil rights activist. She was joined by her sister, Thelma, a graduate of Fisk University, who also became a civil rights activist and child welfare worker in Gary.[26] Carter Wesley, a World War I veteran from Houston, graduated from Fisk University in 1917, saw combat in France, and then attended Northwestern University in Chicago, where he received a law degree in 1922. He then opened a law practice in Muskogee, Oklahoma, before returning to Houston and forming a business partnership with Clifton Richardson in the *Houston Informer*. After a bitter dispute with Richardson, Wesley later took over operations of the newspaper while Richardson bought into the *Houston Defender*.[27]

Henry "Hank" Johnson, who in 1932 became a labor organizer for the Communist Party's International Workers Order and in 1936 for the Congress of Industrial Organizations (CIO) in Chicago's steel and packinghouse industries, recalled that his father was known in Siblo, Texas, as a "bad nigger" who "was always in trouble in the sawmills and logging camps" because he belonged to the IWW. His father, whose expert marksmanship with a six-shooter particularly frightened whites in Siblo, had once taught at Wiley College but had been fired because of his atheism. With the aid of a white friend and neighbor who also belonged to the ɪww, the Johnson family barely escaped a lynching at the hands of a white mob in Siblo, moving then to San Antonio. In 1917, Hank narrowly escaped being beaten by a white gang during the Camp Logan Riot in Houston, where he was living at the time. Soon thereafter, he left Texas.[28]

Black leftists in Texas reinvigorated their political struggle against racism and related social and economic problems in response to the economic crisis of the Great Depression. The revival of labor militancy and President Franklin D. Roosevelt's New Deal helped to breathe new life into black activism. Some black leftists were attracted to the Socialist Party's attempt to encourage interracial unionism through the Southern Tenant Farmers Union (ɪsfu). Created in Arkansas in 1934 in response to the shortcomings of the Agricultural Adjustment Act, the ɪsfu provided an alternative political solution to the deep economic problems that plagued southern agriculture in the 1930s. Due in part to the rise of the cɪo as a rival to the ᴀfʟ, the development of a pro-labor strategy in the ɴᴀᴀcp in the mid-to-late 1930s also gave added punch and coordination to the labor-based organizing campaign against Jim Crow because of the cɪo's more progressive racial policies. For other black leftists, the Communist Party's strong commitment to civil rights increased the appeal of even more radical political alternatives, particularly in the party's Popular Front era.

The failure of the ɪsfu, much weaker in Texas than it was in Arkansas, was not due to lack of effort by Joseph E. Clayton, the black organizer and former employee of the Texas Department of Agriculture who at this time was principal of the school in Littig, a small black community near Manor in eastern Travis County. The *S.T.F.U. News* reported in early 1938 that he had organized six locals in East Texas.[29] H. L. Mitchell, cofounder of the ɪsfu, had gone to Littig on the recommendation of Barney Egan, state director of the cɪo, to invite Clayton to become an organizer for the union. Egan told Mitchell that Clayton, the ɪsfu's most effective organizer in Texas, was a powerful speaker who "could really make the rafters ring."[30]

Elected to the ɪsfu national executive board in February 1938, Clayton promoted the establishment of cooperatives in Littig, which became a cɪo town. He used cɪo literature to teach current events at the local school. Although the ɪsfu did not pay his expenses or provide a salary, he continued on a volunteer basis to organize black farmers in East Texas, endorsing the principle of buyers' and sellers' cooperatives. After he met Carter Wesley at an educational conference on the campus of Prairie View A&M in March 1938, the CIO local in Littig, headed by J. J. Allen, designated the *Houston Informer* as its official newspaper. Clayton also played an important role in unionizing sugar-refinery workers in the company town of Sugar Land. By 1939, 98 percent of the town's employees had joined the CIO. In 1941, the STFU finally gave Clayton an appointment as a general organizer after new locals appeared in the East Texas towns of Chireno and Center.[31]

In Houston, activist Robert Grovey, a barber who headed the Third Ward Civic Club, joined Wesley and his law partners, J. Alston Atkins and James M. Nabrit, in endorsing the CIO as well as AFL-affiliated ILA locals. The *Houston Informer* supported a series of strikes by Houston's black longshoremen in the 1930s and criticized C. W. Rice's *Negro Labor News* for its regular and uncritical support of company unions (ignoring the racist practices of the white-owned companies) and its highly suspect attacks on racism in the CIO and AFL. Houston's black longshoremen, due partly to their achievements within the AFL's segregated ILA locals, did not flock to the CIO's National Maritime Union, despite its more progressive racial policies. In 1935, the *Informer* publicized a recent speech by Grovey in which he had emphasized that black and white ILA members worked "side by side, on the same ship, for the same wages, and under the same working conditions." In an editorial in the newspaper, Atkins praised black longshoremen for organizing a campaign to pay their poll taxes, and for setting up sick funds as well as funds to help widows and children of deceased ILA members. "I would like for somebody to send me the name of a group of Negro teachers, doctors, lawyers, editors, or any other group of so-called educated Negroes," he wrote, "which has been able to do half as much in an organized way."[32]

Grovey joined other black activists in Harris County to continue the ongoing legal campaign against the white primary. Despite the repressive political climate of the 1920s, black activists in Houston, San Antonio, and El Paso, aided by the legal counsel of R. D. Evans and the national office of the NAACP, challenged the white primary. Black newspapers endorsed the court battles and hoped that the campaign would revive the NAACP in the state. After court cases initiated by activists in El Paso (*Nixon v. Herndon*, 1927, and *Nixon v. Condon*, 1932), Carter Wesley and J. Alston Atkins provided counsel for a new attempt spearheaded by Grovey and other Houston activists. Their attempt was more than another mere court battle, though, for they launched a statewide campaign to politically mobilize the black community in Texas regardless of class and other divisions. When the Supreme Court upheld the white primary in *Grovey v. Townsend* (1935),

the stunning defeat drove a wedge between national officers of the
NAACP and the Houston leaders who had initiated the suit. Attorney
R. D. Evans of Waco, and other activists in the state, likewise criticized Houston leaders for usurping the role of the NAACP in the white
primary struggle.[33]

In 1937, the NAACP adopted a more aggressive pro-labor recruitment strategy. At a meeting of the Texas State Conference of Branches
in Dallas, June 18–19, 1937, R. D. Evans urged members not to over-
look labor unions in their activities and recruiting. Delegates passed
a resolution endorsing the labor movement and legislation to amend
the Social Security Act (1935) to include domestic and agricultural
workers, and to end peonage and debt slavery of sharecroppers and
tenant farmers. The shift toward a more labor-based civil rights activism reenergized some local NAACP chapters, particularly in Houston,
where financial problems and factionalism had severely crippled the
local branch since 1931. As Edward L. Snyder, chairman of the Houston chapter's Committee on Legal Address and Investigation, told Roy
Wilkins, assistant secretary of the NAACP, "One thing that has held
the association back, I think it has been the opinion in a great many
quarters that it is a 'High Brow Society' and has not been carried to the
masses. I am happy to say that president [C. F.] Richardson is having
the fullest possible participation from the classes and the masses."[34]

In Dallas, A. Maceo Smith, secretary of the Texas State Conference
of Branches of the NAACP, played an important role in black community activism. As the executive secretary of the Dallas Negro Chamber of Commerce between 1933 and 1939, he promoted not only black
small businesses but also black labor, and he promoted voter registration drives aimed at greater black political empowerment. He also led
efforts to showcase black achievements at the Texas centennial celebration in 1936.[35]

Black labor leaders affiliated with the AFL took the fight against
Jim Crow to the state labor body. Several longshoremen from Beaumont and Houston, in particular, led an unsuccessful campaign to seek
legal redress of race-based grievances at the annual TSFL conventions
in the late 1930s. Black unionists complained about the failure of the
TSFL to hire a black organizer, and they pushed to end racist practices
that excluded black workers from some of its affiliated unions. They
also pushed for a black vice president on the TSFL executive board,
and tried to get the organization to go on record against the white primary. After a relentless battle, they finally achieved one of their goals
in 1947 when the TSFL agreed to amend its constitution to add a black
"vice president at large" to the executive board. Black delegates chose

Houston's Freeman Everett, an ILA community leader who had helped to spearhead the movement for change in the TSFL, to serve in that capacity.[36]

As a strong champion of civil rights, the Communist Party (CP) and a number of organizations in which it played an important role attracted a few Texas black activists, including Cecil B. Robinet, who in 1938 ran as the party's candidate for Texas lieutenant governor on the ticket with gubernatorial candidate Homer Brooks. Robinet, of Houston, also headed the Communist Party's Harris County Commission on Negro Work. Lovett Fort-Whiteman, who was born and raised in Dallas but left to attend Tuskegee Institute in 1906, had joined the IWW and then the CP after World War I. He then traveled to Moscow, where he received training in the mid-twenties. After bitter disappointment and intense sectarian factionalism, he fled the United States for Moscow in 1930. A few years later, Soviet authorities denied his request to return to the United States. Accused of being a counterrevolutionary and Trotskyite, he was exiled to Siberia, where he died of malnutrition in 1939.[37]

Among those attracted to the CP during the Popular Front era was Thyra J. Edwards, who, after leaving Houston in 1920 for Gary, Indiana, became a prominent social worker in Chicago in the 1930s. Her commitment to labor activism and civil rights took her abroad in 1931 to study at the International People's College in Elsinore, Denmark. She also traveled extensively in other Scandinavian and western European nations, as well as the Soviet Union. After working as a union activist for the Brotherhood of Sleeping Car Porters in Chicago and the Progressive Miners of America in the coal fields of southern Illinois, she became a member of the Executive Council of the left-wing National Negro Congress (NNC) when it held its first convention in February 1936. She became friends with a number of distinguished black intellectuals of the era, especially Langston Hughes, Arna Bontemps, and Paul Robeson. She was also a foreign correspondent for Claude Barnett's Associated Negro Press and wrote for a number of black journals.[38]

In 1937 and 1938, Edwards returned to Texas on speaking tours sponsored by the National Religion and Labor Foundation. She gave talks on the campuses of Wiley College, Prairie View A&M, and Houston College for Negroes. In Houston, she praised the accomplishments of local black longshoremen affiliated with the AFL, but especially endorsed the CIO and its progressive racial policies. In Waco she became the first black speaker to address the Texas Conference of Social Welfare Workers in April 1938.[39]

Edwards, a friend of Carter Wesley, who conducted educational travel seminars abroad, was an internationalist with an understanding of the interrelationship of colonialism, imperialism, and fascism. She urged an interracial popular front to combat the expansion of fascism. During the Spanish Civil War she worked with colonies of refugee children uprooted and scarred by the war, and she filed newspaper reports from Spain. Some of her reports appeared in the *Houston Informer* and the *San Antonio Register*. As a field organizer for the Medical Bureau and North American Committee to Aid Spanish Democracy, she raised funds for an ambulance on behalf of the Republican government before Madrid fell to the Hitler-and-Mussolini-sponsored forces of General Francisco Franco. Afterward she worked to aid the resettlement of Spanish Loyalist refugees in Mexico.[40]

The NNC, a Popular Front labor and civil rights organization, whose communist connections strained its relationship with the NAACP, attracted the attention of many black activists in Texas, including the Communist Party's Cecil Robinet, of Houston. The organization included Socialists and other non-Communists, such as its president, A. Philip Randolph, who headed the Brotherhood of Sleeping Car Porters. In 1939, Mason Smith, editor of the *Waco Messenger*, became president of the Texas chapter of the NNC. Among the vice presidents were O. E. Fitzgerald (San Antonio), Ada Bell Dement (Mineral Wells)—who was president of the Texas Association of Colored Women's Clubs, E. L. Snyder (Houston), W. E. Brackee (Fort Worth), and L. M. Hall (Austin). The Texas chapter invited labor representatives from the AFL and CIO as well as liberal politicians such as Maury Maverick of San Antonio, and Dr. Edwin Elliott, regional director of the National Labor Relations Board in Fort Worth, to attend its conferences and address delegates.[41]

The Nazi-Soviet Pact of 1939, which marked the official abandonment of the Popular Front strategy, severely crippled the NNC. Randolph's bitter resignation as president of the NNC in 1940 grew out of the rift over Communist influences in the organization. The CP's abrupt change of course in regard to Nazi aggression disillusioned and embarrassed many in the party who could not defend the pact. By 1941, the Texas chapter of the NNC had virtually disappeared.

During World War II, black Texas women activists carved out an important role in the "Double V" campaign to defeat fascism abroad and win the war against Jim Crow and racism at home. In Houston, Lulu B. White, who had served as acting director of the local NAACP chapter in 1939, became its full-time executive secretary in 1943. Her strong commitment to labor-based civil rights activism helped to reinvigorate Houston's NAACP, and in 1946 she became director of state branches in Texas. Juanita Craft, a maid and seamstress who joined the Dallas chapter of the NAACP in 1935, headed the local membership committee during the war and became a field organizer and youth advisor in 1946.[42]

Thyra Edwards, a target of the Subversive Personnel Committee of the Federal Security Agency, moved to New York, where she became managing editor of the *People's Voice,* a newspaper owned and operated by Adam Clayton Powell Jr. Later that year, she married Murray Gitlin, a white activist and official of the *United Jewish Appeal.* Undaunted by harassment from the Federal Bureau of Investigation, she continued educational and public relations work for the CIO's National Maritime Union, wrote a weekly labor column for the *Houston Informer,* and attended the International Labor Conference in Philadelphia in April 1944. As a radical feminist with an internationalist perspective, she joined the Congress of American Women—the U.S. branch of the recently created Women's International Democratic Federation—in 1946, and served as its recording secretary. Even C. W. Rice, Houston's black conservative newspaper editor, grudgingly acknowledged in 1940 that "there is little doubt in the minds of Houstonians that Miss Edwards has brought more publicity to Houston in the span of her career than numerous other individuals have done in a longer number of years."[43]

The Double V campaign against fascism abroad and Jim Crow at home brought a measure of success, including a legal victory in the battle against the white primary. In *Smith v. Allright* (1944), for example, the U.S. Supreme Court struck down the white primary in Texas. Joseph E. Clayton, who at last received an organizer's salary from the STFU during the war, attended the founding convention of the United Nations in San Francisco as the official representative of the STFU in April 1945. At the end of the war, activists hoped to press forward, building on the momentum of the 1930s and early 1940s, in the struggle for first-class citizenship rights.[44]

Attitudes and conditions in the black community in Texas changed between World War I and World War II. Black Texans essentially accepted World War II; they neither opposed it nor refused to register for the draft. On the other hand, white attitudes toward blacks in Texas saw little shift between the wars. In 1943, Beaumont whites devastated black neighborhoods after a white woman allegedly was accosted by a black man. That same year black troops at Fort Bliss retaliated by attacking white troops for roughing up blacks. Black soldiers faced segregation; their protests met with white retaliation. White objections to the stationing of black troops forced the troops' removal from some communities and kept black soldiers from even arriving in others. Even German prisoners were treated better; Witter Bynner, a non-Texas poet noted:

On a train in Texas German prisoners eat
With white American soldiers, seat by seat,
While black American soldiers sit apart,
The white men eating meat, the black men heart.[45]

As a result, black Texans were determined more than ever to challenge the racial mores, laws, and beliefs of the Lone Star State.

Perhaps more than any one person, an African American professor of English best exemplified the left-wing values that sustained black Texans' struggle from the mid-twenties to the mid-forties. Melvin B. Tolson not only pursued his own strategies for aiding the black race via academics but he also fought for black rights and strategically passed on the gauntlet to his students, some of whom became strong civil rights advocates. Born in Missouri, Tolson received his baccalaureate at Lincoln University and his master's degree from Columbia. He taught at Wiley College in Marshall from 1924 to 1947 when he left Wiley for Langston University. Tolson's award-winning debate teams pressed the black cause by challenging racial mores and stereotypes and by breaking the color line in several states. An accomplished poet, Tolson spent his summers in New York City working on his master's degree and becoming part of, as well as studying, the waning Harlem Renaissance movement.[46]

Tolson worked with and aided the black masses, giving speeches and recruiting farm laborers and sharecroppers for the Southern Tenant Farmer's Union. He spent one three-week period in Arkansas in 1936 doing just that. On at least one occasion he organized a boycott of local stores and was threatened with a lynching. His students, led by James Farmer (the future CORE leader) and Bernard Bell, in 1938 established a chapter of the NAACP on the Wiley campus. An earlier Wiley graduate (1934), Heman Marion Sweatt, also studied with Tolson, and considered Tolson's life and teachings vital when he became the lead proponent of integrating the University of Texas Law School. Although he never joined the Communist Party, Tolson did adhere to democratic socialism and praised radicals. As he asserted, "whenever you hear anybody denounce radicals, remember this: persecuted races get their rights only through the agitation of radicals." Gail K. Beil aptly refers to Tolson as "Texas radical."[47]

In 1944, black Texans achieved a "black victory," as Darlene Clark Hine put it. The decades-long struggle against the white primary was nearly over. In some Texas counties, white men's associations held their own preprimary prior to the Democratic primary, insuring that the black vote in the Democratic primary would not matter. This subterfuge was overturned by the Supreme Court in *Terry v. Adams* (1953) when it ruled that the preprimary tactic was unconstitutional since it made the primary and general elections moot. The specific case arose as a challenge from Fort Bend County. As with *Smith v. Allwright*, the *Terry* decision was initiated by the NAACP. Two black leaders and activists from the county, Arizona Fleming and Willie Melton, fought the preprimary with money, with disdain for Jim Crow, and with dedicated effort. Fleming, who used up most of her money in the effort, was proprietor of the Fort Bend Fraternal Undertaking Company, and Melton was a prosperous farmer. A few years earlier, Fred Lewis, a former Tolson student, had led black resistance to the local white men's association in Harrison County.[48] Finally, after more than half a century, one important means of restricting black suffrage in Texas ended; the white primary existed no more.

The importance of the NAACP in Texas to the challenges of the black community through the forties and fifties cannot be overemphasized. Whites accused black Texas NAACP members and other committed, "left-leaning" leaders, of being communists, radicals, "un-American," et cetera. The NAACP in Texas began in 1912 with the establishment of an apparently short-lived local in Houston; a permanent chapter was organized in 1915 in El Paso. There were thirty or more chapters early in the 1920s, but many failed due to the onslaught of the KKK, white antipathy, and the Depression. Then, in 1936, Dallas businessman A. Maceo Smith set up the Texas State Conference of Branches, NAACP. Soon joined by two hard-working and effective organizers, Lulu B. White of Houston, and Juanita Craft from Dallas, the organization expanded. With committed black Texans, it led the successful attack on the white primary, and developed a plan to attack Jim Crow education and public accommodations, and to dismantle Jim Crow wherever else it existed. But desegregation of the state's schools was not going to be peaceful, for two reasons. First, whites feared integration of the schools even more than Afro-Texan political participation, and, second, black Texans, as Thurgood Marshall remarked, more than blacks in any other state, opposed segregation in education.[49]

When the decision was made to desegregate the all-white University of Texas Law School, the NAACP retained black Dallas attorney W. J. Durham to prepare the case. Durham, the most prominent black lawyer in the state, specialized in civil rights cases, and served on the national board of the NAACP. That organization also raised funds and solicited a plaintiff. They eventually located their plaintiff, due to the efforts of Lulu B. White, in Heman Marion Sweatt, a postal worker in Houston. Sweatt received a B.A. from Wiley College and studied toward a master's degree at Michigan. After he volunteered, Sweatt's family rallied behind him, including his brother John who expressed the somewhat radical opinion that "the only way this white man is going to be whipped is for Uncle Joe Stalin to come over here and just blow the hell out of him." The Texas NAACP was fortunate; Sweatt had the right disposition, background, and connections. A friend of Lulu White, Sweatt's other contacts included his dentist, Lonnie E. Smith, and his barber, Richard R. Grovey, both former participants in the white primary challenges. Carter Wesley, publisher of the *Houston Informer*, supported and otherwise encouraged Sweatt.[50]

Sweatt's father had earlier helped organize national postal employees, and the younger Sweatt worked on numerous issues for the local NAACP. His objectives fit his ground-breaking role. He wanted a law degree, he vehemently opposed segregation, and, as Michael Gillette describes him, he was "a sensitive, determined, and often radical civil rights activist."[51]

Sweatt attempted to register at the University of Texas in 1946. He met all qualifications except for his race, and was rejected. Then began long legal proceedings. Finally in 1950 the U.S. Supreme Court, in *Sweatt v. Painter*, ruled that the University of Texas Law School had to admit Sweatt. The proceedings were difficult years for Sweatt; he developed ulcers, could not work at the post office, underwent an appendectomy, and was divorced. He and his family faced vandalism, hate mail, and strident opposition. He was thirty-seven when he entered law school, emotionally and physically drained. After a year Sweatt dropped out; he later completed a master's degree in social work at Atlanta University.[52]

Perhaps it was the *Sweatt* decision, perhaps it was the times, perhaps it was enlightened officials, perhaps it was the influence of the NAACP, but most likely it was determined black efforts: in the next two years, community colleges in Texas began to be integrated. Three— Texas Southmost College at Brownsville, Howard County Junior College at Big Spring, and Amarillo College—admitted black students in 1951, and a fourth, Del Mar Junior College at Corpus Christi, followed in 1952. In 1951 a black schoolteacher, Annie Taylor, entered Wayland Baptist University, and that four-year liberal arts college became the first in the Confederate South to voluntarily end segregation. Other undergraduate colleges and universities in Texas followed; both the University of Texas and Southern Methodist University desegregated in the fall of 1955. Most of the remaining all-white universities and colleges integrated by the end of the 1950s, with over a half-dozen notable holdouts forced open by lawsuits, or the threat thereof, as late as 1964.[53]

In 1954, the U.S. Supreme Court handed down the path-breaking decision, *Brown v. Board of Education of Topeka,* calling for the integration of segregated schools in the nation, while declaiming that separate but equal education was inherently unequal. White Texans did not willingly desegregate; blacks faced massive resistance in public education. Crises occurred. In 1956, in Mansfield, Governor Allan Shivers sent in the Texas Rangers to ensure that blacks did not enroll or attend classes. The 1954 *Brown* decision affected black Texas greatly, and a separate struggle occurred in virtually every community—heroic African American students, parents, and leaders stood up. Even after a decade, however, only 5 percent of black Texans attended formerly all-white schools. Five years later, by 1970, the number increased to 47 percent.[54]

From politics and education, the civil rights struggle turned to public accommodation and to other remnants of Jim Crow. The push to integrate public accommodations gained momentum during the 1960s. Black Texans' battle for equal access to public accommodations provides a classic example of collective action in the struggle against white supremacy and effort to overturn the oppressive southern way of life. Students carried a major part of the load. Bishop and Wiley College students challenged Marshall segregation with nonviolent demonstrations during 1960. Inspired by Kansas, Oklahoma, and North Carolina students, in March 1960, Texas Southern University (TSU) students participated in lunch-counter sit-ins at Weingarten's supermarkets in Houston; the movement spread in the following months and remained peaceful (on the part of the students, anyway). At the beginning, the spark for the student effort was Eldrewey Stearns, who with TSU student colleagues. including Holly Hogrobrooks, formed the Progressive Youth Association. Stearns, beaten viciously by Houston police in December 1959, energetically led the effort through 1960. While the sit-ins took place, four whites brutally whipped black student Felton Turner; they further tortured Turner by cutting the letters "KKK" on his chest and stomach. Finally, by May 1963, the struggle was over, Houston public accommodations in general were integrated. Similar results followed in other Texas cities.[55]

By the latter 1960s, nonviolence as a civil rights tactic gave way, as the Black Power movement emerged in the Lone Star State. Even on the national level, the movement had a Texas slant when the Congress of Racial Equality (CORE), led by former Texan James Farmer, called for black power. In 1969, Houston native Carl Hampton organized People's Party II in Houston, based on the same black-nationalist ideology and principles as the Black Panther Party with which he had formerly affiliated. Led by Hampton, People's Party II provided free breakfasts, distributed used clothing, sponsored health clinics, monitored reports of police brutality, and carried weapons. The Houston police considered them leftist revolutionaries. In July 1970, after a ten-day confrontation between police and People's Party II, police sharpshooters shot and killed Carl Hampton; they wounded four others, three black and one white. One article refers to this episode as "the police assassination of Carl Hampton."[56]

Other violent episodes occurred in the late 1960s and early 1970s, often a consequence of harassment and brutality directed by white police toward African Americans. In May 1967, for example, TSU students and Houston police engaged in an explosive racial altercation. Students and other participants threw rocks and bottles, shots were fired, and a state of siege existed for several hours. Police eventually stormed a dormitory, tearing it apart in the process. A policeman was killed, likely from a police bullet; 448 students were arrested. As Bernard Friedberg asserts, this "incident is indicative of the total disregard, the degeneration, the ignorance of the plight of the black man" in Houston. Other instances of white-black violence, not always involving police, took place in West Texas—in Midland in 1968 and in Lubbock in 1971.[57]

Riots were not the only outcomes of white police actions. Police and official harassment continued. In Dallas, Ernie McMillan and Matthew Johnson, two Student Nonviolent Coordinating Committee (SNCC) leaders, boycotted white-owned grocery stores. They allegedly caused about $200 in damages and were sentenced to ten years in prison. Ernie McMillan's mother, Eva, thus added prison reform to her list of civil rights activities. Even a black pastor was subject to abuse. In Houston, the Reverend Earl E. Allen, a Methodist minister and former community action agency worker, organized HOPE Development, Inc., with support from local churches and individuals. Though HOPE provided job training, advice to consumers, and youth work, ironically city officials accused Allen of being a "militant" and a "racist." Lee Otis Johnson, a black activist from TSU, received a thirty-year sentence for allegedly handing a marijuana cigarette to an undercover policeman. In 1972, Dallas police pursued a vendetta against black Dallas, killing nine men and wounding eleven, establishing a reign of terror in the black community.[58]

The Texas civil rights movement also became caught up in protests and struggles at Hughes Tool Company. As a direct result, in 1964 the collective bargaining agent for the workers, the segregated Independent Metal Workers Union, was decertified by the National Labor Relations Board. This momentous decision marked one more credit to the spirit of action and protest from black Texans, and meant that no longer could unions discriminate against black employees. For fifty years black workers at Hughes Tool Company not only received lower wages for more difficult labor, their unions were segregated and frequently did not support the rights and grievances of black employees. Segregated Local #2, led by Ivory Davis and Columbus Henry, took the unprecedented step of challenging their own union. As Michael R. Botson shows so well in articles and his book *Labor, Civil Rights, and the Hughes Tool Company*, "after enduring decades of discrimination on the factory floor, a segment of Houston's working class seized the moment and won economic and racial justice for themselves and their brothers and sisters."[59]

By 1974 the successes and struggles of the Texas civil rights movement coalesced in the career of Barbara Jordan. Thanks to the elimination of the white primary, the elimination of the poll tax, the decision in *Baker v. Carr* (one man, one vote), the Voting Rights Act of 1965, and redistricting, Barbara Jordan was elected to the Texas State Senate in 1966. A liberal politician, Jordan worked diligently, served with distinction, and in 1972 was elected to the U.S. House of Representatives from Houston. In 1974 she was a member of the vitally important Judiciary Committee, and during the hearings on whether to impeach the president of the United States, Jordan spoke out courageously and effectively to impeach Richard M. Nixon. The committee agreed, and rather than be impeached, the president resigned.[60]

Barbara Jordan's successes and the resignation of Richard Nixon signaled the end of the modern civil rights movement in the Lone Star State. It also signaled the end of Jim Crow society in the state. For one hundred years, black Texans, with support from groups such as the Populist Party, the Industrial Workers of the World, the NAACP, the CIO, and black nationalists, challenged and overturned the treasured white southern way of life. Even African American "left" activity, however, had not been strong enough to overcome the failure to receive land in the aftermath of the Civil War, and the inability of black Texans to share in a rising prosperity continued. Black Texans remained, in general, an economically impoverished group. Black women barely cracked the glass ceiling. On the other hand, black Texans could point proudly to very real gains over a hundred years; they had attained educational equity, acquired a host of civil and legal rights previously denied them, and earned the right not only to vote but to hold political office. Melvin Tolson's assertion that black Texans needed radicalism proved correct.[61] For one hundred years left-leaning black Texans successfully confronted white supremacy. That in itself is a fitting and courageous monument.

NOTES

The verse in the chapter epigraph is from Melvin B. Tolson, "Dark Sympathy," *Rendezvous with America* (New York: Dodd, Mead, 1944), 39.

1. The most complete discussion of the Brotherhood of Timber Workers is James R. Green, "The Brotherhood of Timber Workers, 1910–1913: A Radical Response to Industrial Capitalism in the Southern U.S.A.," *Past and Present* 60 (August 1973): 161–200. See also Jeff Ferrell, "The Brotherhood of Timber Workers and the Culture of Conflict," *Journal of Folklore Research* 28 (1991): 163–77.

2. James C. Maroney, "Brotherhood of Timber Workers," *The Handbook of Texas Online* (http://www.tshaonline.org/handbook/online/articles/BB/ocbbb.html); Green, "The Brotherhood of Timber Workers, 1910–1913," 161–200 (quote on 200); James R. Green, "Tenant Farmer Discontent and Socialist Protest in Texas, 1901–1917," *Southwestern Historical Quarterly* 81 (1976), 133–54; Charles R. McCord, "A Brief History of the Brotherhood of Timber Workers" (master's thesis, University of Texas, 1959); Jeff Ferrell, "East Texas/western Louisiana Sawmill Towns and the Control of Everyday Life," *Locus* 3, no. 1 (1990), 1–19; Jeff Ferrell and Kevin Ryan, "The Brotherhood of Timber Workers and the Southern Trust: Legal Repression and Worker Response," *Radical America* 19 (July–August 1985), 55–74. After long and expensive legal proceedings, the arrested BTW members were found not guilty. No Operator's Association representatives went to trial, only three briefly had been arrested.

3. There are no books or scholarly articles that review the African American Left in Texas. However, for general accounts that include considerable information, see Alwyn Barr, *Black Texans: A History of African Americans in Texas, 1528–1995*, 2nd ed. (Norman: University of Oklahoma Press, 1996); Alwyn Barr and Robert A. Calvert, eds, *Black Leaders: Texans for Their Times* (Austin: Texas State Historical Association, 1981); Bruce A. Glasrud and James M. Smallwood, eds., *The African American Experience in Texas* (Lubbock: Texas Tech University Press, 2007); Bruce A. Glasrud and Laurie Champion, eds., *Exploring the Afro-Texas Experience: A Bibliography of Secondary Sources about Black Texans* (Alpine, Tex.: SRSU Center for Big Bend Studies, 2000).

4. The Socialist Party in Texas did not actively recruit blacks, thus there was not a close relationship between black Texans and organized Left parties, the Socialists or the Communists. Occasionally white socialist leaders stepped further, and spoke out in racial diatribes with anti-black messages. In "Tom Hickey and the Failure of

Interracial Unity: The Politics of Race, Class, and Gender in the Socialist Party of Texas, 1911–1917," *The White Scourge: Mexicans,
Blacks, and Poor Whites in Texas Cotton Culture* (Berkeley: University of California Press, 1997), 92–117, Neil Foley notes the un-
willingness of Texas socialists to encourage black Texans. See also
Green, "Tenant Farmer Discontent and Socialist Protest in Texas,
1901–1917," 133–54. James R. Green, in *Grass-Roots Socialism:
Radical Movements in the Southwest, 1895–1943* (Baton Rouge:
Louisiana State University Press, 1978), acknowledges that the Socialist Party's "primary focus on winning the support of eligible voters did tend to discourage the recruitment of non white members, as
did the racism of party members" (386).

5.   Lamar L. Kirven, "A Century of Warfare: Black Texans" (PhD diss.,
Indiana University, 1974); Melvin J. Banks, "The Pursuit of Equality:
The Movement for First-Class Citizenship Among Negroes, 1920–
1950" (DSS dissertation, Syracuse University, 1954); Gregg Cantrell,
*Feeding the Wolf: John B. Rayner and the Politics of Race, 1850–
1918* (Wheeling, Ill.: Harlan Davidson, 2001); Darlene Clark Hine,
Black Victory: The Rise and Fall of the White Primary in Texas
(Millwood, N.Y.: KTO Press, 1979).

6.   Paul D. Lack, "Dave: A Rebellious Slave," in *Black Leaders: Texans
for Their Times* (Austin: Texas State Historical Association, 1981),
ed. Alwyn Barr and Robert A. Calvert, 1–18.

7.   Carl H. Moneyhon, *Texas after the Civil War: The Struggle of Reconstruction* (College Station: Texas A&M University Press, 2004); Randolph B. Campbell, *Grass-Roots Reconstruction in Texas, 1865–1880*
(Baton Rouge: Louisiana State University Press, 1997), quote on 111.

8.   The most complete account of the "Millican Riot" and its back-
ground is in Barry A. Crouch, "Reconstructing Brazos County: Race
Relations and the Freedmen's Bureau, 1865–1868," *The Freedmen's
Bureau and Black Texans* (Austin: University of Texas Press, 1992);
102–27, 169–74; see also James M. Smallwood, *Time of Hope, Time
of Despair: Black Texans During Reconstruction* (Port Washington,
N.Y.: Kennikat Press, 1981), 98, 144; *New York Times*, July 30, 1868;
Moneyhon, *Texas after the Civil War*, 95–96.

9.   Merline Pitre, "Ruby, George Thompson," *The Handbook of Texas
Online* (http://www.tshaonline.org/handbook/online/articles/RR/
fru2.html); Merline Pitre, "George T. Ruby: The Party Loyalist,"
*Through Many Dangers Toils and Snares: Black Leadership in
Texas, 1868–1900* (Austin, Tex.: Eakin Press, 1985): 166–73, 238–
40; Carl H. Moneyhon, "George T. Ruby and the Politics of Expedi-
ency in Texas," in *Southern Black Leaders in the Reconstruction
Era*, ed. Howard N. Rabinowitz (Urbana: University of Illinois Press,

1982), 363–92; James M. Smallwood, "G. T. Ruby: Galveston's Black Carpetbagger in Reconstruction Texas," *Houston Review* 5 (Winter 1983), 24–33; Randall B. Woods, "George T. Ruby: A Black Militant in the White Business Community," *Red River Valley Historical Review* 1 (1974), 269–80.

10. Merline Pitre, "Gaines, Matthew," *The Handbook of Texas Online* (http://www.tshaonline.org/handbook/online/articles/GG/fga5 .html); Pitre, "Matthew Gaines: The Militant," *Through Many Dangers Toils and Snares*, 157–65; Ann Patton Malone, "Matt Gaines: Reconstruction Politician," in *Black Leaders*, 49–82. In addition to Pitre, *Through Many Dangers Toils and Snares*, on late-nineteenth-century black politicians, see J. Mason Brewer, *Negro Legislators of Texas and Their Descendants* (Dallas, Tex.: Mathis Publishing, 1935) and the following articles: Alwyn Barr, "Black Legislators of Reconstruction Texas," *Civil War History* 32 (1986), 340–52; Merline Pitre, "The Evolution of Black Political Participation in Reconstruction Texas," *East Texas Historical Journal* 26, no. 1 (1988): 36–45; and Barry A. Crouch, "Hesitant Recognition: Texas Black Politicians, 1865–1900," *East Texas Historical Journal* 31, no. 1 (1993), 41–59.

11. Maud Cuney Hare, *Norris Wright Cuney: A Tribune of the Black People* (New York: Crisis Publishing, 1913); Pitre, "Norris W. Cuney: The Climber of Sorts," *Through Many Dangers Toils and Snares*, 188–97; Virginia Neal Hinze, "Norris Wright Cuney" (master's thesis, Rice University, 1965); Douglas Hales, *A Southern Family in White and Black: The Cuneys of Texas* (College Station: Texas A&M University Press, 2003). On Cuney, the longshoremen, and the Galveston waterfront, see Clifford Farrington, *Biracial Unions on Galveston's Waterfront, 1865–1925* (Austin: Texas State Historical Association, 2007), 51–80.

12. Greg Cantrell, "John B. Rayner: A Study in Black Populist Leadership," *Southern Studies* 24 (Winter 1985): 432–43; Gregg Cantrell, *Feeding the Wolf: John B. Rayner and the Politics of Race, 1850–1918* (Wheeling, Ill.: Harlan Davidson, 2001); Gregg Cantrell, "Rayner, John Baptis," *The Handbook of Texas Online* (http://www .tshaonline.org/handbook/online/articles/RR/fra52.html); Alwyn Barr, "Wade, Melvin," *The Handbook of Texas Online* (http:// www.tshaonline.org/handbook/online/articles/WW/fwa99.html); Donna A. Barnes, *Farmers in Rebellion: The Rise and Fall of the Southern Farmer's Alliance and People's Party in Texas* (Austin: University of Texas Press, 1984).

13. Gregg Cantrell and D. Scott Barton, "Texas Populists and the Failure of Biracial Politics," *Journal of Southern History* 55 (1989), 659–92 (quote on 690). There is no historian who has a firmer grasp of the

nature of Populism and its strengths and weaknesses, especially its effort at creating a biracial political movement, than Cantrell. See also Gregg Cantrell and Kristopher B. Paschal, "Texas Populism at High Tide: Jerome C. Kearby and the Case of the Sixth Congressional District, 1894," *Southwestern Historical Quarterly* 109 (July 2005), 30–70.

14. Sutton E. Griggs, *Imperium in Imperio* (1899; repr. New York: Arno Press, 1969); Bruce A. Glasrud, "Early Black Nationalist Movements in Texas," *Journal of Big Bend Studies* 11 (1999), 159–69.

15. Thad Sitton and James H. Conrad, *Freedom Colonies: Independent Black Texans in the Time of Jim* Crow (Austin: University of Texas Press, 2005); John Gauss, "Give the Blacks Texas," *Civil War Times Illustrated* (May/June 1990), 54–56; Glasrud, "Early Black Nationalist Movements in Texas," 159–69.

16. William E. Bittle and Gilbert L. Geis, "Alfred Charles Sam and African Return: A Case Study in Negro Despair," *Phylon* 23 (1962): 178–94; William E. Bittle and Gilbert L. Geis, *The Longest Way Home: Chief Alfred C. Sam's Back-to-Africa Movement* (Detroit: Wayne State University Press, 1964), quote on 152; Glasrud, "Early Black Nationalist Movements," 163–65 (Parker quote on 164). On black nationalist movements, see also Edwin S. Redkey, *Black Exodus: Black Nationalist and Back-to-Africa Movements, 1890–1910* (New Haven: Yale University Press, 1969).

17. One leftist black Texas woman, Lucy Eldine Parsons, left the state with her husband in 1873 and moved to Chicago. Both became anarchists, joined the International Working People's Association, and in 1886 led a march of eighty thousand people at the beginning of a strike for an eight-hour day. Three days later the Haymarket Riot occurred, and Parsons's husband Albert was among those arrested. He and seven others were found guilty of conspiracy, and all but one sentenced to death. Lucy Parsons continued her revolutionary efforts until her death in 1942. See Carolyn Ashbaugh, *Lucy Parsons, American Revolutionary* (Chicago: Illinois Labor History Society, 1976); Carolyn Ashbaugh, "Parsons, Lucy Eldine," *The Handbook of Texas Online* (http://www.tshaonline.org/handbook/online/articles/PP/fpa68.html).

18. Bruce A. Glasrud, "Time of Transition: Black Women in Early Twentieth-Century Texas, 1900–1930," in *Black Women in Texas History*, ed. Bruce A. Glasrud and Merline Pitre (College Station: Texas A&M University Press, 2008): 99–128; A. Elizabeth Taylor, Ruthe Winegarten, and Judith N. McArthur, *Citizens at Last: The Woman Suffrage Movement in Texas* (Austin, Tex.: Ellen C. Temple, 1987): 127–30, 153–55. One black woman suffragist, Christia Adair

of Kingsville, took a group of black school children to see Republican Warren G. Harding during the 1920 campaign. Harding reached across the black school children to shake hands with whites; Adair switched from being a Republican to a Democrat. Nancy Baker Jones, "Adair, Christia V. Daniels," *The Handbook of Texas Online* (http://www.tshaonline.org/handbook/online/articles/AA/fad19 .html).

19. For a study of black militancy and the NAACP in Texas in the era of World War I, see Steven A. Reich, "Soldiers of Democracy: Black Texans and the Fight for Citizenship, 1917–1921," *Journal of American History* 82 (March 1996), 1478–1504. See Katherine K. K. Walters, "The Great War in Waco, Texas: African Americans, Race Relations, and the White Primary, 1916–1922 (master's thesis, Southwest Texas State University, 2000), especially chapters 2 and 3, for the battle against the white primary in Waco.

20. "Application for Charter," May 31, 1918, reel 19, Papers of the NAACP, Part 12: Selected Branch Files, 1913–1939, Series A: The South, edited by John H. Bracey and August Meier (Bethesda, Md.: University Publications of America, 1991). Correspondence related to the rival Houston groups vying for a charter is also found on this reel.

21. Gregg Andrews, "Black Working-Class Political Activism and Biracial Unionism: Galveston Longshoremen in Jim Crow Texas, 1919–1921," *Journal of Southern History* 74 (August 2008); on black Texas unions, see Ernest Obadele-Starks, *Black Unionism in the Industrial South* (College Station: Texas A&M University Press, 2000); on Pinkney, see also Elizabeth Hayes Turner, *Women, Culture, and Community: Religion and Reform in Galveston, 1880–1920* (New York: Oxford University Press, 1997), 256.

22. Andrews, "Black Working-Class Political Activism and Biracial Unionism"; Reich, "Soldiers of Democracy," 1499–1501.

23. Andrews, "Black Working-Class Political Activism and Biracial Unionism."

24. R.B. Moseley, UNIA Commissioner for Texas, to Marcus Garvey, June 3, 1922, in Robert A. Hill, ed., *Marcus Garvey and Universal Negro Improvement Association Papers: Volume IV, 1 September 1921– 2 September 1922* (Berkeley: University of California Press, 1985), 649–50. For a brief sketch of black nationalism in Texas in the early twentieth century, see Glasrud, "Early Black Nationalist Movements in Texas," 159–69. Mary Rolinson, in *Grassroots Garveyism: The Universal Negro Improvement Association in the Rural South, 1920–1927* (Chapel Hill: University of North Carolina Press, 2007), notes that whatever the reputation of Garvey and the specifics of his

movement, in the rural South it represented a founding cornerstone of pride and militancy that provided a starting point for the civil rights movement of the next generation.

25. Debra A. Reid, "African Americans, Community Building, and the Role of the State in Rural Reform in Texas, 1890s–1930s," in Catherine McNichol Stock, ed., *The Countryside in the Age of the Modern State: Political Histories of Rural America* (Ithaca: Cornell University Press, 2001), 41, 42, 55–65.

26. For a brief sketch of Thyra Edwards, see Elmer P. Martin and Joanne M. Martin, "Thyra J. Edwards: Internationalist Social Worker," in Richard Resh, ed., *Black Accommodation and Confrontation in the Twentieth Century* (Lexington, Mass.: Heath, 1969), 163–76, and Gwynne Gertz, "Edwards, Thyra J.," in Rima Lunin Schultz and Adele Hart, eds., *Women Building Chicago, 1790–1990: A Biographical Dictionary* (Bloomington: Indiana University Press, 2001), 244–48. See Joyce Blackwell, *No Peace Without Freedom: Race and the Women's International League for Peace and Freedom, 1915–1975* (Carbondale, Ill.: Southern Illinois University Press, 2004), 41, 46–47, and passim, for a discussion of Thelma Edwards Marshall.

27. Amilcar Shabazz, "Carter Wesley: Sounding the Ram's Horn for Civil Rights," in Ty Cashion and Jesús F. de la Teja, eds., *The Human Tradition in Texas* (Wilmington, Del.: Scholarly Resources Inc., 2001), 161–76; Darlene Clark Hine, *Black Victory: The Rise and Fall of the White Primary in Texas,* new ed. (1979, Columbia: University of Missouri Press, 2003), 161–62.

28. In 1937, the Works Progress Administration interviewed Johnson. The interview is reproduced in Stephen Brier, "Labor, Politics and Race: A Black Worker's Life," *Labor History* 23 (Summer 1982), 416–21 (quote on 418).

29. *S.T.F.U. News* 1 (April 1938), 5.

30. "Transcribed Interview with H. L. Mitchell and Latane Lambert," by George Norris Green, April 4, 1975, 28, Special Collections Division, University of Texas at Arlington Libraries, Arlington, Texas.

31. "Texas Notes," *Houston Informer,* March 30, 1938; *Negro Labor News,* May 27, 1939; *Tenant Farmer,* May 5, 1941, 3; CIO News (Packinghouse Workers Edition), January 30, 1939. For a brief discussion of Clayton's role in the STFU, see Foley, *The White Scourge,* 190–91.

32. *Houston Informer,* May 25, 1935. On the community-based activism of Houston's longshoremen, see Rebecca Montes, "Working for American Rights: Black, White, and Mexican American Dockworkers in Texas During the Great Depression" (PhD diss., University of Texas at Austin, 2005). Not only was Atkins an activist, he also

wrote a history of the struggle against the white primary; see J. Alston Atkins, *The Texas Negro and His Political Rights: A History of
the Fight of the Negro to Enter the Democratic Primaries of Texas*
(Houston: Webster Publishing, 1932).

33. On the white primary cases, see Hine, *Black Victory*, 111–25, 142–
72, 193–209.

34. Edward L. Snyder to Roy Wilkins, April 26, 1938, reel 20, Papers
of the NAACP, Part 12: Selected Branch Files, 1913–1939, Series A:
The South; Minutes of the Texas State Conference of Branches,
N.A.A.C.P., June 18, 19, 1937, reel 19, Papers of the NAACP, Part 12:
Selected Branch Files, 1913–1939, Series A: The South. See Beth
Tompkins Bates, "A New Crowd Challenges the Agenda of the Old
Guard in the NAACP, 1933–1941," *American Historical Review* 102
(April 1997), 340–77, for a discussion of internal divisions over the
reluctance of the NAACP to embrace a strategy of mobilizing the
black masses.

35. For a thumbnail sketch of Smith, see Neil Sapper, "Smith, Antonio
Maceo," *The Handbook of Texas Online*, http://www.tshaonline
.org/handbook/online/articles/SS/fsm61.html.

36. Texas State Federation of Labor, *Proceedings of the Annual Convention, 1947*, 193–94, 211–12, 221–24, 228. On the fate of resolutions introduced by black union activists at TSFL annual conventions, see, for example, Texas State Federation of Labor, *Proceedings,
1937*, 52; Texas State Federation of Labor, *Proceedings, 1938*, 124–25,
150–51,161–62; Texas State Federation of Labor, *Proceedings, 1939*,
140–42, 176, 178, 191–92.

37. On Robinet, see *Negro Labor News*, November 22, 1938. For the
Texas roots of Fort-Whiteman, see Harvey Klehr, John Earl Haynes,
and Kyrill M. Anderson, *The Soviet World of American Communism* (New Haven: Yale University Press, 1998), 217–25, and Glenda
Elizabeth Gilmore, *Defying Dixie: The Radical Roots of Civil Rights,
1919–1950* (New York: W. W. Norton, 2008), 33 and passim.

38. Martin and Martin, "Thyra J. Edwards," 163–76; Gertz, "Edwards,
Thyra J.," 244–48; Official Proceedings of the NNC Convention Held
in Chicago on February 14, 15, 16, 1936, reel 1 [frame 238], FBI File
on NNC, 1943–1952 (Wilmington, Del.: Scholarly Resources, 1987).

39. *Houston Informer*, May 8, 1937, and March 30, April 9, 27, 1938;
Negro Labor News, April 9, 1938.

40. *Houston Informer*, October 20, November 10, 17, 1937, and June 4,
August 13, 1938.

41. *Negro Labor News*, November 22, 1938, and January 21, February 18,
and March 4, 1939.

42. Merline Pitre, *In Struggle against Jim Crow: Lulu B. White and the*

NAACP, 1900–1957 (College Station: Texas A&M University Press, 1999). For a brief sketch of Craft's life, see Ruth Winegarten, *Black Texas Women: A Sourcebook* (Austin: University of Texas Press, 1996), 244–45. See also Glasrud, "Time of Transition: Black Women in Early Twentieth-Century Texas," 99–128, and Merline Pitre, "At the Crossroads: Black Texas Women, 1930–1954," 129–58, both in Glasrud and Pitre, eds., *Black Women in Texas History.*

43. *The People's Voice,* January 30, 1943; Thyra J. Edwards to Miles Horton, Highlander Folk School, June 21, 1944, Box 11, folder 13, Highlander Research and Education Center Records, Part I, 1917–1978, Subseries: General Correspondence, Wisconsin Historical Society, Madison, Wisconsin; Martin and Martin, "Thyra J. Edwards," 173; *New York Times,* May 26, 1946. The quote is in *Negro Labor News,* April 13, 1940.

44. Hine, *Black Victory,* 231–48; "Transcribed Interview with H.L. Mitchell and Latane Lambert," by George Norris Green, April 4, 1975, 30, Special Collections Division, University of Texas at Arlington Libraries, Arlington, Texas.

45. Bruce A. Glasrud and James M. Smallwood, "The Twentieth Century Experience," in *The African American Experience in Texas: An Anthology,* ed. Bruce A. Glasrud and James M. Smallwood (Lubbock: Texas Tech University Press, 2007): 173–82; James A. Burran, "Violence in an 'Arsenal of Democracy': The Beaumont Race Riot, 1943," *East Texas Historical Journal* 14, no.1 (Spring 1976), 39–51; Barr, *Black Texans,* 187–89; Robert A. Calvert, "The Civil Rights Movement in Texas," in *The Texas Heritage,* ed. Ben Proctor and Archie P. McDonald, 3rd ed. (Wheeling, Ill.: Harlan Davidson, 1998): 167–84 (poem on 167).

46. Gail K Beil, "Melvin B. Tolson—Texas Radical," *East Texas Historical Journal* 40, no. 1 (2002): 26–36; Robert M. Farnsworth, *Melvin B. Tolson, 1898–1966: Plain Talk and Poetic Prophecy* (Columbia: University of Missouri Press, 1983); Joy Flasch, *Melvin B. Tolson* (New York: Twayne, 1972).

47. Farnsworth, *Melvin B. Tolson,* 30–61; Flasch, *Melvin B. Tolson,* 25–47; Anders S. Saustrup, "Tolson, Melvin Beaunorus," *The Handbook of Texas Online* (http://www.tshaonline.org/handbook/online/articles/TT/fto36.html); James Farmer, "Tolstoi and Tolson," *Lay Bare the Heart: An Autobiography of the Civil Rights Movement* (Fort Worth: Texas Christian University Press, 1985): 117–33; Melvin Tolson, "The Death of an Infidel," *Washington Tribune,* April 2, 1938, quote; Beil, "Melvin B. Tolson—Texas Radical," 26.

48. Hine, *Black Victory,* 226–229; Bonni C. Hayes, "Fleming, Arizona," *The Handbook of Texas Online* (http://www.tshaonline.org/

handbook/online/articles/FF/fflmw.html); Beil, "Melvin B. Tolson,"
11; Pauline Yelderman, *The Jay Birds of Fort Bend County: A White Man's Union* (Waco, Tex.: Texian Press, 1979): 207–44; Nina Benware Margraves, "The Jaybird Democratic Association of Fort Bend County: A White Man's Union" (master's thesis, University of Houston, 1955).

49. On the NAACP in Texas, see Nancy Dailey, "History of the Beaumont, Texas, Chapter of the National Association for the Advancement of Colored People, 1918–1970" (master's thesis, Lamar University, 1971); Neil G. Sapper, "The Fall of the NAACP in Texas," *Houston Review* 7 (Summer 1985), 53–68; Michael L. Gillette, "The NAACP in Texas, 1937–1957" (PhD dissertation, University of Texas at Austin, 1984); Michael L. Gillette, "The Rise of the NAACP in Texas," *Southwestern Historical Quarterly* 81 (1978), 393–416; Pitre, *In Struggle against Jim Crow*; Michael L. Gillette, "National Association for the Advancement of Colored People," *The Handbook of Texas Online* (http://www.tshaonline.org/handbook/online/articles/NN/ven1.html); Thurgood Marshall referenced in Michael L. Gillette, "Heman Marion Sweatt: Civil Rights Plaintiff," in *Black Leaders: Texans for Their Times*, 172.

50. Richard Allen Burns, "Durham, William J.," *The Handbook of Texas Online* (http://www.tshaonline.org/handbook/online/articles/DD/fdu46.html); Johnnie Mae Westbrook, "The Sweatt Case: A Study in Minority Strategy in Texas" (master's thesis, Prairie View A&M University, 1953); Gillette, "Heman Marion Sweatt: Civil Rights Plaintiff," 156–88; Gillette, "National Association for the Advancement of Colored People"; Dwonna Goldstone, "African Americans at the School of Law," *Integrating the 40 Acres: The 50-Year Struggle for Racial Equality at the University of Texas* (Athens: University of Georgia Press, 2006): 14–35, 160–65 (quote on 20).

51. Gillette, "Heman Marion Sweatt: Civil Rights Plaintiff," 156–88 (quote 176).

52. W. Page Keeton, "*Sweatt v. Painter,*" *The Handbook of Texas Online* (http://www.tshaonline.org/handbook/online/articles/SS/jrs1.html); Patricia Lefforge Davis, "*Sweatt v. Painter:* Integration in Texas History" (master's thesis, University of Texas at Austin, 1971); Michael L. Gillette, "Blacks Challenge the White University," *Southwestern Historical Quarterly* 86 (1982), 393–416.

53. A number of articles, theses, and reports have been written on collegiate integration in Texas; see especially Amilcar Shabazz, *Advancing Democracy: African Americans and the Struggle for Access and Equity in Higher Education in Texas* (Chapel Hill: University of North Carolina Press, 2004). On the University of Texas, see Gold-

stone, *Integrating the 40 Acres.* Also, Calvert, "The Civil Rights Movement in Texas," *Texas Heritage,* 167–84. Calvert's article, though it needs revision, is still the best single summary of the African American civil rights movement in the Lone Star State. On the holdouts, see Shabazz, *Advancing Democracy,* 210–18.

54. Calvert, "The Civil Rights Movement in Texas," *Texas Heritage,* 167–84. On Mansfield, read Robyn Duff Ladino, *Desegregating Texas Schools: Eisenhower, Shivers, and the Crisis at Mansfield High* (Austin: University of Texas Press, 1996). The process in Houston and Dallas can be found in William Henry Kellar, *Make Haste Slowly: Moderates, Conservatives, and School Desegregation in Houston* (College Station: Texas A&M University Press, 1999); Glenn M. Linden, *Desegregating Schools in Dallas* (Dallas: Three Forks Press, 1995).

55. Though not published, the most thorough study of the struggle to desegregate public accommodations is Martin Kuhlman, "The Civil Rights Movement in Texas: Desegregation of Public Accommodations, 1950–1964" (PhD dissertation, Texas Tech University, 1994). Also see Thomas R. Cole, *No Color Is My Kind: The Life of Eldrewey Stearns and the Integration of Houston* (Austin: University of Texas Press, 1997); F. Kenneth Jensen, "The Houston Sit-In Movement of 1960–61," in *Black Dixie: Afro-Texan History and Culture in Houston,* ed. Howard Beeth and Cary D. Wintz (College Station: Texas A&M University Press, 1992): 211–22; W. Marvin Dulaney, "Whatever Happened to the Civil Rights Movement in Dallas, Texas?" in *Essays on the American Civil Rights Movement,* ed. W. Marvin Dulaney and Kathleen Underwood (College Station: Texas A&M University Press, 1993): 66–95; Robert A. Goldberg, "Racial Change on the Southern Periphery: The Case of San Antonio, Texas, 1960–1965," *Journal of Southern History* 49 (1983), 349–74.

56. Barr, *Black Texans,* 194–95; Calvert, "The Civil Rights Movement," 167–84. In addition to James Farmer, the Black Power movement on the national level has at least one other Texas connection. Black Panther leader Bobby Seale grew up in Dallas, Port Arthur, and San Antonio; the son of a carpenter, he became chair of the Black Panther Party in 1966. See Bobby Seale, *Seize the Time: The Story of the Black Panther Party and Huey P. Newton* (New York: Random House, 1968): 3–12. Charles (BOKO) Freemen, "The Police Assassination of Carl Hampton," It's About Time—Black Panther Party Legacy and Alumni (http://www.itsabouttimebpp.com); Cary D. Wintz, "The Struggle for Dignity: African Americans in Twentieth-Century Texas," in *Twentieth-Century Texas: A Social and Cultural History,* ed. John W. Storey and Mary L. Kelley (Denton: University of North Texas Press, 2008): 69–104.

57. Barr, *Black Texans*, 192–93, 195; Calvert, "The Civil Rights Move-
    ment," 167–84; Bernard Friedberg, "Houston and the TSU Riot," in
    Life Styles in the Black Ghetto, ed. William McCord, John Howard,
    Bernard Friedberg, and Edwin Harwood (New York: W. W. Norton,
    1969): 36–51 (quote on 41); for an overall assessment of the Hous-
    ton police, see Dwight Watson, *Race and the Houston Police De-
    partment, 1930–1990: A Change Did Come* (College Station: Texas
    A&M University Press, 2005).

58. Stefanie Decker, "African American Women in the Civil Rights Era,"
    in *Black Women in Texas History*, 163–64; Barr, *Black Texans*, 191–
    92, 202, 218; Friedberg, "Houston and the TSU Riot," 38–39; Calvert,
    "The Civil Rights Movement," 167–84; Dulaney, "Whatever Hap-
    pened to the Civil Rights Movement in Dallas?" 66–95.

59. Michael R. Botson Jr., "Jim Crow Wearing Steel-Toed Shoes and
    Safety Glasses: Dual Unionism at the Hughes Tool Company, 1918–
    1942," *Houston Review* 16 (1994), 101–16; Michael R. Botson Jr.,
    "No Gold Watch for Jim Crow's Retirement: The Abolition of Seg-
    regated Unionism at Houston's Tool Company," *Southwestern His-
    torical Quarterly* 101 (April 1998), 497–521; Michael R. Botson Jr.,
    Labor, Civil Rights, and the Hughes Tool Company (College Station:
    Texas A&M University Press, 2005), quote on 11.

60. Barbara Jordan and Shelby Hearon, *Barbara Jordan: A Self-Portrait*
    (Garden City, N.Y.: Doubleday, 1979); Mary Beth Rogers, *Barbara
    Jordan: American Hero* (New York: Bantam Books, 1998); Mark
    Odintz, "Jordan, Barbara Charline," *The Handbook of Texas Online*
    (http://www.tshaonline.org/handbook/online/articles/JJ/fjoas.html);
    Jane P. Gooch, "Barbara C. Jordan: Her First Forty Years, A Rhetorical
    Analysis" (master's thesis, Baylor University, 1977).

61. Tolson, "The Death of an Infidel," *Washington Tribune*, April 2,
    1938.

MORE THAN A SOMNOLENT TYPE
Tejanos Resist the Rule of Dominance

Arnoldo De León

◀ Although the majority of Tejanos[1] did not openly challenge the state's economic and political systems, there was an active segment within the community that did dispute the circumstances inhibiting Mexican American yearnings for material betterment and social progress. Beginning in 1836, when Anglo Americans won independence from Mexico, Tejanos faced a ruling class bent on controlling and subordinating them through a combination of force, legal mechanisms, political ties, racist actions, and social custom. Almost from that instance—when Anglo power supplanted Mexico's authority—Tejanos contested white society's license to violate democratic principles and manage the economic system in a conscious effort to maintain a serviceable proletariat. The movement (multifarious though it was) that loosely or collectively questioned the Anglo rule of dominance may be supposed to constitute the Tejano Left.

In practice, few Texas Mexicans raised objections to the democratic ideal. In return for their own commitment (in the form of hard labor, civic duty, military service, and the like) to the state's general tranquility, however, they asked for a fair shake at justice and a chance for life improvement. Obstructed from the democratic promise at almost every turn, they turned to strategies that ranged from the spontaneous and the improvised to the organized and effectively executed.

SPONTANEOUS RESISTANCE

Spontaneous and unplanned outbursts against the social order appear to have been most common in the nineteenth century and early twentieth century, when Anglos disrupted the familiar milieu as they moved into regions of the state numerically dominated by Mexican Americans. One such outbreak occurred in Nacogdoches in the wake of the Texas war for independence, as Anglos in East Texas engaged in the general mistreatment of Texas Mexicans, including attempts to defraud them of their land. Outraged, a small group of Tejanos led by Vicente Córdova ("they had been dogs long enough," according to one angry contemporary) staged an uprising against the new sovereignty, though the revolt proved abortive.[2] Similarly, segments of the Tejano community in South Texas rallied to the banner of Juan Cortina who emerged in the summer and fall of 1859 as the local hero rising to stem the tide of scornful Anglo-Americans arriving in the Rio Grande valley to usurp Texas Mexicans politically and economically.[3] In the El Paso region in 1877, an attempt by Anglo entrepreneurs to take over communally used salt lakes produced an insurgency of native-Mexican-descent citizens bent on retaining access to a natural resource upon which they had depended for generations.[4] Then, in 1891, Tejanos gave succor to Catarino Garza when he and followers retreated into South Texas after failing to unseat Mexico's president Porfirio Díaz; they protected him from Texas Rangers and other law officials (chasing Garza for violating the neutrality laws) because for years Garza had spoken out against the adverse impact that Anglo Texan "progress" had on predominantly Mexican South Texas.[5] Almost a quarter-century later, segments of the Tejano population aided the *sediciosos* (rebels) who in 1915 issued the Plan de San Diego, an ambitious proposal for erecting a republic in the U.S. Southwest for Mexican Americans and Mexicans. Tejanos joined the rebels in attacking Anglo-American establishments, wanting to take revenge for endured wrongs and for the widespread disruption of life caused by changes brought on by the farm revolution then underway in South Texas.[6]

REFORMIST POLITICAL CHALLENGES

More common challenges to the status quo issued from reformist groups.[7] The origins of such movements are difficult to trace precisely; some historians detect progressive ideologies emanating from Tejano communities by the latter decades of the nineteenth century, others do not see them surfacing until the early years of the 1900s, still others not until the 1920s.[8] Disagreement about the beginnings of such ideas aside, this Mexican American generation (which would act as the voice of the community until the 1960s) was quite cognizant of the pervasive mistreatment of their fellow Tejanos and frequently criticized Mexican American victimization. Among other things, progressives held protest meetings, organized communities, launched drives to unify the electorate, and went before the judicial system in an effort to overturn societal transgressions.

Land loss and its impact on Tejano communities (especially on the elites) worried early-twentieth-century, reform-minded Tejanos, but that predicament was not their sole concern. For them, Anglo society placed many obstacles to impede the Tejanos' desire to partake of American opportunity. To deal with such issues, the city of Laredo hosted the Primer Congreso Mexicanista (September 16, 1911), a gathering of Tejano community representatives from throughout Texas, including such far-away places as Houston and San Angelo. There the discussion revolved around such other imperative topics as inferior schooling for Mexican Americans, abuses of the laboring class, and a recent wave of violence. The coordinator of the meeting, newspaper editor Nicasio Idar of *La Cronica*, had hoped the congress would lead to Tejanos being "treated with more respect . . . and given justice when we demand it," but his efforts and that of fellow organizers did not bear fruit, as no record exists that the congress met again.[9]

Tejanos affected by powerful Americanizing forces unfolding early in the century joined the Mexican American progressives of the pre–World War I years in newer reform campaigns during the 1920s. Seduced by the wonders of the age (consumerism, movie shows, dance crazes, teenage fads, and more), converted by a revised school curriculum that had as its intent Americanizing those of foreign birth, and won over by the promises made during World War I for a society that would no longer consider Mexican Americans as stepchildren of the nation, Texas Mexicans felt more at ease insisting on guaranteed rights.[10]

During the 1920s, cohorts of the Mexican American generation appealed for the right to vote without the "white man's primary" or the poll tax disfranchising them. They argued for the privilege to serve on juries, for cases in that era generally were heard by all-white male juries. Tejano reformers called for the freedom to use public facilities and not be restrained by Jim Crow traditions or the constant aspersions that they were a dirty people. These and other demands led to the formation of new, civic-minded associations determined to overturn impediments to full citizenship. Among such organizations was the Order Sons of America (osa), whose members publicized their loyalty to the United States. In no way did they question the American social order; they simply asked why Texans did not live up to constitutional guarantees promised to all. Reform itself, they believed, would affect the needed freedoms and opportunities that Mexican Americans deserved. Unfortunately for reformers, the OSA and organizations like it did not thrive during the 1920s.[11]

The League of United Latin American Citizens (LULAC), founded in 1929, carried forth the goals of middle-class leaders visualizing an open society where Mexican Americans shared freely in the rewards of democracy and free enterprise. Still, in the years immediately preceding World War II, Mexicans faced virulent racism (that categorized them as non-white), obstacles to voting, discrimination in the work place, and a range of other hindrances to social advancement. LULAC treaded carefully during the 1930s in the way it raised objections to the problems that beset Mexican Americans; after all, Anglo Texans did not countenance militant rhetoric or "un-American" behavior. Careful to follow the proper channels of protest (and do so in an acceptable manner), LULAC councils during the Depression and World War II years brought to public notice the plight of laborers (and especially the discrimination that occurred in industrial plants during the war years), city indifference toward conditions in Mexican American neighborhoods, the detestable practice of segregation, and of course, second-class education.[12]

Certainly schooling ranked among LULAC's most urgent concerns. In 1931, consequently, it filed a complaint against the Del Rio school system and won the case of *Independent School District v. Salvatierra.* In *Salvatierra*, a Texas court of civil appeals decided that the segregation of Mexican American children violated the legal code, but agreed with school officials that segregation facilitated the mainstreaming of Spanish-speaking students into the English-language curriculum.[13] In San Antonio, LULAC member Eleuterio Escobar, working independently of LULAC, led a drive in 1934 to upgrade educational facilities for Mexican American children. Organizing several community groups into what came to be called the Liga Pro-defensa Escolar (School Improvement League), Escobar's campaign brought together the media, high-profile Mexican American leaders, and the Texas legislature in a successful movement that produced promises from the school board for new buildings and the remodeling of old structures. Unfortunately, the depression and later World War II priorities stopped construction, but Escobar successfully renewed his campaign for school improvement in the late 1940s.[14]

Also making it part of its mission to solve problems underlined by LULAC (but by no means solved after World War II) was the American GI Forum (AGIF), founded in 1948 by Héctor P. García, a Corpus Christi physician and World War II veteran committed to guaranteeing that the U.S. government extended full benefits to Hispanic ex-servicemen. But a 1949 incident in the South Texas town of Three Rivers centering on the refusal of the local mortician to hold services in his chapel for Félix Longoria, killed in the Philippines in 1945, morphed the GI Forum into a second civil rights association ready to rebuke Texans for perpetuating social ills.[15]

Of priority to the GI Forum, aside from the blatant discrimination that condoned separate funeral services and segregated cemeteries, were standing issues of police harassment, societal indifference toward health problems in the barrios, and the near-total exclusion of Mexican Americans from jury duty. But the age-old problem of inferior schooling preoccupied it the most. In the late 1940s (beginning with *Delgado v. Bastrop,* 1948) and continuing into the 1950s, therefore, the AGIF joined LULAC in a string of court cases that helped desegregate the Texas school system and ended the common practice of detaining Tejano children in beginner classes for three to four years.[16] As to the matter of jury exclusion, the GI Forum financially assisted LULAC in the case of *Hernández v. Texas;* in its decision, the U.S. Supreme Court in 1954 ruled that Texas should not discriminate in jury selection against Mexican Americans (or against "other whites"). Lawyers representing Texas had argued that no discrimination occurred in the state, as Anglos regarded Mexican-origin persons as white, but attorneys for Pete Hernández, the plaintiff, countered that notwithstanding such a consideration, the social norms of the age deemed Mexican Americans as nonwhite, and on that idea Anglos victimized Tejanos. The GI Forum would continue the struggle for Mexican American equality until well into the latter years of the twentieth century.[17]

During the 1960s and 1970s, the strategies used by LULAC and the AGIF of the Mexican American generation gave way (at least momentarily) to the more combative tactics employed by the Chicano generation. This coterie of youths, influenced by World War II events and educated in the United States, now emerged as spokespersons for the oppressed Tejano community. To be sure, other elements across the nation opted for similar confrontational approaches in questioning the credibility of American institutions and 1950s values, but Tejano militants still focused on the lingering problems that beseiged their communities. As it had for ages, poverty plagued many barrio residents (as well as farm workers) during the 1960s and 1970s, as options for finding good-paying jobs remained elusive. High school diplomas eluded young people, many of whom dropped out during their mid-teens to help with household budgets. Even as Jim Crow practices gasped for life, segregation and discrimination persisted in subtle forms. Gerrymandering and at-large elections worked to effectively still Tejano electoral potential. Everyday harassment by local police forces, the Texas Rangers, and the Border Patrol represented reminders to Tejanos that those of Mexican descent, whether native-born or not, were second-class citizens.

Convinced that the tactics used by the Mexican American generation had proven ineffective, encouraged by the rebellious climate of the age, and uplifted by their own youthful idealism, young protesters refused to accept completely the premise of American goodness and of the munificence of U.S. institutions as had previous Tejano generations. Led by the Mexican American Youth Organization (MAYO) founded in 1967, they committed themselves to revising old assumptions about matters centering on race relations, political understandings, and the entrenched belief that certain people were destined for the lower rungs of the economic hierarchy.

MAYO leaders, among them José Angel Gutiérrez, also set out to overturn the old Anglo stereotype of the somnolent Mexican and substitute instead the image of a brash Tejano, confident of a background rooted in both Mexican and American cultures. They took pride in proclaiming themselves "Chicanos" (an in-group term popular in male youth barrio culture).[18] Whereas in previous eras Mexican Americans had downplayed their Mexicanness (stigmatized as it was with backwardness), Chicanos co-opted the symbols of Mexico's greatness—including icons such as Emiliano Zapata and even the Virgen de Guadalupe—and publicly asserted their admiration for them. They did not agonize over being considered nonwhite, either; instead, brown was beautiful. Indeed, they disputed the value of assimilation itself: what good came of Americanization when white society still considered Mexicans as unworthy of the American Dream? MAYO militants talked of separatism and joined other Chicano activists throughout the United States then calling for establishing a homeland somewhere in the Southwest and calling it Aztlán (the ancient land of the Aztecs).

Chicanos during the later 1960s took the United States to task in ways other than questioning the worth of assimilation. MAYO members and their allies embraced brazen methods that the Mexican American generation had once disavowed, including demonstrations, school boycotts, public denunciations of U.S. leaders (at times using obscene language), and committing sacrilegious acts on church properties, because the Church supposedly contributed to Mexican American suffering. Despite their beliefs (and some actions), Chicano activists placed expectations on a democratic process that might give assent to their leftist agenda.

In Texas, the Raza Unida Party (RUP) during the 1970s led the Chicano drive to usher in the intended transformation. Founded initially in Crystal City in January 1970 by José Angel Gutiérrez, who along with his wife Luz and other town supporters subsequently engineered a political coup against the entrenched Anglo ruling-class there, the RUP soon became a statewide political organization, following a meeting in Mission, Texas. In the gubernatorial election of 1972, Ramsey Muñiz, a Corpus Christi attorney, spoke for a liberal platform fixed on bringing about an end to the old inequalities, and the realization of a new society wherein minority groups (including women) would hold a level place with the white majority. It called for such needs as passage of the Equal Rights Amendment, school finance reform, bilingual education, an end to the Texas Rangers (tacitly understood to have been a police body aimed at controlling Mexicans), the elimination of gerrymandering practices that stifled barrio clout, health-care programs, and solutions to urban problems. Despite RUP success in politicizing part of the Mexican American electorate, the party faced an uphill battle against the other two parties throughout the 1970s, and won mainly local races. Its passing after 1978 coincided with the general decline of other reformist struggles across the United States.

What did the Chicano movement leave in its wake? Its politicization of communities produced a cadre of leaders who would continue challenging the Texas establishment on such matters as improved education, poverty in the barrios, and equal representation at all government levels. The Mexican American Legal Defense and Educational Fund (MALDEF) and the Southwest Voter Registration and Education Project (SVREP) have since assumed a conspicuous role in tackling such issues, the former by litigating cases of discrimination and the latter by engaging in drives to improve voter participation. Chicanas, who had been coequals to Chicanos in the Movimiento, overturned the Anglo (if not the Chicano) stereotype of the quiet, passive, and suffering *mujer* (woman). The Chicano movement had heightened the Tejano sense of worth in being of Mexican descent: bilingualism became an asset and not a liability; various Mexican dishes, some of them home specialties, entered the dinner menu in popular restaurant chains; and Latin music, no longer perceived as too "ethnic," emerged as a conduit for corporate advertisers wanting to promote their products and services in the Spanish language. The movement further bolstered a longstanding interest in the Tejano past, an inquisitiveness that fostered a literary renaissance of creative literature and a commitment to historical research.[19]

Still, one observer has recently noted, while the Chicano movement succeeded in having Mexican Americans see themselves differently, it did not completely eliminate those forces that had historically hampered their aspirations.[20] In recent decades, the leadership that has been in the forefront of seeking solutions to perpetual problems has been labeled the Hispanic generation. This cadre, which includes veterans of the Chicano movement, but more prominently those who came of age in the post-movement era—such as state representatives Juan García (D-Corpus Christi) and Pete Gallego (D-Alpine)—has worked closely with other liberal partisans in Texas to protest barriers placed by conservative elements. These include discriminatory redistricting plans, unfair school financing, political stands that prolong adversity for farm workers, English-only sentiments that tend to stigmatize Mexican Americans as un-American, and even the bashing of immigrants that incidentally indicts Mexican American communities for complicity in harboring lawbreakers.[21]

CHALLENGES TO THE CAPITALIST ORDER

Tejanos registered personal displeasure with work conditions, displayed interest in radical ideologies (either Mexico- or U.S.-based) that addressed class oppression, and joined a variety of labor unions in a struggle to achieve material rewards. Certainly such activism existed before 1900, but overt challenges to the economic status quo did not surface before then, and for several reasons. These would include the racist climate of the times that dissuaded Mexican Americans from making bold moves, a hesitancy by mainstream labor organizations to address the problems of Mexican Americans (Anglo workers sometimes saw those of Mexican origin as competitors), and Mexican immigrants' feeling that they had relocated to escape poverty and not to quarrel with American institutions.[22]

Strategies taken by the Immigrant generation (that element within Tejano society which tended to be Mexico-born and that had migrated to Texas during the early decades of the twentieth century) to question the capitalist order during that time tended to be tentative, cautious, and defensive. Generally workers turned to tactics that other powerless people have used to express that displeasure: refusing to work for inconsiderate land owners, impulsively leaving the workplace, physically confronting employers, and forming ethnically oriented workers' associations.[23]

Emilio Zamora, who has extensively studied the Mexican American labor movements of the first two decades of the twentieth century, notes that Mexican Americans and Mexicans turned to more decisive action than mentioned above, and that for a brief period both embraced radical socialist ideologies with roots in both the United States and Mexico. Early in the century, Socialist Party charges that the costs of capitalism were poverty, class oppression, and a disregard for human value, found reception among a segment of the Mexican American and Mexican working masses, for instance.

Professor Zamora finds at least two prominent examples of such involvement with Socialist Party activity in Texas. In Laredo, railway workers belonging to Federal Labor Union #11,953 (an affiliate of the American Federation of Labor) in 1906 and 1907 successfully struck against the Mexican Railway for better wages, though lost overall when the railroad company moved across the river to Nuevo Laredo.[24] Similarly influenced by the Socialist Party, but also by radical ideologies with roots in Mexico, were tenants and farm workers in Central Texas who during the 1910s found the voice of the Renters' Union of America (established in 1911), and its replacement, the Land League of America (1914), appealing. Mexican Americans and Mexicans endorsed the Land League's message that the capitalist system brought misery into the lives of farm tenants, and that land distribution represented one solution to ending such exploitation. For a while, Mexicans and Tejanos succeeded in organizing Land League locals (for some immigrants possessed previous experience working in the Partido Liberal Mexicano, the anarchist party founded in Mexico by Ricardo Flores Magón, which engaged in labor organizing in Texas during the 1910s) to the point that Anglo socialists reversed their perception of Mexicans as stoic peons and began accepting them as almost white and even manlier than Anglo tenants who were cowed by landlords. In the end, however, too many obstacles blocked successful Tejano involvement in the Socialist Party movement. These included race prejudice, inability to pay dues or to organize effectively, and, of course, the general rejection of socialist doctrine by most Texans. Federal repression of the party resulted in the destruction of the socialist movement by the 1920s.[25]

For the most part, however, Mexican Americans elsewhere in the state paid little heed to the socialists. Tejanos seldom talked of replacing capitalism with another economic system, for instance. They reproached employers often, true enough, but made their case on grounds that management tended to be callous and indifferent toward the lot of the worker. That was certainly the case in the West Texas town of El Paso, where the historian Mario T. García unearthed a pattern of sustained labor activity occurring during the period from 1900 to 1920. In the various businesses there, among them the laundry, street car, smelter, and white-collar industries, Mexican-descent workers (many of them immigrants) forcefully remonstrated against their exploitation. They complained about low wages (in almost every workplace), long hours, the use of strikebreakers to undermine job walkouts, and the common practice of paying Anglo Americans more than Mexican Mexicans for performing the same job. To protest such offenses that confronted them, Paseños initiated a series of work stoppages in the city during the first two decades of the twentieth century, among them strikes against the El Paso Street Car Company (1901 and 1905), the smelters (1907 and 1913), the city water department (1911), and laundry establishments (1919). These challenges to the economic status quo at times succeeded, albeit briefly, and at other times failed. Certainly, disagreements with the entrepreneurial class in El Paso continued long past 1920.[26]

In the rural sector, Mexican American field and ranch workers during the 1930s similarly quarreled with an economic system that they believed misused them as it had their immigrant forebears. In West Texas, cotton pickers in El Paso County struck in 1933, complaining of the dismal wages that farmers paid them. But they could not sustain the strike in light of united opposition from the cotton growers, the police, and government authorities. Around San Angelo sheep shearers struck against wool growers in 1934, in a failed attempt to bring an end to certain practices: first, that of fixing the amount paid to shear and tag sheep and goats, and second, that of negotiating not with individual shearers but *capitanes* (contractors) who regularly defrauded them of part of their hard-earned wages.[27] Cotton, onion, and spinach workers in South Texas also complained of numerous abuses inflicted upon them by Anglo farm owners. Their list of grievances included housing woefully unfit for human use, lack of restroom facilities in the fields, miserable pay, exploitation of children, abuses committed under the labor-contractor arrangement, and many other tribulations that produced dire poverty, health problems, and utter despair. Unionizing efforts—even when successful—only produced short-term benefits, given the Depression and the power of the growers.[28]

The dissatisfaction displayed by Mexican Americans in the agrarian sector during the 1930s found parallels among laborers in urban industries. Laundry workers deplored their working conditions: management appeared heedless of the need for safety standards, unconcerned about the lack of proper ventilation in laundry plants, and indifferent toward their employees' needs for bathroom facilities. Those who toiled in the cigar industry in San Antonio likewise rebuked their employers for maintaining a poor environment in the workshop, identifying industrial hazards to employees and bothersome problems like faulty plumbing and leaky roofs. Women in the garment industry of the Alamo City added their own grievances to the complaint list, among them poor lighting, uncomfortable sitting accommodations, and cramped quarters. Pecan shellers, who numbered into the thousands in San Antonio (twenty thousand, according to one estimate), eked out an insufferable livelihood as seasonal workers (pecan shelling slowed down during the summer months), tolerating hot temperatures inside shacks, hours of sitting in one position hunched over on benches, and harmful dust caused by the shelling.[29]

By no means did laborers in urban centers simply grumble about their difficulties. In San Antonio, particularly, they mounted concerted action. A series of strikes during the Depression era resolved to face down economic power. Cigar rollers struck against the Finck Cigar Company in 1933 and 1934, factory hands belonging to the International Ladies Garment Workers Union (ILGWU) struck local garment plants in 1937 and 1938, and, in the most famous of walkouts, the pecan shellers (led by the Mexican American labor leader Emma Tenayuca, a Communist Party member) suspended work at the pecan shelling plants in 1938. These clashes produced few long-term benefits (an ILGWU strike against the Shirlee Frocks Company in 1937 did yield a wage increase); most labor struggles fell victim to a variety of forces, among them shortages of funds to sustain prolonged drives, an antistrike (and antilabor) mentality, and the adverse influence of the Depression.[30]

During the World War II years, labor discontent continued to fester in El Paso against local smelters. Working conditions in the foundries had hardly improved since 1907 and 1913 when workers had last struck them. Smelter workers associated with the International Union of Mine, Mill and Smelter Workers (Mine Mill), expressed dismay with which the two leading smelters in the city, American Smelting and Refining Company and Phelps-Dodge, took advantage of them without fair compensation. Mine Mill members protested housing conditions: they were required to build their own lodging on company land provided them at high rent, despite its high-risk location and filthy surroundings. The companies practiced acts of discrimination against Mexican Americans, allowing better-quality facilities such as restrooms and work stations for Anglos. Workers had to perform hazardous tasks without proper safety precautions in place, risking injuries and the inevitable loss of employment should they be disabled. As had been the case in the industry for years, management assigned Mexican Americans and Mexicans to the most menial jobs and still paid them less, even when they worked alongside Anglos. In 1946, members of the two mills (Locals 501 and 509) felt they had no option other than to strike, and they did so in February. Their effort ended successfully in May; they got the wage increase they demanded, as well as numerous other concessions.[31]

During the 1950s, unionizing activity throughout Texas declined for a number of reasons, among them the antilabor climate pervasive throughout the state and the unrelenting red-baiting used by the establishment against those questioning the economic status quo.[32] These were some of the obstacles that confronted the discontented workers at Economy Furniture Company of Austin, for example, when in 1958 they attempted to unionize. Workers had grown tired of disagreeable practices, among them punishment for time lost (even in the case of family crises), inattention to seniority, a slow promotion process, and a rule penalizing tardiness but not rewarding employees unless they worked fifteen minutes past quitting time. Despite these many grievances, organizers failed in bringing unionization to the Economy Furniture Company.[33]

A strike more than ten years later would lead to victory, however. One historian attributes its success to the climate of the 1960s, as protest had become more legitimate and various elements across society questioned the fairness of the capitalist system, among them Chicano militants who openly supported the strike as being part of "la causa" (the cause). In September 1971, Economy Furniture Company strikers gained recognition of their local (#456 of the Upholsterer's International Union of North America), and management agreed to remedy procedures regarding pay, sick leave, vacations, seniority, and other employee demands.[34]

Women workers in the garment industry had faced resistance from company executives at mid-century similar to what employees at Economy Furniture Company had encountered in 1958. Consequently, strikes against Hortex in El Paso (1952) and Tex-Son of San Antonio (1959–1961) had yielded less-than-satisfying results. Even during the Chicano movement years, garment workers in 1965 and 1971 had faced difficulties in exacting satisfactory contracts from Levi-Straus of El Paso.[35] Into the 1970s, therefore, those tied to the garment trade advanced legitimate grievances. Employers balked at assuming responsibility for extending benefits to women such as reasonable vacation time or for offering them health-care coverage. Many companies provided no adequate maternity leave, necessary bathroom breaks, or suitable clinical health-care facilities on the premises. Women vocalized objections to the preferential treatment given by shift bosses to more attractive employees, alleged sexual harassment, and complained of working under undue stress when supervisors pressured them to meet impractical quotas. These conditions in part explain the decision of the Amalgamated Clothing Workers of America (ACWA) in 1972 to strike against the Farah Manufacturing Company of El Paso.[36]

The Farah strike dragged on for about two years, as the ACWA contended with the same obstacles that labor unions before them had encountered. Management associated striking workers with left-leaning militants, even communists, used the news media to disseminate their version of the struggle, turned to the courts for injunctions against the protesters, and utilized their connections to the local police authorities by arresting strikers or protecting non-strikers. In the end (February 1974), the Farah women won the strike, with management agreeing to address and rectify those wrongs that had prompted the confrontation.[37] The Farah strike would not be the last walkout conducted by Mexican American women against the garment industry in El Paso, however. In 1991, a labor organization by the name of La Mujer Obrera (The Woman Worker), allying itself with the ILGWU, struck four garment companies in the city and won on issues ranging from improved salaries to a new employee-friendly health policy.[38]

No less Herculean were efforts by farm workers during the 1960s and after to get farm owners to address their problems. Farms hands, most of them seasonal workers, faced a dismal life, having to make ends meet with wages well below the poverty line (as late as the 1970s, incomes at times amounted to less than $5 per day). Most were undereducated (more than 80 percent had not finished high school), usually did not own their home (many inhabited hovels in unincorporated sections of border towns), and generally lacked adequate health care. Few, the *campesinos* (farm workers) emphasized, qualified for state services, including unemployment compensation. Moreover, no union represented their cause.[39]

Such circumstances kindled the farm workers' movement that started in the mid-1960s and lasted until the early 1980s. Two unions spoke for the farm workers during the period, but because of philosophical differences worked separately. More in the forefront was the Texas Farm Workers Union (TFWU), led by Tony Orendain, which, in contrast with the United Farm Workers (UFW, its rival, affiliated with the César Chávez–led California farm workers' movement), engaged in greater strike activity (from South Texas to the Panhandle), farm-worker marches, publicity campaigns and press conferences, and lobbying before the state legislature. Both, however, highlighted the need for collective bargaining, for minimum wage standards, and for laws that outlawed practices that imperiled field hands. With the assistance of Mexican American representatives, the state legislature during the 1980s slowly began to heed migrant workers' needs. Ultimately the statehouse outlawed child labor and the use of the short-handled hoe, made provisions for improved facilities on location (such as toilets and better access to water), and included farm hands under worker and unemployment compensation provisions. The UFW remains active today (by the early 1980s the TFWU could no longer sustain itself and

today serves as an advocacy unit and social service organization),
though its approach to gaining improvements for its membership is
more conventional and mainstream.[40]

A CASE OF PRINCIPLE

Over the course of almost two centuries, principle has driven Tejanos to act against Anglo-Texan dominance. Exempting the localized
yet sometimes violent uprisings of the nineteenth century and the
Plan de San Diego episode, however, practically no Tejano-led engage-
ment, campaign, or effort advocated replacing the democratic process or free-enterprise system. Instead movements were against laws,
labor arrangements, well-rooted traditions, and racist beliefs that de-
terred Tejanos from partaking of the democratic and capitalist ideals.
Methods of criticism and confrontation varied according to time and
issue involved, but generally fell within the perimeters of established
norms and entailed litigation, political mobilization efforts, and union
struggles. In the world of the Lone Star State, then, the Tejano Left has
been characterized by a sustained reformist effort on the part of the
disadvantaged to claim their rights as deserving citizens.

NOTES

1. "Tejano" is Spanish for Mexican-descent people living in Texas.
    Throughout the essay, I use various terms that are interchangeable
    with "Tejano," among them "Texas Mexicans," "Mexican Ameri-
    cans," and "Chicanos." When referring to those born in Mexico, I
    use the term "Mexican."
2. Paul D. Lack, "The Córdova Rebellion," in *Tejano Journey, 1770–
    1850*, ed. Gerald E. Poyo (Austin: University of Texas Press, 1996),
    89–109.
3. Jerry Thompson, *Cortina: Defending the Mexican Name in Texas*
    (College Station: Texas A&M University Press, 2007).
4. Paul Cool, "The El Paso Salt War: A Review of the Historical Litera-
    ture," *Journal of Big Bend Studies* 17 (2005); "Law, Race, and the
    Border: The El Paso Salt War of 1877," *Harvard Law Review* 117,
    no. 3 (January 2004), 941; Paul Cool, *Salt Warriors: Insurgency on the
    Rio Grande* (College Station: Texas A&M University Press, 2008).
5. Elliott Young, *Catarino Garza's Revolution on the Texas-Mexico
    Border* (Durham: Duke University Press, 2004), 33–34, 106–108, 131–
    32, 148–50, 155, 228, 234–36.
6. Benjamin Heber Johnson, *Revolution in Texas: How a Forgotten Re-
    bellion and Its Bloody Suppression Turned Mexicans into Americans*

(New Haven: Yale University Press, 2003), 79–82, 90–94; Charles H. Harris and Louis R. Sadler, *The Texas Rangers and the Mexican Revolution: The Bloodiest Decade, 1910–1920* (Albuquerque: University of New Mexico Press, 2004), chap. 3. See further, Richard Ribb, "José Tomás Canales and the Texas Rangers: Myth, Identity, and Power, 1900–1920" (PhD diss., University of Texas, 2001), chap. 3.

7. In his instructive study *Claiming Citizenship: Mexican Americans in Victoria, Texas* (College Station: Texas A&M University Press, 2005), 127–28, Anthony Quiroz argues, "The manner by which Mexican Americans in Victoria challenged the way they had been marginalized and excluded from American beneficence was through institutional avenues, the very model utilized by other disfranchised groups in American politics." The argument advanced in this essay parallels Quiroz's position.

8. Arnoldo De León, "Raza of Middling Status on the *Chaparral*," in *Tejano Epic: Essays in Honor of Félix D. Almaráz Jr.* ed. Arnoldo De León (Austin: Texas State Historical Association, 2005), 59–70; Johnson, *Revolution in Texas*, 42–48; Elliott Young, "Deconstructing *La Raza*: Culture and Ideology of the *Gente Decente* of Laredo, 1904–1911," *Southwestern Historical Quarterly* 98 (October 1984), 226–59; Manuel Peña, *The Texas-Mexican Conjunto: History of a Working Class Music* (Austin: University of Texas Press, 1985), 115, 126; Mario T. García, *Mexican Americans: Leadership, Ideology, and Identity, 1930–1960* (New Haven: Yale University Press, 1989), 13–22.

9. Johnson, *Revolution in Texas*, 52–54. Other works on the Congreso include José E. Limón, "El Primer Congreso Mexicanista de 1911: A Precursor to Contemporary Chicanismo," *Aztlán* 5 (Spring/Fall 1974), 85–118; and José A. Hernández, *Mutual Aid for Survival: The Case of the Mexican American* (Malabar, Fla.: Robert E. Kreiger Publishing Company, 1983), chap. 4.

10. Cynthia E. Orozco, "The Origins of the League of United Latin American Citizens (LULAC) and the Mexican American Civil Rights Movement in Texas with an Analysis of Women's Political Participation in a Gendered Context, 1910–1929" (PhD diss., University of California at Los Angeles, 1992), p92, 95; Peña, *Texas-Mexican Conjunto*, 116; Mario T. García, *Desert Immigrants: The Mexicans of El Paso, 1880–1920* (New Haven: Yale University Press, 1981), 117–22, 211, 213–14, 217–19; Guadalupe San Miguel Jr., "Social and Educational Influences Shaping the Mexican American Mind," *Journal of Midwest History of Education Society* 14 (1986), 58–59.

11. Orozco, "The Origins of the League of United Latin American Citizens," 127–29; Carole E. Christian, "Joining the American Main-

stream: Texas' Mexican Americans During World War I," *Southwestern Historical Quarterly* 92 (April 1989), 589–90.

12. Christian, "Joining the American Mainstream," 591–92; Richard A. García, *Rise of the Mexican American Middle Class: San Antonio, 1929–1941* (College Station: Texas A&M University Press, 1991), 261, 266, 271–72, 275, 281; Benjamín Márquez, LULAC: *The Evolution of a Mexican American Political Organization* (Austin: University of Texas Press, 1993), 17–29; Guadalupe San Miguel Jr., *"Let All of Them Take Heed": Mexican Americans and the Campaign for Educational Equality in Texas, 1910–1981* (Austin: University of Texas Press, 1987), 76, 81; Mario T. García, "Mexican Americans and the Politics of Citizenship," *New Mexico Historical Review*, 59 (April 1984), 188, 198–201.

13. Everett Ross Clinchy, "Equality of Opportunity for Latin Americans in Texas" (PhD diss., Columbia University, 1954), 188–89.

14. García, *Mexican Americans*, chap. 3.

15. Patrick J. Carroll, *Felix Longoria's Wake: Bereavement, Racism, and the Rise of Mexican American Activism* (Austin: University of Texas Press, 2003). See also Ignacio M. García, *Hector P. García: In Relentless Pursuit of Justice* (Houston: Arte Público Press, 2002); Carl Allsup, *The American GI Forum: Origins and Evolution* (Austin: Center for Mexican American Studies, 1982); Henry A. J. Ramos, *The American GI Forum* (Houston: Arte Público Press, 1998).

16. San Miguel, "Let All of Them Take Heed," 117–34.

17. Allsup, *The American GI Forum*, 73–77. See further Ian Haney López, "Race and Colorblindness after *Hernández* and *Brown*," in *"Colored Men" and "Hombres Aquí": Hernández v. Texas and the Emergence of Mexican-American Lawyering*, ed. Michael A. Olivas (Houston: Arte Público Press, 2006): 41–52.

18. "Chicano," in *New Handbook of Texas*, vol. 2, ed. Ron Tyler (Austin: Texas State Historical Association, 1996), 69.

19. I have relied on the following sources in documenting the several aspects of the Chicano movement: Ignacio M. García, *Chicanismo: The Forging of a Militant Ethos among Mexican Americans* (Tucson: University of Arizona Press, 1997), 3, 4, 7–11, 16, 23, 143; Armando Navarro, *Mexican American Youth Organization: Avant-Garde of the Chicano Movement in Texas* (Austin: University of Texas Press, 1995), chaps. 3–7; Armando Navarro, *La Raza Unida Party: A Chicano Challenge to the U.S. Two-Party Dictatorship* (Philadelphia: Temple University Press, 2000), chaps. 1–3; Douglas Foley et al., *From Peones to Politicos: Class and Ethnicity in a South Texas Town, 1900–1987*, rev ed. (Austin: University of Texas Press, 1988), chaps. 5 and 6; John Staples Shockley, *Chicano Revolt in a Texas*

Town (Notre Dame: University of Notre Dame Press, 1974); Ignacio M. García, *United We Win: The Rise and Fall of the Raza Unida Party* (Tucson: Mexican American Studies Resource Center, University of Arizona Press, 1989); José Angel Gutiérrez, *The Making of a Chicano Militant: Lessons from Cristal* (Madison: University of Wisconsin Press, 1998); and Armando Navarro, *The Cristal Experiment* (Madison: University of Wisconsin Press, 1998).

20. Van Gosse, *Rethinking The New Left: An Interpretive History* (New York: Palgrave MacMillan, 2005), 146.

21. García, *Chicanismo*, 9, 15–16, 143–45; Márquez, LULAC, 86–94; Craig A. Kaplowitz, LULAC, *Mexican Americans, and National Policy* (College Station: Texas A&M University Press, 2005).

22. Emilio Zamora, *The World of the Mexican Worker in Texas* (College Station: Texas A&M University Press, 1993), 35, 56–57. See further García, *Desert Immigrants*, 106–107; and Zaragosa Vargas, *Labor Rights are Civil Rights: Mexican American Workers in Twentieth Century America* (Princeton: Princeton University Press, 2005), 18–19.

23. Emilio Zamora, "Chicano Socialist Labor Activity in Texas, 1900–1920," *Aztlán* 6 (Summer 1976), 55–56, 66–70, 198.

24. Ibid., 222, 223, 224–25, 226, 231, 233. Roberto R. Calderón, who has studied mining along the border region for this same time period, notes that FLU #11,953 helped launch Miners Union #12,340. This latter union pressed the mine owners to be fair in assessing the amount of coal the miners collected, to permit workers to purchase outside the company store, and to concede shorter hours. Roberto R. Calderón, *Mexican Coal Mining Labor in Texas and Coahuila, 1880–1930* (College Station: Texas A&M University Press, 2000), 176–96.

25. Zamora, "Chicano Socialist Labor Activity in Texas," 227, 230, 231–32. Further elaboration on FLU #11,953 and the Land League of America is in Zamora, *The World of the Mexican Worker in* Texas, chaps. 5 and 6. Regarding how Anglo socialists came to see Mexican Americans as "almost white," see Neil Foley, *The White Scourge: Mexicans, Blacks, and Poor Whites in Texas Cotton Culture* (Berkeley: University of California Press, 1997), 95–96, 106, 108–109, 113, 114. On the fate of the Socialist Party at the national level, see James Weinstein, *The Decline of Socialism in America, 1912–1925* (New York: Monthly Review Press, 1969).

26. García, *Desert Immigrants*, 106–109.

27. Vargas, *Labor Rights are Civil Rights*, 67–70; Arnoldo De León, "*Los Tasinques* and the Sheep Shearers' Union of North America: A Strike in West Texas, 1934," *West Texas Historical Association Yearbook* 55 (1979), 4, 5, 6, 8.

28. Victor Nelson Cisneros, "*La clase trabajadora en Tejas*, 1920–1940," *Aztlán* 6 (Summer 1975): 244, 247, 248–49; Vargas, *Labor Rights are Civil Rights*, 117–22.

29. Julia Kirk Blackwelder, *Women of the Depression: Caste and Culture in San Antonio, 1929–1939* (College Station: Texas A&M University Press, 1984), 134; Irene Ledesma, "PhD diss., Ohio State University, 1992), 41, 49–59, 68, 69–71.

30. Blackwelder, *Women of the Depression*, 135, 137, 151; Zaragosa Vargas, "Emma Tenayuca: Labor and Civil Rights Organizer of 1930s San Antonio," in *The Human Tradition in America Between the Wars, 1920–1945*, ed. Donald W. Whisenhunt (Wilmington, Del.: Scholarly Resources, 2002), 169–84; Vargas, *Labor Rights are Civil Rights*, 80–83, 123–43; Yolanda Romero, "The Mexican American Frontier Experience in Twentieth Century Northwest Texas" (PhD diss., Texas Tech University, 1993).

31. García, *Mexican Americans*, 176–79, 195–96.

32. Ledesma, "Unlikely Strikers," 157; Anthony Quiroz, "'We Are Not Wetbacks, Meskins, or Slaves, but Human Beings': The Economy Furniture Company Strike of 1968–1971," in *Tejano Epic*, Arnoldo De León ed., 119.

33. Quiroz, "'We Are Not Wetbacks,'" 118–20.

34. Ibid., 118, 120–21, 122, 124–26, 128.

35. Ledesma, "Unlikely Strikers," 51, 137, 138, 139, 142, 157–58, 178–79.

36. Ibid., 51, 152, 179, 182, 184–88. More information may be found in Laurie Coyle et al., "Women at Farah: An Unfinished Story," in *Mexican Women in United States: Struggles Past and Present*, eds. Magdalena Mora and Adelaida Del Castillo (Los Angeles: Chicano Studies Research Publications, 1980), especially 118–21, 139–41.

37. Ledesma, "Unlikely Strikers," 206, 223, 228, 231, 232, 235, 237.

38. Benjamín Márquez, "Organizing Mexican-American Women in the Garment Industry: La Mujer Obrera," *Women & Politics* 15, no. 1 (1995), 66, 74–75.

39. Timothy Paul Bowman, "What About Texas? The Forgotten Cause of Antonio Orendain and the Rio Grande Valley Farm Workers, 1966–1982" (master's thesis, University of Texas at Arlington, 2005), 22, 84, 113; Arnoldo De León, *Mexican Americans in Texas: A Brief History*, 3rd ed. (Wheeling, Ill.: Harlan Davidson, 2009), 1151.

40. James C. Harrington, "From La Casita to LUPE," *Texas Observer* 96 (December 3, 2004), 42–43; Bowman, "What About Texas?" 119; and De León, *Mexican Americans in Texas*, 163.

A MODERN LIBERAL
TRADITION IN TEXAS?

Patrick Cox

◀ The values and goals expressed by liberals in post–World War II Texas originated in the political activism of such movements as the Farmers' Alliance, Populism and organized labor of the late nineteenth century. The modern liberal tradition then emerged in Texas after World War II during decades of dramatic social and economic change. As a result, Texas gained a small degree of distinction from its southern sister states due to the existence of a viable and vocal Lone Star Left. Informed by the traditions and experiences of the political protest movements that existed from the 1870s through the 1930s, this expanded liberal movement grew largely from within the state. The broadly based Farmers' Alliance and Populist movements, the robust Socialist critique, the New Deal, the women's movement, the African American and Hispanic civil rights movements, and the labor movement (the longest-lived movement on the Left), each contributed historic building blocks for the construction of a Texas liberal tradition. This included a conviction that government should play a role in the economy and in society. The rights of working people, racial and ethnic minorities, and women eventually became part of the mid-to-late-twentieth-century liberal agenda.

Gunnar Myrdal wrote in *An American Dilemma* in 1944 that "southern liberalism gets its power from outside the South." Southern liberals themselves were both critics and defenders of the South, according to his assessment. They spoke of the area as "hopelessly backward," but also "flattered" it "in the most extravagant terms of regional mythology." Myrdal concluded that the southern liberal was "inclined to stress the need for patience and to exalt the cautious approach, the slow change, the organic nature of social growth." Since Myrdal, other southern observers have also argued that national—not southern—forces defined and shaped the struggle over civil rights, economic justice, and social equality in the South. Labor unions, the National Association for the Advancement of Colored People (NAACP), private foundations, church organizations, and many other northern-based institutions did indeed provide leadership and support for the liberal movement in the South. Nevertheless, while many southern liberals sought and found support from outside the South, in the Lone Star State reformers looked to one another and the work of their historic predecessors in their challenge to conservative southern politics and economics. As a result of the efforts of the state's homegrown liberal leadership, Texas evinced a more moderate—or at least more diverse—identity than in the rest of the South. Conservatism remained firmly entrenched, dominated by the state's business community and elected officials reluctant to challenge, or sympathetic to, the status quo. However, some Texas liberals contradicted the patient, slow change that Myrdal described.[1]

Noted Southern historian Numan Bartley concluded that by the mid 1950s, the southern liberal was disappearing at a rapid rate. Southern liberals who advocated racial and economic reforms met widespread resistance and skepticism. "By defining liberalism not in terms of the redistribution of wealth, power and privilege but as an issue of individual morality, the new American left sharply narrowed the liberal agenda," Bartley concluded. Middle-class white southerners, grandchildren of the Populist movement and Progressivism, and beneficiaries of the New Deal, turned in their liberal credentials after World War II when confronted with challenges to white supremacy. The vast majority of southern elected officials, from the courthouse to Washington, D.C., retreated to safely conservative positions. Even the more outspoken southern newspaper editors shifted their alignment as race became more of a factor in the postwar liberal movement. "Even the word liberal began to disappear from the southern political lexicon," Bartley writes.[2]

Liberalism in Texas—and this is an important distinction—advocated change, but only so much as could be absorbed by the existing traditional political system. Texas liberals sought democratization, civil rights, and racial equality. They envisioned a pluralistic society within a market-based economy, while retaining some of the egalitarian flavor of their nineteenth century Populist forbears, albeit situated in an increasingly homogeneous society influenced by corporate power.

Like the rest of the South during the first eight decades of the twentieth century, Texas was virtually a one-party state. The Democratic Party dominated the political scene—a lasting vestige of the post–Civil War struggle over race, property, and power. Texas and the other southern states maintained their white, conservative elites in power through a political system distinctive from the rest of the nation. Political scientist V. O. Key noted in his monumental *Southern Politics in State and Nation* that the one-party order sustained itself through the bonds of kinship, localism, corruption, racial discrimination, and a number of other practices that made the South the least democratic society in the nation. Nevertheless, the gathering mid-century storm over civil rights changed the social and political atmosphere in Texas where both race and class became crucial catalysts in generating the cornerstone of the liberal movement in the post–World War II era.[3]

World War II transformed the state despite its rural image. The population and economy were poised for a major transition. After 1950, nearly two thirds of the 7.7 million Texans lived in towns and cities, the first decade for an urban majority. The sudden change came as a result of the rapid industrialization fueled by federal spending immediately prior to and during World War II. Agricultural mechanization meant fewer farm jobs; the war meant more opportunities in the armed forces; and service, manufacturing, and construction industries lured people to Texas cities during World War II. The trend continued through the postwar economic boom and into the Cold War era. But this expansion came at a cost. The state government's low-tax, low-service, cheap-labor, and anti-union policies, along with its nonexistent environmental protection, inexpensive utilities, and business-friendly state and local governments, increased opportunities for some but created new issues that became rallying cries of liberals. Interestingly, most of the migration to the state's urban centers came from nearby rural areas with little immigration from other states. Although classified as urbanites, these recently uprooted country people brought their rural culture—and politics—with them to the new cities. While the largest cities, like Houston and Dallas, touted their steel skylines and sudden wealth, their residents were still mostly rural Texans in city clothes.[4]

Texas during the decade of the 1950s experienced a slow, uneven transition to its new cosmopolitan image. The state's economy linked to industrialization and urban centers changed much faster than individual attitudes. The political culture remained tradition-bound, as Texas was still a one-party state whose working classes and city residents went largely underrepresented while minorities were merely seen and not heard. In rural Texas, the railroad tracks separated whites from black and brown people. The new urban Texas also maintained this separation, as African Americans and Mexican Americans resided in divided communities, confined by legal and de facto segregation. In practice and in law in the early 1950s, race separated schools, public facilities, private businesses, and the entire culture. In the 1940s, Supreme Court rulings began to knock down some barriers, beginning with the all-white Democratic primary. Little movement toward racial equality occurred, however, as "whites only" signs appeared in rural and urban Texas and even in locales with few minority residents. With the exception of Mexican Americans tied to South Texas political machines, only a handful of minorities legitimately participated in the democratic process. The 1950s would bring serious challenges to white supremacy in Texas and the rest of the South, but as the decade began it was business as usual in politics and society.[5]

In the years following World War II, a number of liberals joined forces to confront the conservative Democratic establishment in the state. Calling themselves the "Texas Loyal Democrats," these activists included independent oil man J. R. Parten, Dickinson banker Walter Hall, former state representative Fagan Dixon, Austin attorney Creekmore Fath, former suffrage leader and longtime Democratic activist Minnie Fisher Cunningham, former San Antonio congressman Maury Maverick Sr., and a number of others.[6]

In 1946, former University of Texas president Homer Price Rainey, fired in 1944 by conservative UT regents over his defense of academic freedom, led a coalition of liberals, labor, and minorities in a bid for governor. Beauford Jester, a member of the Railroad Commission, assembled a moderate and conservative Democratic force to defeat Rainey. Jester vowed to collar the power of labor unions, to fight communism, and to uphold states' rights. These issues set the stage for some of the postwar divisions that would split Texas Democrats. What began as a philosophical battle and intra-party dispute evolved into a political free-for-all that drew larger numbers of dissatisfied Democrats to the Texas Loyal faction. Within a few years, Ralph Yarborough, a Democratic activist and former district judge, would emerge as the group's standard-bearer, challenging Allan Shivers for the governorship in 1952 and 1954.[7]

In the late 1940s, President Harry Truman proposed to widen federal jurisdiction on civil rights by strengthening the Fair Employment Practices Act. Northern Democrats in Congress also pushed to restrict poll taxes and to enact tougher anti-lynching laws, with southern congressional Democrats consistently opposing these efforts. The 1948 Democratic National Convention also passed a civil rights plank, and,

in spite of considerable conservative effort in Texas, Truman still easily carried the state. Allan Shivers led the pro-business, segregationist, conservative establishment of the Texas Democratic Party upon
becoming governor after Jester's death in 1949. Shivers capitalized on
the Tidelands controversy by criticizing the Truman administration
and the Supreme Court decisions that favored federal ownership of the
submerged lands off the Texas coast. In 1951 he accused the Truman
administration of an attempt to "nationalize" the oil industry, and
further charged the federal government with violating states' rights.
Shivers's language on states' rights previewed his future opposition to
federal enforcement of racial equality in Texas.[8]

Shivers aligned himself with the other southern governors in opposition to civil rights from the outset, with public support for segregation and states' rights. Additionally, he successfully led his "Shiver-
crats" to carry the state for Republican Dwight D. Eisenhower in 1952.
Although buoyed by his political success, Shivers was also forcing the
liberal/left faction of the Texas Democratic Party to take a stand. The
Texas Loyal Democrats and a growing group of other dissenters began
openly opposing the traditional low-tax, low-service, segregationist
agenda. By 1954, the long-smoldering issue of racial discrimination
would burst into a full-fledged wildfire that swept Texas and the entire
South. The catalyst for the national wildfire, as well as the political
battle between the two Texas Democratic factions, was the U.S. Supreme Court's 1954 *Brown* decision.[9]

Following the *Brown* decision, liberals pressured the UT administration and state legislators to permit integration at the state's flag-
ship university. The university's board of regents and the university
administration continued to place restrictions on minority students
for a number of years. Notably, the active opposition by those in the
liberal movement both on and off the campus maintained a constant
criticism of discriminatory practices for the next decade. Although the
university claimed it was officially integrated, many programs, services and activities remained off-limits to minorities by rule and custom. Yet with the significant involvement of students of this era, an
important precedent was set for the activist years of the 1960s.

Shivers and other Texas politicians exploited the racial tensions
generated by desegregation. Shivers, facing a tough reelection primary
battle, urged resistance to *Brown* generally and specifically encouraged those violently resisting desegregation of Mansfield schools in
North Central Texas. There, enraged mobs of between three hundred
and four hundred white people roamed the town and surrounded the
city's high school on August 30 and 31, 1956, to block the enrollment
of three African American students. Whites symbolically hung images

of three blacks, and local officials allowed the black-faced effigies to remain hanging in front of the Mansfield High campus for days. Rather than maintain order and enforce the law, Shivers praised Mansfield's mob and violated a federal court order by dispatching Texas Rangers to prevent desegregation.[10]

Just before Mansfield, Shivers had successfully placed three inflammatory referenda on the Democratic primary ballot. Democratic voters were asked whether they favored repeal of compulsory school attendance laws "when white and Negro children are mixed in public schools"; whether they supported strengthening the state law barring intermarriage between whites and blacks; and whether they backed the use of "interposition" to "halt illegal federal encroachment" on states' rights. The referenda passed by overwhelming majorities, but, as historian George Green points out, the aggregate numbers belie the real and growing opposition to Shivers's shrill stands. Cracks were appearing in the solid face of white supremacy, with a third of Texas gubernatorial voters abstaining from the referenda, and with three counties—including San Antonio's Bexar—even refusing to place the referenda on the ballot. State-sponsored enthusiasm for supporting massive resistance passed with Shivers's departure from office in 1957 and the arrival of new legislative leadership determined to shift the focus of the debate. Liberals continued to gain steam in the fight against segregation.[11]

Following Yarborough's narrow loss to Shivers in the 1954 Democratic primary, a new publication emerged that would serve as the voice of the liberal movement in Texas for years to come. Frankie Randolph and others founded the *Texas Observer* in 1954. The founders represented a who's who of the liberal movement in the 1950s, including, in addition to Randolph, Mark Adams, Jesse Andrews, Jack and Margaret Carter, Lillian Collier, Minnie Fisher Cunningham, Chris Dixie, Robert "Bob" Eckhardt, Don and Ruth Ellinger, Creekmore Fath, Franklin and Huldah Jones, Otto Mullinax, J. R. Parten, and Fred and Venola Schmidt. They wanted a publication that would cover issues largely ignored by the state's daily newspapers, including business abuse, labor rights, government corruption, and the struggle for racial equality—and the fight against that equality by the Ku Klux Klan and White Citizens' Councils. Randolph enlisted a young Ronnie Dugger to serve as the publication's first editor. Dugger and his colleagues and successors brought national attention to the paper. They included such acclaimed writers as Bob Sherrill, Billy Lee Brammer, Willie Morris, Jim Hightower, Kaye Northcott, and Molly Ivins. The publication has served as the semi-official voice of the liberal movement in Texas for the subsequent five decades. Liberals inside and outside Texas came to see the *Texas Observer* as the moral voice of the state.[12]

Ronnie Dugger was given complete editorial control and declared the *Observer* to be politically independent. Notably, the founding group included no minorities, although those alliances would expand in the civil rights movement of the 1950s and 1960s.[13]

Dugger wrote in an early column about the definition of a liberal in Texas, "Surely the liberal is dedicated to human liberty, to the rights of the individual, to the human instead of the formal." Dugger's *Observer* attacked corrupt politicians, exposed the discrepancies in "separate but equal" facilities in the state, and advocated wholesale political changes in the state. The *Texas Observer* quickly became recognized for its hard-hitting, well-researched articles that major news publications in the state often avoided. The alternative paper also covered news from minority organizations and recognized rising political stars in the minority community.[14]

Willie Morris, who would become a liberal icon while editing *Harper's* in the 1960s, served as one of the most renowned editors of the *Texas Observer*. Although the publication suffered through many crises, Morris wrote, "it was good to know that any week's issue would be read, and read closely, by most members of the state legislature, the two U.S. Senators, the governor, the Speaker of the U.S. House, and the Vice-President of the United States (who not only read it, I was to learn, but underlined it with a ball-point pen)." Morris added that the staff also served as "intermediaries in fights, some of them not specifically philosophical, between the liberals." Morris praised Ronnie Dugger for inspiring his successors at the publication. Dugger imbued the *Observer* veterans with a "'commitment' in its most human sense. . . . He taught those of us who passed through en route to our more personal work how to view public life as an ethical process, how to be fair."[15]

The critical role played by women leaders in the modern liberal movement has only recently garnered recognition by historians. Some liberal leaders of the civil rights era had also worked for women's suffrage and social and economic reforms during the Great Depression. Frankie Randolph was at the epicenter of the modern liberal movement. She was one of the founders of the Houston Junior League, and an active member of the League of Women Voters and many charitable organizations. In Houston she fought for urban planning, public housing, and improved services for low-income areas. By the 1950s she publicly fought to end the poll tax and racial segregation. She worked closely with Senator Ralph Yarborough and other liberal and labor leaders throughout the state. Through her support of the *Texas*

Observer and the Democrats of Texas, she became one of the most influential leaders in the liberal movement until her death in 1972.[16]

Frankie Randolph, the "Eleanor Roosevelt of Texas," made her mark in Democratic politics. At the state Democratic convention in 1956, a sufficient number of liberals won election as delegates to elect Randolph as a national committeewoman. Uniting with backers of Lyndon Johnson, the liberals also ousted supporters of outgoing Governor Alan Shivers, thus effectively ending his influence with Texas Democrats. Similar to his 1954 campaign against Yarborough, Shivers attempted to retain control of the Democratic Party by denouncing Johnson and Rayburn as "ultra liberals" who were captives of the NAACP, the CIO, and the liberal Americans for Democratic Action. However, at the tumultuous fall 1956 state convention, the Johnson forces turned the tables on the liberal Democratic delegates, as they seized complete control of the Democratic Party machinery. Johnson's forces installed many Shivers conservatives and ousted veteran liberal Democrats, keeping them from gaining control of the state Democratic Party. As historian George Green noted about the animosity that was generated in the political fight, "from that point on in Texas's political history, it was an article of faith among Texas liberals, who had entertained some doubts about Lyndon since 1948, that Johnson could never be trusted." In late 1956, Randolph, Bob Eckhardt, and other liberals formed the Democrats of Texas (DOT) in order to operate independently of Johnson and Rayburn.[17]

A close associate of Randolph's joined with her in the fight against Shivers's conservatives and the Johnson-Rayburn faction. Minnie Fisher Cunningham served as a longtime reformer whose work began with the women's suffrage movement and continued into the postwar liberal movement. Cunningham—"Minnie Fish" to her many friends and admirers—helped found the League of Women Voters, was the first woman in Texas to run both for the U.S. Senate and for governor. A strong supporter of Roosevelt's New Deal program in the 1930s, she maintained her leadership into the 1940s and 1950s. She encouraged white liberals to expand their ranks to include minorities. In the battles for civil rights and economic justice, she forged coalitions between minorities, women, organized labor, and other reformers. She became known as the "conscience of Texas politics," someone who applied moral standards to the battles over public policy. She became close friends with Ralph Yarborough and Eckhardt who represented the Texas liberal movement in Washington.[18]

Another wealthy Texan provided leadership and financial support to the liberal movement in the state. Although he never ran for public office, lifelong Democrat J. R. Parten served as one of the most active liberal leaders over seven decades. He served as one of James Allred's chief advisors during the 1930s, became a close friend of Congressman Sam Rayburn, worked with the Loyal Democrats to unseat Shivers's delegation in 1952, and joined with Frankie Randolph in establishing the *Texas Observer*. Parten also established a close relationship with Ralph Yarborough. In the 1960s and 1970s, Parten joined with an informal triumvirate of wealthy liberal Democratic fund-raisers, that included Waco insurance executive Bernard Rapoport and Walter Hall, to support liberal Democrats for local, state, and federal offices. Parten was a consistent activist in support of liberal policies.[19]

In 1956 Parten even confronted Lyndon Johnson when the senator's pragmatic forces ousted many of the state's liberal Democrats. When he discovered that Randolph and other Houston Democrats had been locked out of the convention, Parten openly challenged Johnson behind the stage. Parten told Johnson that the senator had made "the biggest mistake of his life" when turning against Randolph. Johnson countered that "Frankie Randolph and her gang of 'red hots' should have stayed in line last May (during the spring Democratic convention)." Parten later warned Rayburn, "Johnson's making wounds that will take many years to heal." Johnson, with his take-no-prisoners tactics, won at the convention. Parten, Randolph, Yarborough, and other influential liberal leaders believed that Johnson's betrayal led liberal Democrats and many Democratic candidates to defeat in 1956. This seemingly irreversible defeat was soon followed, however, by a series of triumphs for Texas liberals.[20]

The year 1957 marked a significant change in Texas, as the state began to follow a separate path from its southern neighbors. While across much of the South state legislatures enacted over 450 segregationist laws aimed at obstructing the *Brown* decision and targeting the NAACP, in Texas a more subtle, "moderate course" emerged as early as 1957. Even though integration and other economic opportunities moved slowly, Texas began to follow a more moderate track on these issues. Throughout the South, massive resistance made its impact on restricting opportunities and improving the overall condition of all southerners.[21]

The 1957 special election for the U.S. Senate resulted in a breakthrough for Ralph Yarborough and the liberal movement in Texas. Following Senator Price Daniel's razor-thin victory over Yarborough in the 1956 gubernatorial campaign, Daniel had to resign his Senate seat to be sworn in as governor. Yarborough immediately became a favorite to replace Daniel. However, the state's daily newspapers fanned the fires between the rival Democratic factions. "Neither Johnson nor Rayburn want Yarborough to win that Senate race," columnist Dick

West of the *Dallas Morning News* wrote. Both Speaker Rayburn and Senate Majority Leader Johnson were "middle of the road" politicians who disliked the "wild-eyed radicalism" of Yarborough's supporters. West maintained that the Johnson-Rayburn team wanted to prevent Yarborough Democrats and the "extreme-liberal bloc" from becoming stronger. However, Johnson also wanted to be his party's presidential nominee in 1960, and knew that he needed to curry favor with liberals back in Texas in order to strengthen his standing with liberals throughout the nation, even as he sought to find the middle ground between northern liberals and southern conservatives.[22]

A total of twenty-two candidates filed for the vacant U.S. Senate seat in 1957. In the crowded special election, the winning candidate only needed to finish with the largest number of votes—not a majority—and there was no runoff. By this time, Yarborough was in the fifth year of his nearly nonstop campaign. "He is fighting a war in a cause he believes in his soul is just," Yarborough's campaign literature proclaimed. In his public appearances, Yarborough selected safe issues, while his campaign workers concentrated on voter turnout. He called for budget cuts, favored an income tax reduction, and maintained his longtime support for farm programs, soil conservation, and drought relief. He endorsed continuation of the oil depletion allowance for the nation's petroleum producers. Yarborough's victory brought joy to liberal Democrats and represented the first major political victory of an avowed liberal candidate. He would soon be tested with the first civil rights legislation since Reconstruction.[23]

By 1957, the *Brown* case put many elected officials with liberal tendencies on the hot seat. Speaker Sam Rayburn, along with Jim Wright, a young congressman from Fort Worth, and Jack Brooks, another new member from Beaumont, were among the Texas congressmen who refused to sign the "Southern Manifesto." Senators Lyndon Johnson and Ralph Yarborough also refused pressure to join their southern cohorts in the Senate. Outside of Texas, the vast majority of southerners in Congress, including veteran New Deal members, united behind the declaration that denounced the Supreme Court for overturning racial segregation. The document stated that the court decision was an abuse of judicial power, and it encouraged resistance to integration. Southerners would soon have much more to deal with on the civil rights issue.[24]

Initiated by President Eisenhower to address political divisions prompted by the *Brown* decision, the Civil Rights Act of 1957 stood as the first civil rights legislation since the end of Reconstruction. The president adopted the 1947 recommendations of President Truman's Civil Rights Committee. The proposal divided southerners and launched a fierce debate in Congress. The legislation served as a cata-lyst for the liberal movement in Texas. With the coordinated leader-ship of House Speaker Sam Rayburn and Senator Lyndon Johnson, the bill passed, albeit with significant compromises. Johnson, a frequent target of Texas liberals in the 1950s, took great pride in his opposi-tion to the Southern Manifesto and support for the Civil Rights Act of 1957. Vice President Hubert Humphrey later recalled in an interview how Johnson felt about his votes: "'I want you to notice who signed the Southern Manifesto and who didn't. Now all your bomb throwers over there think I am the worst thing that came down here. They won't cooperate' and so on. 'But they're all cheering Bill Fulbright. Why do they cheer Bill Fulbright? Because they think he's got great connec-tions overseas. He's a Rhodes Scholar, and he's got the Fulbright Act' and so on and so on. And he'd go on. He said, 'He [Fulbright] signed the Southern Manifesto, didn't he? He signed that Southern Manifesto. I didn't.' Oh, many times he'd mention that. He was very proud of the fact that he didn't sign it. Also, he used it."[25]

Along with Johnson, Speaker Sam Rayburn also exhibited a new attitude toward civil rights. Not long after the *Brown* decision, Ray-burn stated, "If you had been on that Court, you'd have voted exactly as they voted—if you were an honest man." Rayburn began working with other House liberals to address civil rights issues, particularly voting rights. Rayburn's Northeast Texas district was generally char-acterized as pro-segregationist, but Rayburn believed that he had the standing with his constituents to weather any criticism. He worked to streamline the process for the adoption of the 1957 civil rights bill in the House, and worked closely with Johnson to ensure final passage. Witnessing the change in postwar America and taking note of growing liberal support for Democratic initiatives, Rayburn saw the political wisdom in moving forward on civil rights. As the political godfather to Johnson, Rayburn also wanted his protégé to be the next Democratic presidential nominee in 1960. But, as with the United States at large, Texas was experiencing rapid social changes in the 1950s and Texas politicians who wanted to succeed on the national stage would have to recognize the importance of new alliances being constructed in the state.[26]

New alliances between liberal and minority communities in Texas produced remarkable leaders. Henry B. Gonzalez emerged as an orga-nizer and principal in the Mexican American community who drew significant support from liberals in Texas. Gonzalez served as a unify-ing figure that united the minority community and Anglo liberals dur-ing the 1950s. First elected to the San Antonio City Council in 1953, Gonzalez counted supporters both inside and outside the minority precincts. His popularity led to his election as a state senator in 1956, the first Hispanic Texan ever elected to that office.[27]

While in the Texas Senate, Gonzalez drew national attention for his opposition to a series of bills that aimed at thwarting the Supreme Court's *Brown* decision. In the 1957 regular session, Gonzalez set the record for a filibuster. In 1958, Gonzalez received support from the Democrats of Texas, Senator Ralph Yarborough, and many other liberal activists in his unsuccessful bid for governor. Gonzalez became a cochair of the "Viva Kennedy" campaign in 1960, in which the Democratic ticket of John F. Kennedy and Lyndon B. Johnson narrowly carried Texas. Gonzalez soon won election to the U.S. House of Representatives in a special election in 1961. From his position in Congress, Gonzalez established his reputation as a spokesman and leader of liberal efforts until he retired in 1998.[28]

Lyndon Johnson proves to be the most difficult political leader to analyze during this period. Johnson biographer Robert Dallek maintains that the Texas senator's presidential ambitions guided his political decisions during the 1950s. Johnson strove to become the "liberal nationalist" leader whose moderation would bridge the differences between liberals and conservatives. Johnson's conflict with Texas liberals derived less from his policy stands than from his abusive tactics. Many Texas liberals, uniting behind Ralph Yarborough as their standard bearer, detested the overbearing Johnson. Yet the growing influence of the liberal movement in Texas, especially after Yarborough's election to the Senate in 1957, resulted in a coherent force at home. While Johnson had to find the middle course as Senate majority leader, he also had to contend with the persistent voices from the Left in the Lone Star State.[29]

In his study of the liberal-conservative division in Texas, Chandler Davidson identifies the liberal resurgence after World War II as one of the "critical moments" when divisions over race and economic issues came to the forefront. The issues that pointed in the direction of fairness and opportunity, the moral compass of the liberal agenda, motivated large numbers of Texans. "Were it not for the under representation of the progressives' natural constituency in the electorate, they would have won more victories than history records," writes Davidson. Discriminatory election laws and practices discouraged poor people's participation. In addition, conservative candidates were traditionally better financed and on cozy terms with the state's media in this era. And at the heart of it all, Davidson maintains, writing twenty-five years after *Brown*, the politics of race and class lie interwoven at the core of Texas political culture, influencing policy decisions concerning an array of complex social issues such as education, health care, justice, and public services.[30]

If the impact of the Texas liberal movement in the years after World War II is measured solely by electoral success, then the record would be largely unimpressive. With the notable exceptions of electing Yarborough, Eckhardt, and Gonzalez to Congress, on the surface Texas politics seem typical for a conservative southern state. Notwithstanding this, a case can be made for the liberal agenda significantly influencing the public policy in Texas.

By 1957, the liberal movement in Texas could point to a number of achievements and successes in the public-policy arena. A recognizable demarcation separated Texas from other southern states confronting the civil rights challenge. Although racism was widespread in the state, most Texas congressmen had not signed the Southern Manifesto nor enlisted the strategy of open resistance, as was the case in many other southern states. Texas liberals pressured candidates and officeholders to at least moderate their stands on segregation. With the success of Ralph Yarborough, Bob Eckhardt, Henry Gonzalez, and other liberals in the late 1950s, conservative and moderate officeholders understood that they had to recognize the liberal movement in Texas as a legitimate political and moral force. Furthermore, national leaders such as Sam Rayburn and Lyndon Johnson, despite their confrontations with Texas liberals, followed a more moderate, national Democratic trend during this era. While liberals could not capture a convincing majority, the electorate and public sentiment responded to a degree that made Texas more moderate than its southern counterparts. The Texas liberal movement, however, soon followed the national pattern that developed in the late 1960s and the early 1970s in moving from class and economic issues, and instead embracing identity politics.

Perhaps in the final analysis the most momentous accomplishment of the 1950s Texas liberal movement was its influence on Lyndon Johnson. In spite of his ongoing battles with liberals at home and northern liberals in his own party, LBJ provided leadership for landmark legislation through his support for civil rights, voting rights, his War on Poverty program, and his attempts to create a "great society" that provided greater benefits and protections for all Americans. The impetus within Johnson to push through such measures sprang from a variety of sources, not least of all the legacy of eighty years of work by his Hill Country forebears. Although LBJ would seldom acknowledge the influence, the Texas liberal movement proved to be a guiding hand in pushing this grandson of Texas Populism toward a more liberal agenda.

NOTES

1. Gunnar Myrdal, *An American Dilemma: The Negro Problem and Modern Democracy* (New York: Harper & Brothers, 1944), 456, 466. A number of historians and studies support this thesis of outside support as the foundation for southern liberals. These include the landmark studies of V. O. Key's *Southern Politics in State and Nation* (Knoxville: University of Tennessee Press, 1984, c. 1949); John Dollard, *Case and Class in a Southern Town* (New Haven, Yale University Press, 1937); and Numan Bartley, *The New South, 1945–1980* (Baton Rouge: LSU Press, 1995).

2. Bartley, *New South*, 70–73.

3. Key, *Southern Politics*, 254–61.

4. Robert A. Calvert, "Texas Since World War II," *The Handbook of Texas Online* (http://www.tshaonline.org/handbook/online/articles/TT/npt2.html).

5. *Texas Almanac, 1952–53* (Dallas: A. H. Belo Corporation, 1951), 58–67; Ricky F. Dobbs, *Yellow Dogs and Republicans: Allan Shivers and Texas Two-Party Politics* (College Station: Texas A&M University Press, 2005).

6. George Norris Green, *The Establishment in Texas Politics, 1938–1957* (Westport, Ct.: Greenwood Press, 1979), 141–47; Don Carleton, *A Breed So Rare* (Austin: Texas State Historical Association, 1998), 410–15.

7. Patrick Cox, *Ralph W. Yarborough: The People's Senator* (Austin: University of Texas Press, 2001), 98–99; Green, *The Establishment in Texas Politics*, 86–92; George N. Green, "Rainey, Homer Price," *The Handbook of Texas Online*, http://www.tshaonline.org/handbook/online/articles/RR/fra54.html (accessed August 24, 2008).

8. Green, *The Establishment in Texas Politics*, 110–12.

9. Green, *The Establishment in Texas Politics*, 141–47.

10. *The New Handbook of Texas*, 1996, s.v., "Mansfield School Desegregation Incident." The best and fullest account of the Mansfield's desegregation trauma can be found in Robin Duff Ladino, *Desegregating Texas Schools: Eisenhower, Shivers, and the Crisis at Mansfield High* (Austin: University of Texas Press, 1996). For Shivers's public stands opposing desegregation, see Dobbs, *Yellow Dogs and Republicans*, and Patrick Cox, *Ralph W. Yarborough, The People's Senator* (Austin: University of Texas Press, 2001).

11. Green, *The Establishment in Texas*, 187–89. Calvert and De León, *Texas: A History* (Wheeling, Ill.: Harlan Davidson, 1996), 388–91. For more on the interrelated ideas of nullification and interposition, con-

sult Garry Wills, *A Necessary Evil: A History of American Distrust of Government* (New York: Simon and Schuster, 1990), 123–78.

12. "About Us," *Texas Observer*, http://www.texasobserver.org/about.php.

13. "The Texas Observer," *The Handbook of Texas Online*, http://www.tshaonline.org/handbook/online/articles/TT/edt12.html (accessed May 10, 2009).

14. *Texas Observer*, May 2, 1955.

15. Willie Morris, *North Toward Home* (Boston: Houghton Mifflin Company, 1967), 201–202.

16. "Randolph, Frankie Carter," *The Handbook of Texas Online*, http://www.tshaonline.org/handbook/online/articles/RR/fra34.html (accessed May 10, 2009); Ann Fears Crawford, *Frankie: Mrs. R. D. Randolph and Texas Liberal Politics* (Waco: Eakin Press, 1999).

17. Cox, *Ralph W. Yarborough*, 111–12; Green, *Establishment in Texas Politics*, 178; Gary A. Keith, *Eckhardt: There Once Was a Congressman from Texas* (Austin: University of Texas Press, 2007), 134–38.

18. Judith N. McArthur and Harold L. Smith, *Minnie Fisher Cunningham: A Suffragist's Life in Politics* (Oxford: Oxford University Press, 2003), 204–206.

19. Don E. Carleton, "Parten, Jubal Richard," *The Handbook of Texas Online*, http://www.tshaonline.org/handbook/online/articles/PP/fpa93.html (accessed May 10, 2009).

20. Don Carleton, *A Breed So Rare: The Life of J.R. Parten, Liberal Texas Oil Man, 1896–1992* (Austin: Texas State Historical Association, 1998), 472.

21. Bartley, *New South*, 220–60.

22. Cox, *Ralph W. Yarborough*, 144–49; *Dallas Morning News*, February 11, 1957; Dallek, *Lone Star Rising*, 509–10; Robert A. Caro, *Master of the Senate: The Years of LBJ* (New York: Knopf, 2003).

23. Cox, *Ralph W. Yarborough*, 142–43.

24. Randall Wood, *LBJ: Architect of American Ambition* (New York: Free Pres, 2006), 325–28; for the most detailed narrative of the 1957 Civil Rights Act and Lyndon Johnson's political strategy in the 1950s, see Caro, *Master of the Senate*, 910–1012.

25. Transcript, Hubert H. Humphrey Oral History Interview III, June 21, 1977, by Michael L. Gillette, Internet copy, LBJ Library (University of Texas, Austin, Texas), 8. http://www.lbjlib.utexas.edu/johnson/archives.hom/oralhistory.hom/humphrey/humphr03.pdf.

26. D. B. Hardeman and Donald C. Bacon, *Rayburn, A Biography* (Austin: Texas Monthly Press, 1987), 420.

27. "Henry B. Gonzalez: Voice of the People," Dolph Briscoe Center for American History, University of Texas, http://www.cah.utexas.edu/

feature/0611/bio.php; Eugene Rodriguez Jr., *Henry B. Gonzalez: A Political Profile* (New York: Arno Press, 1976).

28. "Henry B. Gonzalez: Voice of the People"; Julie Leininger Pycior, "Henry B. Gonzalez," in *Profiles in Power: Twentieth-Century Texans in Washington*, ed. Kenneth E. Hendrickson, Michael L. Collins, and Patrick Cox (Austin: University of Texas Press, 1993), 294–308.

29. Robert Dallek, *Lone Star Rising: Lyndon Johnson and His Times, 1908 – 1960* (New York: Oxford University Press, 1991), 510–12.

30. Chandler Davidson, *Race and Class in Texas Politics* (Princeton: Princeton University Press, 1990), 32, 270–71.

ABOUT THE CONTRIBUTORS

GREGG ANDREWS, labor historian and former NEH Fellow at Texas State University, is the author of *Shoulder to Shoulder? The American Federation of Labor, the United States, and the Mexican Revolution, 1910–1924* (1991), *City of Dust: A Cement Company Town in the Land of Tom Sawyer* (1996), and *Insane Sisters: Or, the Price Paid for Challenging a Company Town* (1999). In 2008 his article "Black Working-Class Political Activism and Biracial Unionism: Galveston Longshoremen in Jim Crow Texas, 1919–1921" was published in the *Journal of Southern History*. He is currently finishing a biography of Thyra J. Edwards, a black radical feminist and labor and civil rights activist in the 1930s and 1940s who grew up in Houston.

DONNA BARNES is associate professor of sociology at the University of Wyoming. She is the author of *Farmers in Rebellion: The Rise and Fall of the Southern Farmers Alliance and People's Party in Texas* (1984) and has recently completed a manuscript, *The Unredeemed*, on the Louisiana Farmers' Union and People's Party in Louisiana.

MICHAEL R. BOTSON JR. is a former union steelworker turned historian. He received his PhD from the University of Houston in 1999 and is professor of history at Houston Community College. His articles on labor and civil rights have appeared in the *Houston Review*, *Southwestern Historical Quarterly*, *Steel Labor*, and the *Houston Chronicle*, and his book *Labor, Civil Rights, and the Hughes Tool Company* received the Texas Historical Commission's T. R. Fehrenbach Award in 2005.

PETER H. BUCKINGHAM previously taught at three different Texas universities but is now professor of American history at Linfield College in Oregon. He is writing a biography of "Red Tom" Hickey and the Texas socialist movement. He is the author of several books, including *International Normalcy: America's Open Door Peace with the Former Central Powers, 1921–1929; Woodrow Wilson: A Bibliography of His Times and Presidency; America Sees Red: Anti-Communism in America, 1870s to 1980s; Rebel against Injustice: The Life of Frank P. O'Hare;* and (ed.) *Expectations for the Millennium: American Socialist Visions of the Future.*

GREGG CANTRELL holds the Erma and Ralph Lowe Chair in History at Texas Christian University. He is author of *Kenneth and John B. Rayner and the Limits of Southern Dissent* and *Stephen F. Austin, Empresario of Texas.* He is currently writing a history of the Texas Populist Party. Cantrell is a two-time winner of the T. R. Fehrenbach Book Award.

PATRICK COX is associate director of the Dolph Briscoe Center for American History (University of Texas at Austin) and author of numerous publications, including the award-winning *Ralph W. Yarborough: The People's Senator* (2002). His most recent book, coauthored with Michael Phillips, is *First among Equals: A History of the Texas House Speakers* (2010). Cox is a fellow of the Texas State Historical Association.

DAVID O'DONALD CULLEN, professor of history, Collin College, and Rockefeller Foundation Grant recipient, is the author of numerous historical essays, including "Back to the Future: Eugenics, A Bibliographic Essay" in the *Public Historian: A Journal of Public Policy* and "Populism" in the *Encyclopedia of American Social Movements.* He is coauthor of "The Communist Party of the United States and African American Political Candidates" in *The African American Presidency: From Douglass to Obama* (2010).

ARNOLDO DE LEÓN is the C. J. "Red" Davidson Professor of History at Angelo State University, a fellow of the Texas State Historical Association, and a member of the Texas Institute of Letters. Among his many publications are *North to Aztlan: A History of Mexican Ameri-*

cans in the United States; *Mexican Americans in Texas: A Brief History*; *They Called Them Greasers: Anglo Attitudes Towards Mexicans in Texas, 1821–1900*; and *The Tejano Community, 1836–1900*. He is currently completing a book on Hispanics in U.S. sports.

BRUCE A. GLASRUD, an independent historian residing in Seguin, Texas, is professor emeritus of history, California State University, East Bay, retired dean, School of Arts and Sciences, Sul Ross State University, and a fellow of the Texas State Historical Association. A specialist in the history of blacks in the West, Glasrud has authored or co-authored more than thirteen books, including *Black Women in Texas History* (winner of the 2009 Texas State Historical Association's Liz Carpenter Award), *The African American West: A Century of Short Stories*, and *Buffalo Soldiers in the West*.

GEORGE NORRIS GREEN is professor of history at the University of Texas at Arlington, and cofounder of the Texas Labor and Political Archives. He is the author of *The Establishment in Texas Politics* and various articles on Texas labor and politics. He is a former president of the Texas State Historical Association.

JUDITH N. MCARTHUR, lecturer in history, University of Houston–Victoria, authored *Creating the New Woman: The Rise of Southern Women's Progressive Culture in Texas, 1893–1918* (1998) and co-authored *Minnie Fisher Cunningham: A Suffragist's Life in Politics* (2003) which won the 2003 T. R. Fehrenbach Book Award.

CARL MONEYHON is a professor of history at the University of Arkansas at Little Rock. A specialist in the American Civil War and Reconstruction, he has written extensively on the Texas experience during these years. His most recent work on the topic is *Texas after the Civil War: The Struggle of Reconstruction* (2004).

HAROLD L. SMITH, professor of history, University of Houston–Victoria, authored *The British Women's Suffrage Campaign 1866–1928* (2007) and coauthored *Minnie Fisher Cunningham: A Suffragist's Life in Politics* (2003) which won the 2003 T. R. Fehrenbach Book Award.

KYLE G. WILKISON, professor of history, Collin College, writes about poor people and the working class. His book *Yeomen, Sharecroppers and Socialists: Plain Folk Protest in Texas, 1870–1914* (2008) won the T. R. Fehrenbach Book Award.

INDEX